Mastering Cloudflare

Optimizing Security, Performance, and Reliability for the Web

Robert Johnson

Published by HiTeX Press

For permissions and other inquiries, write to:
P.O. Box 3132, Framingham, MA 01701, USA

Contents

Introduction

In the contemporary digital environment, where the internet infrastructure experiences both unprecedented growth and increasing complexity, ensuring security, performance, and reliability is paramount for online presence. This book, "Mastering Cloudflare: Optimizing Security, Performance, and Reliability for the Web," presents a comprehensive examination of one of the leading platforms designed to enhance these essential aspects of web services—Cloudflare.

Cloudflare has emerged as a critical solution for mitigating threats, enhancing performance, and maintaining high levels of availability across the web. Originally founded in 2009 as a project to develop a more secure, faster internet infrastructure, Cloudflare has evolved significantly. Its suite of products addresses a wide spectrum of needs, from protecting websites from Distributed Denial of Service (DDoS) attacks to enabling faster page loads, to providing seamless and efficient content delivery through its expansive network of data centers globally.

For individuals and organizations alike, mastering the intricacies of Cloudflare's offerings is not merely advantageous but essential. Whether you are a web developer, IT professional, or a security consultant, understanding how to leverage Cloudflare's capabilities can profoundly impact your ability to deliver speedy, secure, and reliable web experiences. This book seeks to guide you systematically through the core elements of Cloudflare, structured to build knowledge progressively from foundational concepts to advanced configurations.

The contents are organized to provide a clear progression. Early chapters introduce fundamental aspects of Cloudflare, such as its basic services and DNS management. The discussion extends to explore how Cloudflare's security mechanisms mitigate threats like DDoS attacks and offers detailed insights into performance optimization techniques. Furthermore, the book ventures into specialized areas such as Cloudflare Workers for edge computing and offers deep dives into content delivery mechanisms.

Every feature and concept is elucidated with practical approaches in mind, ensuring that readers can apply their learning effectively to real-world scenarios. Each chapter not only explicates a component of Cloudflare but also presents case studies, troubleshooting tips, and best practices to ensure that the knowledge is both theoretical and profoundly practical.

In addressing Cloudflare's comprehensive set of tools and features, this book also acknowledges the broader context of web operations. Thus, readers are equally presented with insights into integrating Cloudflare into existing systems, ensuring compatibility and maximized efficacy.

As you engage with these chapters, expect to develop a robust understanding of how to harness the full potential of Cloudflare to secure, accelerate, and optimize web applications. The objective is clear: equip you with the expertise necessary to confidently deploy Cloudflare as an integral component of your web infrastructure strategy, ensuring that your online presence is not only resilient but also competitive in an ever-evolving digital landscape.

"Mastering Cloudflare: Optimizing Security, Performance, and Reliability for the Web" intends to be an authoritative resource, indispensable for anyone intent on enhancing their knowledge and control over web services with Cloudflare. Welcome to your exploration of a technology that stands at the forefront of shaping the future of the internet.

8

Chapter 1

Introduction to Cloudflare

Cloudflare stands as a pivotal player in the realm of web infrastructure, known for its comprehensive services that enhance security, performance, and reliability. This chapter delves into the core elements of Cloudflare, explaining its significance and the array of tools it offers for web optimization. Readers will gain insights into Cloudflare's operational mechanics, a walkthrough of its service offerings, and initial setup procedures, forming a foundational understanding of how Cloudflare acts to mediate and improve web interactions for both providers and users alike.

1.1   Overview of Cloudflare

Cloudflare is a pivotal player in the domain of web infrastructure and web security services. From its inception, it has positioned itself as a necessity for internet entities aiming to achieve better performance, heightened security, and increased reliability of their services. In this section, we delve into what Cloudflare is, tracing its historical developments and highlighting its significant contributions to modern web infrastructure.

Cloudflare commenced operations with the mission of enhancing the web experience for users globally by providing a suite of services that protect and accelerate any website online. Established in 2009 by Matthew Prince, Lee Holloway, and Michelle Zatlyn, it quickly grew to become a cornerstone in the internet infrastructure landscape. The company aimed to solve issues related to internet infrastructure that were previously costly and complex to manage, such as distributed denial-of-service (DDoS) attacks, web loading speeds, and content delivery.

Historically, internet users faced significant challenges with regards to performance and security. Websites were particularly vulnerable to malicious activities such as hacking and DDoS attacks, which could lead to disruptions and data breaches. Furthermore, content delivery was often sluggish, especially for websites hosted on servers located far from the end user's geographical location. Cloudflare emerged to address these challenges through an integrated approach that leverages reverse proxying, caching, and distributed computing.

Cloudflare's architecture is predicated on the concept of a content delivery network (CDN), which it enhances with unique features. Unlike traditional CDNs that primarily focus on content acceleration, Cloudflare combines this with formidable web security solutions. The network comprises data centers spread across the globe, forming a large, distributed system that responds to user requests in a highly efficient manner. By temporarily storing (caching) content on servers closer to the user, Cloudflare reduces latency, decreases server load, and diminishes bandwidth usage.

An essential feature of Cloudflare's offering is its use of reverse proxy technology. In the traditional web model, user requests traverse the internet to reach the web server hosting the desired site. With Cloudflare, requests are intercepted by a global network of reverse proxy servers that evaluate and optimize traffic to ensure it reaches the destination efficiently. The reverse proxy also provides a layer of security by preventing bad traffic from reaching the origin server.

```
import socket

def start_proxy():
    # Define backend server address
```

```
backend_address = ('backend.server.com', 80)

# Create server socket
server_socket = socket.socket(socket.AF_INET, socket.SOCK_STREAM)
server_socket.bind(('localhost', 8080))
server_socket.listen(5)
print("Proxy server listening on port 8080...")

while True:
    # Accept connection from client
    client_socket, client_address = server_socket.accept()
    print(f"Received connection from {client_address}")

    # Connect to the backend server
    backend_socket = socket.socket(socket.AF_INET, socket.SOCK_STREAM)
    backend_socket.connect(backend_address)

    # Forward request to the backend
    request = client_socket.recv(4096)
    backend_socket.send(request)

    # Receive response from the backend and send it to the client
    response = backend_socket.recv(4096)
    client_socket.send(response)

    # Close sockets
    client_socket.close()
    backend_socket.close()

start_proxy()
```

In this simplistic Python example, a reverse proxy is emulated to demonstrate the basic idea of rerouting client requests via an intermediary. While real-world implementations like Cloudflare are much more sophisticated, the fundamental principle of redirecting and managing traffic remains consistent.

Cloudflare further enhances its service offering with performance improvement tools. For effective web acceleration, Cloudflare uses a proprietary protocol, Argo Smart Routing, to direct traffic through the fastest and most reliable network paths. By dynamically evaluating path efficiency and rerouting traffic as needed, Argo minimizes latency and provides a smoother user experience.

Security is a foundational pillar of Cloudflare's infrastructure. At its core, Cloudflare provides protection against DDoS attacks, SQL injection, cross-site scripting (XSS), and other common vulnerabilities. By analyzing incoming traffic patterns, Cloudflare detects and mitigates potential threats before they reach the web server. A noteworthy feature is the Web Application Firewall (WAF), which employs heuristic analysis to filter malicious HTTP traffic and protect web applications.

```yaml
- id: 1001
  description: Block XSS Attack Patterns
  action: block
  filters:
    - field: query
      operator: contains
      value: <script>
    - field: method
      operator: equals
      value: POST
```

In the YAML snippet above, a basic conceptual WAF rule is illustrated. The rule is configured to block requests containing the string '<script>' in the query, typically associated with XSS attacks.

Cloudflare's DNS service, 1.1.1.1, represents one of the fastest public DNS resolvers available, providing privacy-oriented features and rapid DNS resolution. This service underscores Cloudflare's dedication to boosting security and performance from the ground up, starting with DNS lookup processes. In addition to standard DNS record management, it supports DNSSEC, which ensures queries are answered with authenticated records.

Moreover, Cloudflare provides SSL/TLS encryption, a critical component of online security. By offering automatic HTTPS connections, Cloudflare ensures data transmitted between users and web servers remains encrypted and secure. This feature obviates the need for complex SSL certificate management on behalf of the website owner, simplifying the integration of encryption standards.

The incorporation of serverless computing with Cloudflare Workers further exemplifies its innovative strides. By running JavaScript applications at the network edge, Cloudflare Workers allow developers to deploy scalable applications that are less dependent on centralized servers. This serverless model offers a significant reduction in response times and enhances scalability for rapid development and iteration.

```javascript
// A simple Cloudflare Worker that responds with a Hello message
addEventListener('fetch', event => {
  event.respondWith(handleRequest(event.request))
})

async function handleRequest(request) {
  return new Response('Hello! This is a response from Cloudflare Worker.',
```

12

```
    { status: 200, headers: { 'Content-Type': 'text/plain' } })
}
```

This lightweight Cloudflare Workers script exemplifies a simple edge computing operation, responding to requests with a static message. It highlights how developers can leverage serverless functions to manage tasks closer to the user's location, reducing latency and server dependency.

Cloudflare's journey from a startup to an indispensable internet infrastructure provider illustrates how strategic technological advancements can redefine industry standards. Its comprehensive security and performance solutions empower websites with capabilities that were traditionally complex and financially prohibitive. As the internet evolves, Cloudflare continuously adapts its offerings, ensuring it remains relevant and indispensable in safeguarding and optimizing web interactions.

The breadth of services that Cloudflare provides is continuously expanding to encompass novel challenges and opportunities in the web security and performance domains. By staying at the forefront of technological advancements, Cloudflare has cemented its reputation as a guardian of digital assets across various industries, establishing a legacy built on innovation and resilience.

1.2   Cloudflare Services and Products

Cloudflare offers a comprehensive suite of services and products that address the multifaceted needs of modern web infrastructure. These offerings enhance security, performance, and reliability for websites of all sizes, from personal blogs to large corporate networks. This section delves into the various services and products that Cloudflare provides, highlighting their features and applications.

Central to Cloudflare's services is its globally distributed Content Delivery Network (CDN), which improves the performance and reliability of websites by caching content in data centers worldwide. By storing copies of site resources at nodes closer to users, Cloudflare reduces latency, minimizes bandwidth usage, and increases the speed at which content is delivered. This feature is particularly beneficial for websites with a global audience, where geographical distance from the server can significantly impact loading times.

```
def cache_control(response):
    # Set cache headers
    response.headers['Cache-Control'] = 'public, max-age=31536000'
    response.headers['ETag'] = 'example-etag'
    return response

# Example of applying caching to a web response
response = some_web_framework_response()
cached_response = cache_control(response)
```

The code snippet demonstrates how caching headers can be set in a Python web application, thereby facilitating interaction with Cloudflare's CDN, which uses such headers to serve cached content efficiently.

Security is a cornerstone of Cloudflare's product line, beginning with its renowned DDoS Protection service. DDoS attacks can cripple web infrastructure by overwhelming it with traffic, causing services to become unavailable. Cloudflare mitigates such threats using its vast network capacity and real-time traffic analysis, ensuring that legitimate traffic reaches clients while malicious activity is identified and blocked.

Web Application Firewall (WAF) is another critical component of Cloudflare's security suite. It defends against common threats such as SQL injection, cross-site scripting (XSS), and zero-day attacks. The WAF applies rule-based filters and machine learning techniques to differentiate between legitimate and potentially harmful requests, ensuring the integrity and confidentiality of web applications.

```
{
  "description": "Basic XSS Filter",
  "rules": [
    {
      "action": "block",
      "expression": "(http.request.uri.query contains \"<script>\")"
    }
  ]
}
```

This JSON representation illustrates a basic WAF configuration rule designed to detect and block potential XSS attacks using Cloudflare's API, reinforcing application security against common exploits.

14

Cloudflare's Argo Smart Routing significantly augments web performance by optimizing internet paths. This service evaluates network latency and congestion to determine the most efficient route for data packets, reducing latency and packet loss. Argo's adaptive routing improves reliability and speed, ensuring user requests take the fastest possible paths across the internet.

In addition to core CDN and security services, Cloudflare also offers enhanced DNS services through its public DNS resolver, 1.1.1.1. Considered one of the fastest and most private DNS servers, it emphasizes speed, privacy, and encryption to secure users' DNS queries from interception. With DNSSEC support, Cloudflare ensures DNS queries return authentic responses, negating the risk of cache poisoning attacks.

SSL/TLS encryption is a vital part of Cloudflare's security offerings, ensuring data privacy and integrity between users and servers. Cloudflare simplifies SSL management by automatically providing SSL certificates and ensuring HTTPS connections are available without complex setups. This service not only improves user trust by displaying the secure padlock icon but also enhances search engine optimization (SEO) due to the prioritization search engines give to secure sites.

Cloudflare Workers enable serverless computing, allowing developers to execute JavaScript applications at the network edge. These Workers are designed for high scalability and low latency by running code closest to the user. This positioning reduces round-trip time to servers and enables developers to build dynamic applications that are both responsive and geographically distributed.

```
addEventListener('fetch', event => {
  event.respondWith(handleRequest(event.request))
})

async function handleRequest(request) {
  const jsonResponse = JSON.stringify({ message: "Hello, World!" })
  return new Response(jsonResponse, {
    headers: { 'content-type': 'application/json' },
  })
}
```

This example illustrates a simple Cloudflare Worker script that responds to requests with a JSON payload, showcasing how edge computing can be utilized for quick, scalable serverless operations.

Further extending its suite, Cloudflare Stream provides a powerful platform for managing and distributing video content. This service integrates encoding, storage, and a global CDN in a seamless package, supporting video streaming with minimal delay. Stream handles complexities associated with video distribution, requiring minimal backend configuration while ensuring high quality and adaptive bitrate streaming.

Cloudflare's product lineup also includes Access and Zero Trust Network Access (ZTNA), which allows organizations to secure internal applications without the need for traditional VPNs. This model improves security by applying stringent identity and access control measures, seamlessly integrating with single sign-on (SSO) providers and enforcing authentication protocols.

For automation and customization, Cloudflare's API provides comprehensive access to its features. Users can programmatically manage services, configure settings, and gather analytics using this API, allowing deep integration with existing workflows and systems. By exploiting RESTful principles, Cloudflare's API eases the integration process with various programming languages and environments.

```
curl -X GET "https://api.cloudflare.com/client/v4/zones/:zone_id/dns_records" \
  -H "Authorization: Bearer YOUR_API_TOKEN" \
  -H "Content-Type: application/json"
```

The command demonstrates how to interact with Cloudflare's API using curl to fetch DNS records. This automation capability exemplifies Cloudflare's commitment to providing flexible infrastructure tools for developers.

Cloudflare's continued expansion into new services, such as Cloudflare R2 for object storage, demonstrates its dedication to broadening its product ecosystem. R2 offers scalable and performant object storage without egress fees, standing as a viable alternative to traditional cloud storage solutions that often include hidden costs.

Each of these services and products illustrates Cloudflare's integrated approach to not only solving present-day performance and security challenges but also redefining how websites and applications operate over the internet. Designed to be user-friendly while providing robust protection and optimization tools, Cloudflare's offerings support a vast array of industries, securing everything from e-commerce platforms and governmental portals to financial services and personal websites. Through continual innovation and enhancement, Cloudflare remains a leader in web infrastructure solutions, ensuring that it meets the demand of the evolving digital landscape.

1.3 How Cloudflare Works

Cloudflare operates as a multifaceted network service provider, employing an intricate infrastructure to manage and optimize web traffic. Positioned as an intermediary between users and servers, Cloudflare enhances web operations through a combination of traffic optimization, security measures, and load management. Understanding how Cloudflare functions sheds light on its role in modernizing and securing the web experience.

At the heart of Cloudflare's operation is its globally distributed Content Delivery Network (CDN). The CDN comprises an extensive array of data centers distributed across strategic locations worldwide. These data centers cache content from origin servers and serve cached content to users from the nearest node. This approach significantly reduces latency, as requests are fulfilled by local nodes rather than distant origin servers.

The process begins when an end-user makes a request to a Cloudflare-enabled website. This request is routed through Cloudflare's network, arriving first at one of its reverse proxy servers. These proxies play a crucial role in Cloudflare's operation, acting as checkpoints that examine and manage incoming and outgoing traffic.

Cloudflare's proxy servers utilize DNS to ascertain the optimal path for rerouting requests between the point of origin and destination. This intelligent request routing forms the cornerstone of Cloudflare's performance enhancement services. Leveraging the Anycast network technology, a single IP address is advertised from multiple locations, allowing user requests to be routed to the nearest or most optimal data center dynamically.

```
curl -X GET "https://mywebsite.com" --resolve mywebsite.com:443:203.0.113.1
```

In the bash script, the '–resolve' option forces the DNS resolution to a specific IP, demonstrating how DNS requests can be explicitly routed.

17

One of Cloudflare's primary advantages is its advanced caching mechanism. When Cloudflare receives a request for a resource, it checks if the resource is cached in the local node. If the content exists in the cache and is still valid (not expired), Cloudflare returns the cached version to the user, dramatically enhancing the load speed. This caching not only improves performance but also alleviates server load and minimizes bandwidth consumption.

The security aspect is intertwined with Cloudflare's core functionalities. Security services begin at a fundamental level with DDoS protection. Cloudflare measures against DDoS attacks by distributing incoming traffic across its network, effectively absorbing and mitigating attack attempts. Through traffic analysis and rate-limiting, Cloudflare identifies potentially harmful requests, blocking them before they can reach the origin server.

Web Application Firewall (WAF) capabilities are built into the Cloudflare fabric, functioning to protect web applications from threats such as SQL injection and XSS. WAF inspects incoming requests against predefined security rules and algorithms to identify and block malicious requests.

```
rules:
  - description: Prevent SQL Injection
    action: block
    condition:
      request:
        query: "(SELECT|UNION|INSERT|DELETE|UPDATE|;|--)"
```

Presented above is a YAML configuration example showing a basic WAF rule to thwart SQL injections, configured to identify SQL syntax patterns often used in attacks.

The TLS termination process is another critical component. Cloudflare handles SSL/TLS connections at their edge nodes, offloading the cryptographic overhead from origin servers. This offload translates to significant server performance improvements while simultaneously simplifying certificate management through full HTTPS support. Cloudflare manages SSL scenarios by facilitating the options of Full, Flexible, and Off SSL modes, adjusting to the encrypted connection requirements between a visitor's browser and Cloudflare, and between Cloudflare and the origin server.

A fascinating aspect of Cloudflare's operations is the optimization protocol, Argo Smart Routing. This protocol dynamically chooses the fastest and most efficient path for internet traffic, rerouting as necessary to avoid congested routes. This dynamic adaptation reduces latency and packet loss, ensuring that web pages are delivered promptly to the end user.

Cloudflare plays a transformative role at the network edge through Cloudflare Workers. Running JavaScript-powered scripts closer to the user enhances performance by cutting down on server round trips and processing times. Workers support a multitude of applications, from simple page modification and redirection tasks to complex API and microservice functionalities.

```
// Cloudflare Worker that redirects users based on country code
addEventListener('fetch', event => {
  event.respondWith(handleRequest(event.request))
})

async function handleRequest(request) {
  const country = request.headers.get('CF-IPCountry')
  let response

  if (country === 'JP') {
    response = Response.redirect('https://jp.example.com', 302)
  } else {
    response = Response.redirect('https://global.example.com', 302)
  }

  return response
}
```

This JavaScript code illustrates redirection based on the user's geolocation, showcasing how Cloudflare Workers are leveraged to deploy logic at the edge for improved localization and personalization.

Beyond regular traffic handling, Cloudflare also has built-in mechanisms for ensuring redundancy and resilience. Should a server or data center become unavailable, Anycast facilitates efficient traffic rerouting, sending requests to alternative nodes without noticeable downtime, maintaining business continuity.

Cloudflare's Zero Trust services illustrate the growing need for granular access control and enhanced security in accessing internal applications. By leveraging identity-centric models, Cloudflare facilitates secure and authenticated user access without relying on traditional perimeter-oriented security methods.

Clients can engage with Cloudflare services programmatically through its extensive API offerings. This API provides users with the ability to automate account management, configure settings, update security protocols, and retrieve analytical data. Through this interface, Cloudflare offers extensive customization, enabling users to craft workflows tailored to unique operational needs.

```python
import requests

def list_dns_records(zone_id, api_token):
    url = f"https://api.cloudflare.com/client/v4/zones/{zone_id}/dns_records"
    headers = {
        "Authorization": f"Bearer {api_token}",
        "Content-Type": "application/json"
    }
    response = requests.get(url, headers=headers)

    if response.status_code == 200:
        return response.json()
    else:
        raise Exception("API request failed with status code: " + str(response.
            status_code))

# Example usage
response_data = list_dns_records("your_zone_id", "your_api_token")
```

The Python script demonstrates how to interact with Cloudflare's API to manage DNS records, reflecting the flexibility available to developers managing their Cloudflare accounts.

In internet edge processing, Cloudflare's efforts are directed towards advancing services that enhance website speeds while mitigating infrastructure burdens. By continuously innovating, Cloudflare garners its reputation as not only an enabler of rapid web service delivery but also as a pioneering guardian against the ever-escalating threats of cyber attacks. Through a blend of intelligent routing, reliability, and robust security, Cloudflare remains a crucial participant in shaping the resilient and efficient digital experiences of the future.

1.4 Benefits of Using Cloudflare

Cloudflare provides an array of benefits that make it an attractive solution for a variety of organizations seeking to enhance their web applications' performance, security, and reliability. Its comprehensive feature set addresses key aspects of web management while offering a seamless user experience. This section explores the manifold advantages of integrating Cloudflare into web services, from operational efficiency improvements to robust security enhancements.

A primary benefit of employing Cloudflare is the significant improvement in website performance, achieved through its extensive Content Delivery Network (CDN). With data centers strategically located across the globe, Cloudflare dramatically reduces the geographical latency encountered in traditional web hosting environments. It ensures that user requests are served by the closest available node, resulting in faster load times. The reduction in site latency not only enhances user experience but also positively impacts SEO rankings, as search engines favor fast-loading sites.

Through advanced caching techniques, Cloudflare stores static content at its edge servers, reducing server load and bandwidth usage. Sites witness an immediate enhancement in responsiveness, while also benefiting from a reduction in operational costs as bandwidth demands decrease.

```
<meta http-equiv="Cache-Control" content="public, max-age=31536000" />
<meta http-equiv="ETag" content="W/'abc123'" />
```

The HTML example illustrates how 'Cache-Control' and 'ETag' headers can be applied, encouraging efficient caching practices that Cloudflare utilizes to optimize delivery speed.

Beyond performance, Cloudflare delivers substantial security enhancements, positioning itself as a critical guardian against digital threats. It offers free and automatic SSL/TLS encryption, securing data in transit and fostering user trust by displaying the secure padlock icon in browsers. This security measure protects sensitive data and prevents tampering or interception by malicious actors.

Cloudflare's DDoS protection service is instrumental in safeguarding web applications against the peril of large-scale attack attempts designed to overwhelm and incapacitate services. By leveraging its vast network capacity and intelligent traffic filtering, Cloudflare diffuses these threats, ensuring service continuity even under attack.

The Web Application Firewall (WAF) is another pivotal security feature that provides defense against common threats such as cross-site scripting (XSS) and SQL injection. By applying a refined set of pre-configured rules and utilizing machine learning for threat detection, Cloudflare's WAF performs deep inspection of incoming requests, blocking malicious actors before they can exploit vulnerabilities.

```
<rule>
  <matchPattern>request.uri.query</matchPattern>
  <operator>contains</operator>
  <value><script></value>
  <action>block</action>
</rule>
```

The XML snippet demonstrates a fundamental WAF rule to prevent XSS attacks, showcasing how pattern matching can block attempts to inject scripts into web applications.

Cloudflare's traffic optimization tools, such as Argo Smart Routing, present another substantial benefit by dynamically selecting the fastest and most reliable paths for data transmission. These optimizations decrease latency, significantly improving user experiences. Such enhancements are particularly valuable for global businesses where every millisecond of network efficiency translates to enhanced customer satisfaction and retention rates.

Moreover, Cloudflare's support for HTTP/3 and QUIC protocols represents its commitment to pioneering web performance improvements. These protocols facilitate quicker, more reliable connections, particularly for mobile networks where packet loss is more common. As the internet infrastructure continues to evolve, support for emerging standards puts web properties ahead of the curve in performance and compatibility.

Another key benefit is Cloudflare's analytics services, providing vital insights into web traffic patterns, potential threats, and performance metrics. The objectivity and detail offered by Cloudflare's analytics empower site administrators to make data-driven decisions, enhancing site security and efficiency. Insights into which rules are most frequently triggered or which threats are most common allow for tailored cybersecurity strategies that adapt to evolving threat landscapes.

Leveraging Cloudflare Workers, a powerful edge computing platform, provides additional advantages by running scripts directly at the network edge. By engaging in serverless computing, applications can execute logic closer to the end user, reducing latency and enabling innovative use cases, such as A/B testing, custom routing, and payload manipulation.

```
addEventListener('fetch', event => {
  event.respondWith(fetchAndModify(event.request))
})

async function fetchAndModify(request) {
  const response = await fetch(request)
  const body = await response.text()
  const updatedBody = body.replace('Hello, World!', 'Hello, Cloudflare!')
  return new Response(updatedBody, {
    headers: { 'content-type': 'text/html' }
  })
}
```

This JavaScript example shows how Cloudflare Workers can alter content before delivering it, demonstrating personalization capabilities that can lead to a richer user experience by tailoring interactions in real time.

Scalability is another key benefit of Cloudflare's platform. As web traffic increases, Cloudflare's infrastructure scales smoothly, handling increased loads without requiring corresponding increases in resource provisioning from the client's end. This scalability translates into predictable costs and enhances operational efficiency by reducing the need for overprovisioning server hardware.

From an administration perspective, Cloudflare simplifies DNS management and SSL certificate handling. Automated processes reduce administrative overhead and the burden of manual configuration, enabling efficient management of complex digital properties with minimal operational friction. By centralizing these processes, administrative consistency and accuracy are maintained across multi-domain infrastructures.

Lastly, Cloudflare facilitates robust integration capabilities via its powerful API, allowing developers to programmatically access and manage Cloudflare's suite of services. This integration is invaluable for businesses aiming to incorporate Cloudflare functionality into CI/CD pipelines, automate security and performance configurations, and tailor services to align with corporate IT policies.

```
import json
import requests

def update_a_record(zone_id, record_id, api_token, record_name, new_ip):
```

23

```
    url = f"https://api.cloudflare.com/client/v4/zones/{zone_id}/dns_records/{
        record_id}"
    headers = {
        "Authorization": f"Bearer {api_token}",
        "Content-Type": "application/json"
    }
    data = {
        "type": "A",
        "name": record_name,
        "content": new_ip,
        "ttl": 120,
        "proxied": True
    }
    response = requests.put(url, headers=headers, data=json.dumps(data))
    return response.json()

# Example usage
response_data = update_a_record('your_zone_id', 'your_record_id', '
    your_api_token', 'subdomain.example.com', '192.0.2.1')
```

The Python script showcases how Cloudflare's API can be used to auto-mate DNS record management, a task often required in dynamic and large-scale infrastructures.

The myriad benefits of using Cloudflare extend far beyond simple web performance improvements. They encompass vital security enhance-ments, cost-efficiency, scalability, and administrative ease. By employ-ing Cloudflare, organizations not only increase the speed and reliability of their digital properties but also gain a formidable partner in securing these assets against an ever-growing spectrum of cyber threats.

1.5 Basic Cloudflare Setup

Implementing Cloudflare into your web infrastructure involves a straightforward setup process, yet this integration yields considerable benefits in terms of performance and security. This section provides a detailed walkthrough of the essential steps involved in setting up Cloudflare for a website, accompanied by insightful analysis and detailed code examples where necessary. By understanding the intricacies of this setup, users can maximize the potential of Cloudflare's extensive suite of services.

The initial step in setting up Cloudflare is to create an account on the Cloudflare platform, which is accessible from their official website.

Upon registering and logging into your account, the Cloudflare dashboard serves as the control center, offering users a comprehensive view of their domains and associated settings.

The next phase involves adding a website to your Cloudflare account. By entering your website's domain, Cloudflare automatically scans the existing DNS records associated with that domain. This automated scanning facilitates the integration process by identifying critical records such as A, AAAA, CNAME, MX, and TXT records.

To demonstrate this process, consider a simple addition of a site to Cloudflare using their API. The API provides functionality to add, manage, and configure a domain programmatically.

```
import requests

def add_site_to_cloudflare(api_token, domain_name):
    url = "https://api.cloudflare.com/client/v4/zones"
    headers = {
        "Authorization": f"Bearer {api_token}",
        "Content-Type": "application/json"
    }
    data = {
        "name": domain_name,
        "account": {"id": "your_account_id"},
        "type": "full"
    }
    response = requests.post(url, headers=headers, json=data)
    return response.json()

# Replace 'your_api_token', 'your_account_id', and 'your_domain.com' with actual
    values
response_data = add_site_to_cloudflare("your_api_token", "your_domain.com")
```

In this script, a site is added to Cloudflare using the API through a POST request, establishing the foundation for further configuration.

Once the domain is successfully added to Cloudflare, the next crucial step is updating the DNS nameservers. Cloudflare provides two unique nameservers for each newly added domain. Users need to log into their domain registrar's platform and update their domain's nameserver settings to the ones provided by Cloudflare. This update can take up to 48 hours to propagate fully across global DNS servers, although it often completes much sooner.

By configuring the nameservers correctly, traffic directed at the domain first routes through Cloudflare before reaching the origin server. This configuration is fundamental, as Cloudflare's security and performance features rely on this intermediary positioning.

After DNS propagation, users can begin configuring specific settings within the Cloudflare dashboard. One essential feature enabled by default is SSL/TLS support, which ensures secure data transmission. Cloudflare's flexible SSL options allow users to choose how connections are encrypted between Cloudflare and end users, as well as between Cloudflare and the origin server. These options include Flexible, Full, and Full (strict).

In addition to SSL configuration, users can optimize performance through Cloudflare's "Speed" section in the dashboard. Features like "Auto Minify" compress HTML, CSS, and JavaScript files, reducing file sizes and thereby reducing load times. Another powerful feature, "Rocket Loader", improves page load times by managing the asynchronous loading of all JavaScript resources to ensure efficient rendering without delays.

```
<!-- Example HTML comment demonstrating compressed source code -->
<!-- Use Cloudflare's dashboard to enable Auto Minify for HTML -->
<!DOCTYPE html><html><head><title>Minified Example</title></head><body
    ><h1>Hello, World!</h1></body></html>
```

The HTML snippet reflects how enabling Auto Minify can compress inline HTML code. This reduction ostensibly enhances loading speeds and decreases resource consumption.

Security settings in Cloudflare provide customizable protection against various threats. The Web Application Firewall (WAF) can be configured to protect against OWASP Top 10 vulnerabilities, and the managed rulesets maintain vigilance against newly identified threats. By setting an appropriate security level via the "Firewall" tab, websites can adjust their sensitivity to traffic patterns, ensuring legitimate user access while blocking suspect activities.

Another significant aspect of Cloudflare setup is the Page Rules feature. Page Rules allow users to define nuanced behaviour for URL patterns on their webpage. These rules can modify settings such as redirect logic, caching levels, or security settings based on specific conditions.

```
1. Navigate to the "Page "Rules tab in the Cloudflare dashboard.
2. Click on "Create Page "Rule.
3. Enter the URL pattern: "www.example.com"/*.
4. Choose "Cache Level: Cache "Everything.
5. Select "Forwarding URL" with a 301 redirect (if applicable).
```

6. Click "Save and "Deploy.

The step-by-step guide displays how to establish a page rule for caching every resource under a specified domain. Page rules offer powerful, customizable options that extend the platform's capabilities.

Cloudflare also enables users to leverage analytics for insightful trends and security monitoring. The "Analytics" section of the dashboard provides data on traffic requests, bandwidth usage, threat analysis, and performance improvements. Insights drawn from these analytics aid administrators in making informed adjustments to optimize the efficacy of Cloudflare settings continuously.

Furthermore, one notable feature is the Domain Name System Security Extensions (DNSSEC) availability. Enabling DNSSEC strengthens DNS integrity by ensuring that responses to DNS queries originate from authoritative sources, mitigating the risk of cache poisoning and replay attacks. Enabling DNSSEC involves a validation process between Cloudflare and the domain registrar that requires updating the DNS with specific records.

1. Go to the ""DNS section in Cloudflare dashboard.
2. Find the ""DNSSEC section and click "Enable "DNSSEC.
3. Note the DS record details provided by Cloudflare.
4. Access your domain registrar and input the DS record to complete linkage.

The instructions elucidate enabling DNSSEC, a critical process that solidifies the trust framework underpinning DNS transactions.

Cloudflare's platform supports automation through its Restful API, allowing developers finer control over their setup. Automating DNS updates, record management, or WAF configurations through code streamlines the operational overhead and aligns cloud properties with DevOps practices.

```
import requests

def update_dns_record(zone_id, record_id, api_token, record_name, record_type):
    url = f"https://api.cloudflare.com/client/v4/zones/{zone_id}/dns_records/{
        record_id}"
    headers = {
        "Authorization": f"Bearer {api_token}",
        "Content-Type": "application/json"
    }
    data = {
        "type": record_type,
        "name": record_name,
```

```
        "content": "192.0.2.1",
        "ttl": 3600
    }
    response = requests.put(url, headers=headers, json=data)
    return response.json()

# Update DNS A record
response_data = update_dns_record("zone_id", "record_id", "api_token", "example.
    com", "A")
```

The script illustrates updating a DNS A record via Cloudflare's API. This automation proves invaluable in fast-paced environments or when managing numerous domains.

By thoroughly configuring these settings, users can harness Cloudflare's full potential to create a secure, efficient, and reliable web experience. The synergy between Cloudflare's intuitive dashboard, robust security mechanisms, performance optimizations, and expansive API flexibility empowers administrators to protect and scale their web properties with precision and ease. With careful consideration and strategic implementation, Cloudflare can become an integral component of web management, contributing significantly to a competitive digital presence.

Chapter 2

Understanding DNS and its Role in Cloudflare

This chapter explores the pivotal function of the Domain Name System (DNS) within internet operations, emphasizing its integral role in Cloudflare's service architecture. It provides an in-depth look at DNS components, processes, and functionalities, shedding light on how DNS underpins web accessibility by translating domain names into IP addresses. The chapter further examines how Cloudflare enhances DNS performance and security through advanced features, and guides users through configuring DNS settings within the Cloudflare environment to optimize both site reliability and protection.

2.1 What is DNS?

The Domain Name System (DNS) is a hierarchical and decentralized naming system for computers, services, or any resource connected to the Internet or a private network. It is extensively utilized in mapping human-friendly domain names, such as www.example.com, to the numerical IP addresses needed for locating and identifying computer services and devices with the underlying network protocols. By abstracting away the complex numerical addresses, DNS facilitates easier navigation for internet users.

DNS operates on a distributed database model where each domain is managed by a primary authority. The entire system is a collective, decentralized mechanism composed of millions of distributed domains interconnected through name servers.

The overall architecture of DNS is essential for Internet infrastructure, and it fundamentally consolidates a global network of DNS servers tasked with storing domain name information at various hierarchical levels. This vast network ensures seamless translation of domain names into IP addresses. Each component within the DNS framework is meticulously designed to interact in ways that enhance efficiency and reliability.

DNS functions as a pivotal component of network applications, enabling user-friendly interaction with services scattered across various geographical locations. To understand the functionality of DNS, consider the following critical stages and parts:

- **Domain Names:** Domain names serve as the anchor for DNS operation. They are structured in layers of hierarchy represented as a sequence of labels separated by dots (e.g., *www.example.com*). A typical domain name consists of two primary segments: a top-level domain (TLD), such as *com*, *org*, or *net*, and a second-level domain which is typically the individual or organization's name.

- **DNS Zones and Records:** A DNS zone is a portion of the DNS namespace administered by a specific organization or administrator. The zone file contains mappings of domain names to IP addresses using different record types, such as A (address) records, MX (mail exchange) records, and CNAME (canonical name) records. Each record specifies parameters associated with the domain name.

- **Name Servers:** These are servers specifically designated to re-

30

solve domain names into IP addresses. They are categorized primarily as authoritative or recursive. Authoritative name servers answer queries about domains for which they are responsible. Recursive name servers, on the other hand, handle requests from clients seeking to resolve domain names efficiently, determining the full path to the necessary data.

DNS's complexity lies in its ability to utilize distributed systems to manage these entities on the global scale, overcoming the challenges associated with maintaining a consistent and comprehensive dataset.

The DNS resolution mechanism is a multi-step process that exhibits significant intricacy in executing seemingly instantaneous DNS queries. A typical DNS query progresses through a tiered structure, beginning at the requesting client's device and radiating outward to additional name servers within the DNS chain.

```python
import socket

def resolve_domain_name(domain_name):
    try:
        ip_address = socket.gethostbyname(domain_name)
        print(f"Domain Name: {domain_name}, IP Address: {ip_address}")
    except socket.error as err:
        print(f"Error resolving domain {domain_name}: {err}")

# Example usage
resolve_domain_name('www.example.com')
```

This simple example uses Python to perform a DNS query, converting a domain name into an IP address using the built-in socket library. The function gethostbyname is called to resolve the provided domain name, illustrating the typical process that a user-initiated DNS query might undergo.

The DNS query flow begins with a user entering a domain name into a web browser. The request then propagates through the following stages:

- **Local Cache Resolution:** The initial step checks the client's local DNS cache, where previously queried domain name/IP address combinations might already be stored, enabling expedited resolutions.

- **Resolving Server Query:** If the requested domain isn't found

31

locally, the query moves to a recursive resolver, often maintained by the user's Internet Service Provider (ISP). The recursive resolver searches its cache or reaches out to other DNS servers as needed.

- **Iterative Resolution:** In cases where recursive resolvers lack authoritative information, the query is funneled through multiple name servers in a tiered, iterative process. The query may pass from root name servers to top-level domain name servers (TLD servers), and finally to authoritative name servers until the information is uncovered.

- **Final Resolution and Reply:** Upon gathering the required data, the recursive resolver transmits the resolved IP address back to the client device, which finalizes the request process and permits the client to access the specified web resource via a connection to the resolved IP address.

The importance of DNS to the overall structure of internet protocols cannot be overstated. It enables humans to utilize memorable domain names as a proxy for complex IP addresses that detail the underlying physical network infrastructure. As an integral aspect of networking, DNS must handle a variety of challenges, such as managing high query loads, providing redundancy, and ensuring rapid performance.

DNS also forms the basis for many critical network protocols and is designed to be robust against variable operational loads owing to its distributed architecture. This distributes the processing load across multiple servers, diminishing potential bottlenecks and enhancing fault resilience.

To probe deeper into DNS performance, deeper analysis involves understanding how elements like time-to-live (TTL) values impact cache efficiency, or how DNSSEC (DNS Security Extensions) provides integrity and authenticity to DNS data.

The DNS architecture's adaptability facilitates scalability and operational growth without compromising performance. Innovative features such as anycast routing have been integrated into many DNS systems, allowing multiple servers to share the same IP address, enhancing both redundancy and global response times through geographical distribution. This becomes essential in managing the high query volumes characterizing modern-day DNS traffic.

Given the rising volume of DNS queries and the ever-increasing number of resources connected to the Internet, maintaining DNS system integrity is especially critical. Thus, advanced DNS solutions implement complex algorithms to streamline query resolution, minimize latency, and ensure accuracy in domain name/IP address translations.

DNS remains equally significant in facilitating network security protocols. It plays an enabler role in the implementation of DNSSEC, which enhances security by providing cryptographic verifications of name records. This mitigates vulnerabilities like cache poisoning by ensuring data has not been altered in transit, considering the Internet's ever-evolving threat landscape.

Through understanding DNS's foundational role, one gains a comprehensive view of its operation and necessity within the broader scope of Internet infrastructure, emphasizing the irreplaceable position it holds in translating user intent into actionable network queries.

2.2 DNS Components and Terminology

Understanding the Domain Name System (DNS) necessitates familiarity with its components and a grasp of the associated terminology, which underpin the operational framework of this critical internet infrastructure. DNS functions as a robust, distributed system, tasked with resolving domain names to IP addresses, hence facilitating seamless internet navigation. The structured DNS hierarchy and its key components ensure robust resolution capabilities, providing both scalability and redundancy.

The foremost elements of DNS consist of domains, DNS zones, name servers, and the various record types integral to the system's operation. Each of these components interacts seamlessly to ensure efficient query resolution while managing scaling requirements posed by the ever-expanding internet landscape.

Domain Names: At the core of DNS are domain names, serving as human-friendly identifiers translatable to numerical IP addresses.

Structured as labels segmented by dots, domain names are hierarchical and signal domain relationships from most to least specific. Domain names culminate in top-level domains (TLDs), such as *.com, .org, .net*, or specialized country-code TLDs like *.uk* or *.fr*. The hierarchy in domain names is integral to resolution processes, defining parent-child relationships among domains.

DNS Zones: A DNS zone represents a portion of the DNS namespace managed by an authoritative entity. Zones define domain subsets that are administratively bound into a cohesive management domain. Practical application of DNS zones allows delegation of administrative control, facilitating scalability and distributed management across various geographic or functional boundaries. The zone file comprises definitions for the domains managed within that zone, including name-to-IP mappings and other directives.

Zone Files and Resource Records (RRs): Central to DNS's operation are zone files, which contain a series of resource records (RRs) that define domain relationships or directives such as mappings between domain names and IP addresses. Resource records are composed of fields that specify the domain name, the type of record, possibly associated data, and time-to-live (TTL) values, which dictate caching durations.

Record Types: The versatility of DNS is reflected in the variety of record types it supports, each designed to handle differing lookup needs. Key record types include:

- **A Record:** Maps a domain name to an IPv4 address. Essential for basic domain resolution.

- **AAAA Record:** Associates a domain name with an IPv6 address, essential due to the proliferation of IPv6 adoption.

- **CNAME Record:** Canonical name records permit aliasing of a domain, allowing multiple domain names to map to a single resource.

- **MX Record:** Mail exchange records direct email to mail servers, crucial for orchestrating email services.

- **NS Record:** Name server records indicate which servers are re-

34

sponsible for domain management, thereby defining administrative boundaries.

- **TXT Record:** Permits storage of arbitrary text strings within a domain's dataset; often used for appended metadata or verification data.

- **SOA Record:** The start of authority denotes a zone's origin and introduces metadata, including serial numbers, refresh intervals, and administrator contact information.

The following example utilizes Python's DNS library to query specific DNS record types, illustrating how such queries can be implemented programmatically:

```
import dns.resolver

def query_dns_records(domain_name, record_type):
    try:
        answers = dns.resolver.resolve(domain_name, record_type)
        for answer in answers:
            print(f"{domain_name} {record_type} record: {answer.to_text()}")
    except dns.resolver.NoAnswer:
        print(f"No {record_type} record found for {domain_name}.")
    except Exception as e:
        print(f"Error querying {record_type} record for {domain_name}: {e}")

# Example usages
query_dns_records('example.com', 'A')
query_dns_records('example.com', 'AAAA')
```

Name Servers: DNS relies on meticulously categorized name servers to perform query resolution efficiently. Servers are delineated primarily as:

- **Authoritative Name Servers:** These servers provide definitive answers to DNS queries based on data stored locally. When a query matches a domain managed by an authoritative server, it can confirm the mappings specified.

- **Recursive Name Servers:** These act as intermediaries, receiving queries from clients and systematically interrogating other name servers to return requisite data. Recursive servers are pivotal in caching responses, minimizing resolution times, and optimizing load distribution.

- **Root Name Servers:** Occupying the pinnacle of the DNS hierarchy, these servers direct queries for top-level domains, facilitating DNS navigation by connecting recursive queries to TLD servers.

- **TLD Name Servers:** Top-Level Domain name servers route queries further down into the DNS hierarchy by maintaining records of second-level domain addresses beneath the respective TLD.

The architecture of DNS is inherently layered, with each branch or component designed to facilitate efficient querying throughout the hierarchy. By operating within a multi-layer recursive query path, DNS achieves balance between data availability, query resolution, and security.

DNS Caching: Crucial to DNS performance is the concept of caching, whereby query results are temporarily stored by recursive servers or client systems. This mitigation technique diminishes the need to repeatedly query authoritative servers, thereby reducing latency and server load. TTL values within resource records strictly govern cache duration, ensuring data remains timely while optimizing efficiency.

DNSSEC: To counteract vulnerabilities inherent to traditional DNS, such as cache poisoning or spoofing, DNS Security Extensions (DNSSEC) were introduced. DNSSEC incorporates cryptographic signatures to each response, empowering DNS resolvers to verify data integrity and authenticity. This fundamental upgrade addresses security challenges by ensuring that DNS data received is identifiably untampered.

The broad terms and concepts within DNS contribute to a system both intrinsically scalable and resilient. DNS's continued evolution reflects the adaptation to the demands of web growth, with developments in protocols and technology ensuring its ability to handle increased loads and threats.

As the bedrock of Internet interaction, DNS components and terminology form an intertwined schema, supporting crucial communication processes and enabling the seamless function of web services. By understanding these terms and their interactions, one gains insight into the pivotal role DNS plays within both current and future internet frameworks.

2.3   DNS Resolution Process

The Domain Name System (DNS) resolution process is a fundamental aspect of the internet's infrastructure, serving as a translator between human-readable domain names and machine-understandable IP addresses. This translation enables users to easily access websites without the need to memorize complex numerical IP addresses. The DNS resolution process involves several stages and components, each playing a crucial role in efficiently converting a domain name into its corresponding IP address.

DNS resolution is typically initiated by a query generated by a client's request, such as a web browser needing to resolve the domain name typed into the address bar. This query embarks on a journey through a hierarchy of DNS servers, involving recursive and iterative methods, until the specific record information is obtained.

- **1. Initial Client Request:** The resolution process begins when a user enters a domain name, such as www.example.com, in a web browser. The browser first checks its local cache to see if it has recently resolved this domain name. If a cached record is found and is still valid based on its time-to-live (TTL) value, the browser uses the cached IP address to establish a connection to the server.

- **2. Recursive Resolver Query:** If the domain is not found in the local cache, the browser forwards the query to a recursive resolver, often operated by the user's Internet Service Provider (ISP) or configured third-party DNS providers like Google DNS or Cloudflare DNS. The recursive resolver is responsible for navigating the DNS hierarchy to resolve the query on behalf of the client. The recursive resolver begins this process by checking its own cached data. Should the data not exist or be expired, the resolver must retrieve the information through a set of queries starting at the highest level of the DNS hierarchy.

- **3. Root Name Server Query:** The recursive resolver sends an iterative query to one of the thirteen recognized root name

37

servers. Root servers maintain information about top-level domain (TLD) servers. This query does not immediately resolve the domain but instead guides the resolver towards the appropriate TLD name server by returning a referral to the relevant TLD server.

- **4. TLD Name Server Query:** Upon receiving a referral from the root name server, the recursive resolver queries the appropriate TLD name server. For www.example.com, this would be a .com TLD server. The TLD server does not hold complete information for the domain name but knows where to direct the resolver for more specific details by providing referral records that point to authoritative name servers responsible for the queried domain.

- **5. Authoritative Name Server Query:** The recursive resolver, now equipped with the address of an authoritative name server, queries this server for the specific IP address of the desired domain. An authoritative name server holds complete and definitive answers for domains within its scope of authority — essentially the endpoint for the query process.

- **6. IP Address Retrieval and Finalization:** The authoritative server responds with the requested records, such as the A record for IPv4 addresses or the AAAA record for IPv6 addresses. The recursive resolver caches this information for future queries, subject to the TTL of the records returned, and forwards the address back to the requesting client.

Upon receiving the IP address, the client can initiate a connection to the server hosting the website, thereby completing the DNS resolution process. This entire process is remarkably swift, typically achieving domain resolution within milliseconds, despite the distances and complexities involved.

Coding Example: Simulating DNS Resolution in Python

The Python standard library offers basic DNS resolution capabilities via the socket module, while the dnspython module expands these capabilities considerably, enabling nuanced interactions with DNS records.

```
import dns.resolver
```

```
def dns_resolution(domain):
    # Starting the DNS resolution process
    print(f"Resolving the domain: {domain}")

    # Querying for A record to get the IPv4 address
    try:
        answer = dns.resolver.resolve(domain, 'A')
        for ip in answer:
            print(f"IPv4 address for {domain}: {ip.to_text()}")
    except dns.resolver.NoAnswer:
        print("No A record found.")

    # Querying for the NS record to find authoritative name servers
    try:
        ns_answer = dns.resolver.resolve(domain, 'NS')
        print(f"Authoritative Name Servers for {domain}:")
        for ns in ns_answer:
            print(ns.to_text())
    except dns.resolver.NoAnswer:
        print("No NS record found.")

# Example domain
dns_resolution('example.com')
```

This Python script demonstrates how to resolve a domain name to its corresponding IPv4 address using the dnspython library. It also queries the authoritative name servers, showcasing the two main steps involved in the resolution process.

- **DNS Caching:** Caching is a vital aspect of DNS, helping minimize latency and reduce server load by storing resolved queries temporarily. Both recursive resolvers and client systems employ caching mechanisms to optimize performance. The TTL value specified in DNS records determines how long a cache entry remains valid. Efficient caching significantly improves the user experience by enabling faster domain resolutions.

- **Security Considerations in DNS Resolution:** Protecting the DNS resolution process from attack vectors like cache poisoning and Man-in-the-Middle (MITM) attacks is critical. Cache poisoning involves corrupting a DNS resolver's cached data, potentially redirecting users to malicious sites. DNS Security Extensions (DNSSEC) guard against such exploits by authenticating the origin of DNS data using public key cryptography. DNSSEC ensures that the response received by a resolver has not been altered in transit, preserving data integrity and authenticity.

39

While the DNS resolution process consists of multiple steps and involves numerous entities within the DNS hierarchy, its elegant design ensures comprehensive service delivery. By understanding the nuances involved in DNS resolution, one gains insights into both its fundamental role in internet operations and the challenges it faces, from ensuring efficient performance to securing the integrity of its processes amidst a constantly evolving digital landscape.

2.4   Cloudflare's DNS Features

Cloudflare, an American web infrastructure and website security company, has developed a formidable suite of DNS-related features that enhance website performance, security, and manageability. These offerings cater to a wide range of users, from individual developers to large enterprises, and are designed to address modern internet challenges, such as speed of DNS queries, resistance to attacks, and the need for a reliable and scalable infrastructure.

Cloudflare operates one of the world's largest and fastest global networks, with millions of internet properties across more than 200 cities in over 100 countries, facilitating rapid DNS resolution and delivering a suite of advanced features. These features are aimed at enhancing internet security and performance through various mechanisms, including managed DNS services, DNS Security Extensions (DNSSEC), CNAME flattening, load balancing, and more.

- **Managed DNS Services:** Cloudflare provides a highly reliable and resilient managed DNS service. By leveraging a network capable of handling an enormous volume of DNS queries, Cloudflare ensures that resolution times are kept to an absolute minimum. The service is designed with automatic failover and load balancing to guarantee that queries are answered promptly, even under duress or hardware failures. Cloudflare's DNS edge caches dynamically handle millions of requests per second, which significantly reduces latency.

  An advantage of Cloudflare's managed DNS is the ease of administration. Users can manage their DNS settings through an intuitive web dashboard or programmatically via the Cloudflare API.

40

This versatility allows for seamless domain management, record updates, and configuration changes.

- **DNS Security Features:** DNSSEC is a prominent feature in Cloudflare's security toolkit, ensuring the authenticity and integrity of DNS responses. By signing DNS data with cryptographic signatures, DNSSEC protects against man-in-the-middle attacks and prevents cache poisoning. Cloudflare's support for DNSSEC is straightforward to enable through its dashboard, allowing domain owners to secure their DNS architecture without complex setup processes.

  Cloudflare's DNS security capabilities extend to a suite of features that prevent Distributed Denial of Service (DDoS) attacks. By leveraging its extensive global network, Cloudflare absorbs and mitigates DDoS attacks by distributing the attack load across its infrastructure, preventing concentrated impacts on any single point.

- **CNAME Flattening:** A unique feature offered by Cloudflare is CNAME flattening. In traditional DNS setups, CNAME records cannot exist at the apex of a domain (such as example.com), but only as subdomains (like www.example.com). This is because a CNAME cannot coexist with other record types like NS or MX at the zone apex. CNAME flattening resolves this limitation by returning an IP address directly for non-existent CNAME records at the root, essentially 'flattening' the CNAME into an A record. This process provides more flexibility in domain configuration and prevents potential DNS resolution issues associated with CNAME records.

- **Global Anycast Network:** Cloudflare's DNS service employs an anycast network architecture, meaning that DNS queries are automatically routed to the nearest data center with the capacity to respond. This ensures minimal latency and rapid response times, irrespective of the user's geographical location. Anycast also provides inherent failover capabilities, as queries can seamlessly reroute to alternate sites in the event of a data center experiencing downtime or high traffic loads.

- **Load Balancing and Redundancy:** For businesses requiring resilient and distributed architectures, Cloudflare's DNS service

41

offers advanced traffic load balancing capabilities. By diverting traffic from overwhelmed or unresponsive servers to those available and performing optimally, load balancing significantly improves service reliability.

Cloudflare's traffic steering is customizable, with features such as geographic routing, failover support, and latency-based routing helping optimize the user experience by directing requests according to pre-defined criteria. These advanced controls ensure that content delivery is consistent and reliable globally.

- **DNS Analytics and Insights:** Cloudflare provides DNS analytics, giving users visibility into their DNS traffic patterns. Insights can uncover trends, monitor performance, and reveal unusual activity potentially indicating security breaches or operational issues. Having access to comprehensive analytics tools helps maintain domain integrity and optimize DNS configuration to adapt to changing traffic demands.

Python Script to Interact with Cloudflare API:

Cloudflare offers a robust API enabling programmatic management of DNS records. The following example illustrates how to interact with Cloudflare to list DNS records using Python:

```python
import requests

# Define your Cloudflare API details
api_token = 'your_api_token'
zone_id = 'your_zone_id'

def list_dns_records():
    url = f"https://api.cloudflare.com/client/v4/zones/{zone_id}/dns_records"
    headers = {
        'Authorization': f'Bearer {api_token}',
        'Content-Type': 'application/json',
    }

    response = requests.get(url, headers=headers)

    if response.status_code == 200:
        records = response.json().get('result', [])
        for record in records:
            print(f"Type: {record['type']}, Name: {record['name']}, Content: {record['
                content']}")
    else:
        print(f"Failed to retrieve DNS records: {response.status_code}")

# Fetch and print DNS records
```

42

```
list_dns_records()
```

This script enables listing DNS records for a specified zone in Cloud-flare. By modifying the requests sent to the Cloudflare API, users can manage records with great flexibility, automating tasks like record addition, modification, or removal.

Cloudflare's DNS features extend beyond basic resolution and configuration. Its innovative approaches, rooted in a deep understanding of modern internet challenges, provide users with more than just basic connectivity. They avail a comprehensive toolkit, coupling security with performance and enriching the user experience with flexibility and manageability. With Cloudflare, not only is DNS resolution extremely efficient, but it is fortified to withstand a spectrum of threats, as befits any service underpinning today's digital domains. As Cloudflare continues expanding its services, users benefit from state-of-the-art DNS technologies ensuring secure, fast, and reliable internet new frontiers.

2.5   Configuring DNS with Cloudflare

Configuring DNS with Cloudflare involves setting up and managing DNS records through Cloudflare's comprehensive platform, enabling enhanced performance, security, and manageability for web domains. Cloudflare's user-friendly dashboard and powerful API provide domain administrators the tools necessary to manage their DNS infrastructure effectively, ensuring seamless resolution and robust protection against threats. Utilizing Cloudflare's DNS services also improves website speed through advanced caching and optimization techniques, all within a globally distributed network.

The process of configuring DNS with Cloudflare involves several critical steps that domain owners need to understand and execute precisely. These steps include setting up a Cloudflare account, adding a domain to Cloudflare, configuring DNS records, implementing security features, optimally managing traffic, and leveraging analytical tools for monitoring performance.

1. Setting up a Cloudflare Account: The initial step in utilizing

Cloudflare's DNS services involves creating an account on Cloudflare's platform. This requires registering with a valid email address and creating a secure password. Upon verification of the account, users gain access to Cloudflare's dashboard, from which they can manage and configure DNS settings.

2. Adding a Domain to Cloudflare: Once an account is created, the next action is to add a domain. This involves entering the domain name within the Cloudflare dashboard and following the guided setup process. Cloudflare performs an automatic scan to detect existing DNS records associated with the domain. Users should review these records and make necessary adjustments to ensure they align with the desired configuration.

```python
import requests

api_token = 'your_api_token'
email = 'your_email@example.com'
domain_name = 'example.com'

def add_domain_to_cloudflare():
    url = 'https://api.cloudflare.com/client/v4/zones'
    headers = {
        'X-Auth-Email': email,
        'X-Auth-Key': api_token,
        'Content-Type': 'application/json',
    }
    data = {
        'name': domain_name,
        'jump_start': True
    }

    response = requests.post(url, json=data, headers=headers)

    if response.status_code == 200:
        result = response.json().get('result', {})
        print(f"Domain '{domain_name}' added successfully. Status: {result['status']}")

    else:
        print(f"Failed to add domain: {response.status_code}")

# Adding a domain to Cloudflare
add_domain_to_cloudflare()
```

This script demonstrates how to add a domain to Cloudflare using its API, providing domain administrators with a programmatic approach to cloud-based DNS management.

3. Configuring DNS Records: After the domain is registered with Cloudflare, configuring DNS records is the next task. Common DNS record types include A, AAAA, CNAME, MX, and TXT. Each record type serves specific purposes within the DNS framework. Cloudflare's dashboard allows for easy addition, modification, and removal of these records.

- **A Record:** Maps a domain or subdomain to an IPv4 address. Domain owners often route main domain traffic to a web server using this record type.

- **AAAA Record:** Similar to the A record, but maps to IPv6 addresses, supporting modern networks increasingly adopting IPv6.

- **CNAME Record:** Routes domain traffic to another domain, often favored for subdomains as an alias.

- **MX Record:** Directs email sent to a domain to the correct mail server.

- **TXT Record:** Stores text information, often used for domain verification and providing metadata.

4. Enabling DNS Security Features: Cloudflare supports advanced DNS security features like DNSSEC, which enhances trust in DNS responses by using cryptographic signatures to validate authenticity. Enabling DNSSEC via Cloudflare is straightforward through its dashboard, providing detailed guidance on key management and setup.

5. Optimizing Traffic with Cloudflare: Cloudflare's powerful traffic management features, such as load balancing and Anycast network routing, can significantly enhance user experience by routing traffic optimally. These features help manage heavy loads and ensure that users experience minimal latency regardless of their geographical location. Administrators can define and apply traffic management rules through the Cloudflare interface to meet specific requirements.

6. Monitoring and Analytics: Cloudflare offers analytics tools that provide insights into DNS activity, helping diagnose issues, understand traffic patterns, and identify potential security threats. By leveraging this data, administrators can optimize DNS configurations, identify discrepancies, and make informed decisions to enhance domain performance and security.

Implementing these steps through Cloudflare's interface and API ensures robust control over DNS management, allowing domain owners the flexibility to meet evolving requirements.

Example: Managing DNS Records Programmatically

To illustrate the management of DNS records programmatically, consider a Python script that updates an A record for a domain by interacting with Cloudflare's API:

```python
import requests

api_token = 'your_api_token'
zone_id = 'your_zone_id'
dns_record_id = 'your_dns_record_id'
new_ip = '203.0.113.123'

def update_a_record():
    url = f"https://api.cloudflare.com/client/v4/zones/{zone_id}/dns_records/{
        dns_record_id}"
    headers = {
        'Authorization': f'Bearer {api_token}',
        'Content-Type': 'application/json',
    }
    data = {
        'type': 'A',
        'name': 'example.com',
        'content': new_ip,
        'ttl': 120,
        'proxied': True,
    }

    response = requests.put(url, json=data, headers=headers)

    if response.status_code == 200:
        print(f"A record updated successfully to IP: {new_ip}")
    else:
        print(f"Failed to update A record: {response.status_code}")

# Run the update
update_a_record()
```

This Python script interacts with the Cloudflare API to update an A record, facilitating dynamic DNS management suitable for environments where IP addresses may change or for automating regular updates.

Utilizing Cloudflare's suite of DNS tools delivers comprehensive domain management capabilities to administrators. Its user-friendly

46

platform ensures that the complexities of DNS management are simplified, while still providing robust security measures and performance enhancements. Cloudflare continues to set industry standards, reflecting innovative solutions to meet the demands of a continuously growing and evolving digital landscape, achieving optimal web presence through efficient, secure, and flexible DNS configurations.

2.6   Security Implications of DNS

The Domain Name System (DNS), while an essential component of the internet's infrastructure, is a frequent target for security threats due to its pivotal role in facilitating web activities. DNS is responsible for translating human-friendly domain names into numerical IP addresses that machines use to communicate, making it a fundamental part of the network layer. Yet, its open, distributed nature presents unique challenges and vulnerabilities that can be exploited by malicious actors. Understanding the security implications of DNS is critical for implementing effective defensive measures and ensuring the integrity and availability of DNS services.

- **1. DNS Spoofing (Cache Poisoning):** One of the most notorious DNS vulnerabilities is cache poisoning, or DNS spoofing. This attack involves corrupting the DNS cache of a resolver by providing it with falsified information. When other users query this resolver, they are provided with incorrect IP addresses, redirecting them to malicious servers. Attackers often exploit this to steal sensitive information, deliver malware, or facilitate phishing schemes.

  Mitigating DNS spoofing requires enhancing the security of DNS transactions through mechanisms such as DNS Security Extensions (DNSSEC), which authenticate DNS responses using cryptographic signatures, ensuring that data has not been tampered with during transit.

- **2. Distributed Denial of Service (DDoS) Attacks:** DNS infrastructure can be susceptible to DDoS attacks, where overwhelming numbers of requests flood DNS servers, intending to

47

exhaust resources and render them inoperative. DDoS attacks can heavily impact domain resolution, leading to service unavailability and significant downtime for targeted domains.

Protective measures against DDoS include utilizing advanced DNS services like Cloudflare which incorporate DDoS protection at scale. By leveraging vast, distributed networks, these services can absorb traffic spikes and prevent them from overwhelming individual DNS servers.

- **3. DNS Tunneling:** DNS tunneling involves misusing DNS traffic to covertly pass data or commands. Attackers may encode data within DNS queries and responses, bypassing Internet filtering policies and moving data unnoticed by network security measures. Through this method, hackers can exfiltrate sensitive data or communicate with compromised hosts.

Detection of DNS tunneling requires traffic analysis and anomaly detection techniques, using tools that monitor DNS traffic patterns to identify and block suspicious activity. Effective monitoring coupled with security intelligence systems allows defenders to recognize and mitigate these threats promptly.

- **Example: Monitoring DNS Traffic for Anomalies with Python:**

Monitoring DNS logs for unusual patterns can help identify potential security threats. The following example demonstrates how to parse DNS query logs using Python to detect anomalies:

```python
import re

def parse_dns_logs(log_file):
    pattern = re.compile(r'(\d+\.\d+\.\d+\.\d+) .* query: ([^\s]+) ')
    with open(log_file, 'r') as logs:
        suspicious_queries = {}
        for line in logs:
            match = pattern.search(line)
            if match:
                ip, domain = match.groups()
                if domain.endswith('.xyz') or 'malicious' in domain:
                    suspicious_queries.setdefault(ip, []).append(domain)

    for ip, queries in suspicious_queries.items():
        print(f"Suspicious activity from IP {ip}:")
        for domain in queries:
            print(f" - {domain}")
```

48

```
# Assuming 'dns_logs.txt' contains DNS query logs
parse_dns_logs('dns_logs.txt')
```

This script parses a DNS log file, identifying queries to suspicious domains based on heuristics, such as unexpected TLDs or known malicious keywords, which might indicate potential tunneling or infiltration efforts.

- **4. Man-In-The-Middle (MITM) Attacks:** In a DNS MITM attack, an attacker intercepts communication between a client and the DNS resolver, substituting genuine responses with falsified ones. Successful attacks can redirect users to counterfeit sites, facilitating data theft or malware distribution. DNSSEC is an effective countermeasure, providing authentication for DNS responses and negating MITM threats by ensuring DNS data integrity.

- **5. DNS Amplification Attacks:** A form of reflection-based DDoS attack, DNS amplification exploits the disparity between query and response sizes. Attackers transmit smaller queries spoofing the victim's IP to open DNS resolvers, which respond with significantly larger payloads. This reflection attack overwhelms the victim through sheer data volume.

  Defending against amplification attacks involves configuring DNS servers to reject requests from open, unauthenticated sources and employing rate limiting and network-level filtering. Leveraging secure DNS resolvers with built-in safeguards further mitigates this threat.

- **Cloudflare's Role in Securing DNS:** Cloudflare offers a comprehensive suite of DNS security features designed to combat these vulnerabilities. Its DNSSEC support safeguards against tampering, ensuring that users receive accurate, tamper-free DNS responses. Additionally, Cloudflare's protective DNS resolvers are leveraged to absorb and deflect DDoS attacks directed at DNS infrastructures, ensuring both performance and uptime are maintained during attacks.

  By integrating global threat intelligence and AI-powered detection into their infrastructure, Cloudflare dynamically identifies

49

emerging threats and adapts its defenses, maintaining robust protection for domains subscribed to its services.

- **Implementing DNS Security Best Practices:**

  - **Enable DNSSEC:** Ensures the authenticity and integrity of DNS data, which is crucial for defending against several forms of DNS attacks.

  - **Use Reputable Managed DNS Services:** Providers like Cloudflare offer built-in security features that protect against DDoS and other threats.

  - **Regularly Monitor DNS Traffic:** Implement log monitoring tools to detect abnormal patterns, indicative of potential security breaches.

  - **Harden DNS Infrastructure:** Use firewalls and IDS/IPS to guard DNS servers and segment network traffic to reduce attack surfaces.

  - **Educate Users:** Inform clients and employees about phishing risks and safe browsing practices to prevent inadvertent exploitation.

The security implications of DNS underscore the importance of rigorous defense strategies to safeguard this critical component of internet infrastructure. By implementing robust DNS security measures and leveraging solutions offered by leaders like Cloudflare, organizations can protect their domains from prevalent threats, ensuring the integrity and availability of their web services while maintaining user trust. The dynamic nature of these challenges dictates that constant vigilance and adaptation remain central to DNS security practices, as the landscape of cyber threats continues to evolve.

Chapter 3

Cloudflare Security Features and Implementation

This chapter offers a detailed examination of Cloudflare's robust security features, which are designed to safeguard web applications from a plethora of online threats. It discusses the implementation of essential security tools such as the Web Application Firewall (WAF), SSL/TLS encryption, and bot management controls. By understanding these features, users will learn how to effectively configure their security settings in Cloudflare, reinforcing their web environments against vulnerabilities and ensuring data integrity. Furthermore, the chapter provides insights into advanced security practices, enhancing awareness and response capabilities to potential cyber threats.

3.1   Overview of Cloudflare Security

Cloudflare is a widely recognized platform that plays a critical role in enhancing the security posture of web applications by providing innovative and robust security solutions. At the core of Cloudflare's offering is a suite of services that provide protection against a multitude of online threats, thereby ensuring the integrity, availability, and confidentiality of web applications. This section provides a comprehensive overview of these security services, emphasizing the mechanisms through which Cloudflare fortifies websites against numerous potential vulnerabilities.

Cloudflare operates a global network designed to calibrate and deploy security measures against a vast array of threats. Its distributed nature allows it to efficiently filter malicious traffic, ensuring that legitimate user requests are processed while malicious attempts are thwarted. The potency of Cloudflare's security measures can be attributed to its in-depth threat intelligence, which stems from its extensive network, handling massive volumes of internet traffic daily.

- One of the fundamental aspects of Cloudflare's security apparatus is its ability to provide protection against Distributed Denial of Service (DDoS) attacks. These attacks aim to render services unavailable by overwhelming them with a flood of illegitimate requests. Cloudflare's network is capable of absorbing and mitigating such distributed attacks by leveraging its vast infrastructure to distribute the request load, thus ensuring service continuity. At the core of this defense mechanism is the ability to dynamically adjust the filtering criteria based on real-time threat analysis.

- Equally important is Cloudflare's Web Application Firewall (WAF), which monitors and filters HTTP traffic between a web application and the Internet. The WAF protects against numerous attack vectors, such as SQL injection, cross-site scripting (XSS), and other OWASP Top 10 threats. This is achieved through a set of configurable rules that allow for adaptive responses to novel threat patterns.

- Transport Layer Security (TLS) is crucial for securing data in transit. Cloudflare's implementation of SSL/TLS ensures that all data exchanged between users and servers is encrypted, providing confidentiality and integrity against eavesdropping and data tampering. Cloudflare offers Flexible, Full, and Strict modes of SSL verification, which provide varying levels of encryption to accommodate diverse security requirements of web applications.

Below is an example of how SSL/TLS settings can be configured to enforce secure communications:

```
# Command to generate a certificate signing request (CSR)
openssl req -new -newkey rsa:2048 -nodes -keyout cloudflare.key -out cloudflare.csr
```

This command generates a CSR and a 2048-bit RSA private key, which are essential in obtaining an SSL certificate from a Certificate Authority (CA). Cloudflare further simplifies certificate management by automating renewal processes and providing support for advanced configurations such as Origin CA and Full (Strict) mode.

- An integral component of maintaining application integrity is controlling bot activity. Malicious bots can perform unauthorized actions, such as scraping data, attempting brute-force logins, or executing DDoS attacks. Cloudflare's Bot Management utilizes machine learning algorithms to differentiate between legitimate bots, such as search engine crawlers, and malicious ones, enabling precise and adaptive mitigation strategies.

The ability to leverage machine learning is manifested in the following pattern recognition approach:

```
# Example of a simple bot detection algorithm
from sklearn.cluster import KMeans

def is_bot_activity(ip_requests):
    model = KMeans(n_clusters=2)
    model.fit(ip_requests)
    labels = model.labels_
    return sum(labels) > (len(labels) // 2)
```

This illustrative example shows how clustering algorithms can be utilized to identify anomalies in request patterns, thus flagging potential bot activity. Cloudflare's advanced analytics further refine these approaches by integrating extensive threat intelligence data aggregated globally.

53

- Rate limiting is a proactive measure employed by Cloudflare that controls request frequency from unique users, mitigating threat vectors such as brute-force attempts and API abuse. Through user-defined rules, it is possible to fine-tune the threshold levels to strike a balance between security and user experience.

The implementation of rate limiting may include defining custom thresholds as follows:

```
# Define a simple rate limiting logic
class RateLimiter:
    def __init__(self, calls_per_minute):
        self.calls_per_minute = calls_per_minute
        self.last_called = {}

    def is_allowed(self, user_id):
        current_time = time.time()
        if user_id in self.last_called:
            elapsed_time = current_time - self.last_called[user_id]
            if elapsed_time > 60 / self.calls_per_minute:
                self.last_called[user_id] = current_time
                return True
        else:
            self.last_called[user_id] = current_time
            return True
        return False
```

This code snippet illustrates a basic implementation of a rate limiter which ensures that calls from a user are limited in a time-bound manner, reflecting a straightforward rule that Cloudflare might enhance with its extensive infrastructure and analytics.

- Cloudflare provides extensive logging capabilities, which serve as a cornerstone for security analysis. Logs offer valuable insights into access patterns, attack attempts, and system performance. By leveraging Cloudflare logs, administrators can perform deep forensics, identifying trends or behaviors indicative of advanced persistent threats (APT).

These logs are structured to facilitate parsing and can be integrated into Security Information and Event Management (SIEM) systems for continuous monitoring and enhanced incident response:

```
# Example of command to tail logs for monitoring
tail -f /var/log/cloudflare/security.log | grep "THREAT"
```

The aforementioned command demonstrates real-time extraction of potential threats from security logs, a typical part of routine security operations.

Cloudflare's comprehensive approach to security includes other robust features such as secure origin protection and edge certificate management, ensuring that public-facing interfaces are only part of an extensive, integrated security posture. The dynamic capabilities of Cloudflare to preemptively address security concerns and mitigate ongoing threats underscore its position as a leader in cloud-based security solutions for web applications.

3.2   Web Application Firewall (WAF)

The Web Application Firewall (WAF) provided by Cloudflare is an essential component of the comprehensive suite of security tools aimed at protecting web applications from a broad spectrum of attack vectors. The WAF is a sophisticated security mechanism designed to inspect and filter HTTP traffic traveling to and from a web service, thereby safeguarding applications against malicious activities, such as SQL injection, cross-site scripting (XSS), and other exploits categorized under the OWASP Top 10 vulnerabilities. This section elucidates the intricacies of how Cloudflare's WAF operates, detailing its configuration, rulesets, and effectiveness in fortifying web applications.

The fundamental purpose of a WAF is to serve as a barrier between web applications and end-users, analyzing incoming requests to identify and block potential threats before they can reach the application server. Cloudflare's WAF is particularly powerful due to its ability to leverage a globally distributed network for comprehensive threat detection and its use of real-time threat intelligence to adapt to emerging security challenges.

- **Architecture and Functionality**

  Cloudflare's WAF operates as part of a layered security model, filtering traffic at the edge of its network before it reaches the origin server. The architecture of the WAF involves both static and dynamic rule sets, which include pre-configured rules based on known vulnerabilities and the ability to customize rules to address unique threats specific to a web application's deployment.

The inspection process primarily involves deep packet inspection (DPI), whereby each incoming data packet is thoroughly analyzed. The WAF utilizes signature-based, anomaly-based, and behavior-based detection mechanisms in unison to identify malevolent payloads embedded within HTTP requests.

Below is an example of defining a regex-based rule for detecting SQL injection attempts:

```
# Example of a WAF rule to block common SQL injection payloads
SecRule REQUEST_URI "@rx select.*from.*users" "id:1001,phase:1,deny,
    status:403,msg:'SQL Injection Detected'"
```

The rule effectively inspects the URL of incoming requests for patterns notoriously used in SQL injection attacks and takes corrective action by denying the request and logging the incident for further analysis.

- **Rule Management and Customization**

The ability to manage and customize rule sets is a hallmark of Cloudflare's WAF. Users can enable or disable specific rules based on their threat landscape and compliance requirements. The WAF supports custom rules written in a manner that aligns with ModSecurity syntax, a widely adopted standard in the field of web application security.

An example illustrating this modularity is the creation of a custom rule to prevent XSS attacks:

```
# Custom WAF rule to block typical XSS attack vectors
SecRule ARGS "<script>" "id:1002,phase:2,deny,status:403,msg:'XSS
    Attempt Detected'"
```

This rule scans incoming request parameters for the presence of embedded script tags, which are a common vector for XSS attacks, and consequently blocks requests that contain such payloads.

- **Managed Rulesets and Adaptive Security**

Cloudflare's WAF includes access to a comprehensive managed ruleset library that capitalizes on regularly updated threat intelligence. These rulesets encompass a broad range of signatures for

56

known vulnerabilities and exploit patterns, offering robust protection against zero-day vulnerabilities as they are identified in the wild.

In addition to static signatures, the WAF employs machine learning algorithms to adaptively update its rules based on evolving threat patterns. The adaptive capabilities facilitate proactive defense against novel attack vectors not yet cataloged in traditional rule bases.

- **Performance and Scalability**

  Performance is a significant consideration for any web security implementation. Cloudflare's WAF is optimized to minimize latency, ensuring that security checks do not impede application performance. The WAF leverages Cloudflare's edge network infrastructure to distribute the processing load, allowing inspections to be handled swiftly at locations geographically close to the end-users, thus reducing round-trip times.

  Furthermore, the scalability of Cloudflare's WAF is evident in its ability to handle billions of requests daily without degrading performance. This scalability ensures that irrespective of the size of the web application or the volume of traffic, Cloudflare's WAF can maintain effective security protocols.

- **Integration and Automation**

  Integration of Cloudflare's WAF into existing DevOps workflows can be managed seamlessly via its robust API. Automation of rule deployments, log analysis, and incident response can thus be efficiently orchestrated, promoting an agile security operations framework. Infrastructure as Code (IaC) strategies can incorporate WAF configurations, favoring consistent and repeatable deployment practices.

  An illustrative example of utilizing Cloudflare's API to automate the enabling of a specific WAF rule is provided below:

```
import requests

# Enable a specific WAF rule via Cloudflare's API
API_TOKEN = 'exampleToken'
ZONE_ID = 'exampleZoneId'
RULE_ID = 'exampleRuleId'
```

```
url = f"https://api.cloudflare.com/client/v4/zones/{ZONE_ID}/firewall/
    waf/packages/{RULE_ID}"
headers = {
    "Authorization": f"Bearer {API_TOKEN}",
    "Content-Type": "application/json"
}

payload = {"mode": "on"}

response = requests.patch(url, json=payload, headers=headers)

print(response.json())
```

This example demonstrates how Python and Cloudflare's API can automate security policy adjustments, thus reducing manual overhead and potential human errors.

- **Monitoring and Reporting**

  Continuous monitoring and detailed reporting are crucial aspects of maintaining an effective security posture. Cloudflare's WAF provides access to extensive analytics that offers insights into traffic patterns, detected threats, and the effectiveness of security policies.

  ```
  # Example command to extract specific WAF events from logs
  grep "XSS Attempt Detected" /var/log/cloudflare/waf.log
  ```

  This command filters log entries to highlight detected XSS attempts, aiding in forensic analysis and alerting security teams to ongoing attack campaigns. Integration with SIEM tools extends the monitoring capabilities to enable real-time detection and response.

- **Adaptive Countermeasures and Incident Response**

  Finally, in the event of a security incident, Cloudflare's WAF can be configured to implement adaptive countermeasures, including rate limiting, IP address blacklisting, and geographical blocking, to prevent further exploitation of vulnerabilities. Efficient incident response necessitates a well-coordinated plan supported by automation tools to rapidly neutralize threats and restore normal operations, minimizing potential damage and service disruption.

The aforementioned features of Cloudflare's WAF demonstrate its critical role in defending modern web applications against malicious entities, thus reinforcing the overall security architecture. Its ability to provide protective measures that scale with application demands, alongside its adaptability and integration capabilities, make Cloudflare's WAF an indispensable tool in the security arsenal of enterprises globally.

3.3 SSL/TLS Encryption and Management

The significance of Secure Sockets Layer (SSL) and Transport Layer Security (TLS) in securing online communications cannot be overstated. These protocols establish a secure channel for data transmission over the internet, ensuring confidentiality, integrity, and authenticity of data exchange between clients and servers. Cloudflare's deployment of SSL/TLS provides robust security features that facilitate seamless encryption, certificate issuance, and management across its vast network infrastructure. This section delves into the details of SSL/TLS encryption as implemented by Cloudflare, examining the protocols, configurations, and management techniques that underpin secure communications.

- **Understanding SSL/TLS Fundamentals**

  SSL and its successor, TLS, are cryptographic protocols that use a combination of asymmetric and symmetric encryption to secure data exchanges. During a typical SSL/TLS handshake, which is initiated when a client connects to a server, several critical steps occur:

  - Negotiation of Protocol Version: The client and server agree on the highest version of SSL/TLS they both support.

  - Cipher Suite Agreement: Both parties select a cipher suite, a set of algorithms that will be used for encryption, key exchange, and message authentication.

  - Authentication and Pre-Master Secret Exchange: The server provides a digital certificate to authenticate its identity. If verified, a pre-master secret, encrypted with the server's public key, is sent by the client.

— Session Key Generation: The pre-master secret is used by both parties to generate session keys for encrypting data.

— Secure Data Transmission: Finally, the client and server use the agreed-upon algorithms and keys to encrypt and decrypt data.

- **Cloudflare's Encryption Modes**

Cloudflare offers different SSL/TLS encryption modes catering to varying security needs and legacy compatibility:

— Flexible SSL: Encrypts traffic between the client and Cloudflare, but not between Cloudflare and the origin server. Suitable for environments where full end-to-end encryption is not feasible.

— Full SSL: Ensures that encryption is maintained between both the client-Cloudflare and Cloudflare-origin server connections, requiring at least a self-signed certificate at the origin.

— Full (Strict) SSL: Mandates the use of a validated certificate on the origin server, providing the highest level of security by verifying server authenticity.

- **Certificate Issuance and Management**

Cloudflare simplifies certificate management through its Origin CA service, allowing for the issuance of certificates directly from its dashboard. This service automates certificate lifecycle events such as issuance and renewal, thus reducing administrative overhead and ensuring continuous security.

Example command to generate a certificate request using OpenSSL:

```
openssl req -new -newkey rsa:2048 -nodes -keyout origin.key -out origin.csr
```

The command generates a 2048-bit RSA private key and a certificate signing request (CSR), the latter of which is needed to obtain a certificate from a Certificate Authority.

Cloudflare supports advanced certificate configurations such as SAN (Subject Alternative Name) and wildcard certificates, allowing multiple domain/subdomain protection under a single certificate, optimizing management and cost efficiency.

- **TLS Configuration Best Practices**

  To ensure optimal security, it is crucial to follow TLS configuration best practices, which include:

  - Protocol Versioning: Preferentially disable obsolete protocols (e.g., SSLv2, SSLv3) and promote the use of modern versions like TLS 1.2 and TLS 1.3.
  - Cipher Suite Selection: Opt for cipher suites that offer forward secrecy and eschew those with known vulnerabilities. Recommended cipher suites typically include AES 256 GCM and ChaCha20 Poly1305.
  - Certificate Transparency: Utilize tools like Certificate Transparency (CT) logs to monitor newly issued certificates, detecting misissuance promptly.

- **Enhancing Security with HTTP/2 and HSTS**

  The adoption of HTTP/2 protocol by Cloudflare enhances performance through multiplexing and header compression while maintaining encrypted connections. Further bolstering secure communications, HTTP Strict Transport Security (HSTS) can be enabled, instructing browsers to initiate connections only over HTTPS, thus preventing downgrade attacks.

  The following example demonstrates how to enable HSTS via Cloudflare's dashboard or API:

```
{
    "strict_transport_security": {
        "enforce": true,
        "max_age": 31536000,
        "includeSubdomains": true,
        "preload": true
    }
}
```

  This configuration enforces HSTS with a max age directive of one year and preloads instructions for browser compliance.

61

- **TLS 1.3 and Future Protocols**

  TLS 1.3 represents a significant advancement in cryptographic protocols, designed to expedite handshakes while eliminating antiquated features susceptible to vulnerabilities. Cloudflare's early adoption of TLS 1.3 embodies its commitment to leveraging cutting-edge technologies to enhance security. Benefits of TLS 1.3 include reduced handshake latency and streamlined cipher suites, promoting robust communications without compromising on speed or user experience.

- **Monitoring and Analytics**

  Robust monitoring tools and detailed analytics are vital for maintaining secure TLS deployments. Cloudflare provides real-time visibility into SSL analytics, traffic patterns, and detects irregularities that may signify attacks such as Man-in-the-Middle (MitM) attempts.

  Below is a simple method to filter suspicious SSL handshake failures from server logs:

  ```
  grep "SSL handshake failure" /var/log/nginx/error.log
  ```

  This command highlights handshake failures, which may warrant further investigation into potential compromised connections.

- **Automating Security with Cloudflare's API**

  Automation is a pillar for managing dynamic security landscapes efficiently. Cloudflare's RESTful API grants programmatic access to SSL configurations, certificate management, and other security features, fostering an environment where Infrastructure as Code (IaC) principles can thrive.

  Example showing the automation of SSL/TLS settings through Cloudflare's API:

  ```
  import requests

  API_TOKEN = 'exampleToken'
  ZONE_ID = 'exampleZoneId'

  headers = {
      "Authorization": f"Bearer {API_TOKEN}",
  ```

```
    "Content-Type": "application/json"
}

url = f"https://api.cloudflare.com/client/v4/zones/{ZONE_ID}/settings/ssl
   "
response = requests.patch(url, json={"value": "full"}, headers=headers)

print(response.json())
```

This Python snippet showcases modifying the SSL mode to "full," ensuring end-to-end encryption.

- **Challenges and Future Directions in SSL/TLS**

  Despite its robustness, SSL/TLS is not impervious to threats. Attack vectors such as SSL Stripping, Logjam, and BEAST exploit implementation weaknesses or rely on downgrading attacks to bypass encryption mechanisms. Constant vigilance and adherence to best practices are imperative, alongside the continuous evolution of the SSL/TLS protocol to address new vulnerabilities.

  Cloudflare's proactive approach in integrating emerging technologies and security insights ensures that it remains at the forefront of secure communication innovation. By embracing concepts such as quantum-safe cryptography and Zero Trust architectures, Cloudflare is well-positioned to confront future challenges in data encryption and transmission.

  Cloudflare's implementation of SSL/TLS encryption embodies a comprehensive strategy to safeguard web communications. Through strategic certificate management, adherence to best practices, and integration of the latest cryptographic advancements, Cloudflare provides an unparalleled encryption solution that fosters secure interactions in a continuously evolving digital ecosystem.

3.4   Bot Management and Mitigation

In the digital age, automated bots have become an intrinsic part of internet operations, performing tasks such as indexing content for search engines, monitoring web performance, and executing scraping scripts.

While many bots are benign and useful, a significant number are malicious, posing threats to web security, integrity, and performance. Malicious bots conduct activities like credential stuffing, data scraping, and Distributed Denial of Service (DDoS) attacks, which necessitate effective bot management and mitigation strategies. This section delves into the sophisticated mechanisms employed by Cloudflare to identify, manage, and mitigate malicious bot traffic, safeguarding the health and security of web applications.

- **Understanding the Bot Landscape**

To effectively manage bots, it is crucial to distinguish between good bots, like web crawlers from legitimate search engines, and malicious bots that execute harmful activities. Malicious bots are often programmed to mimic human behavior and circumvent basic detection methods, leveraging complex arbitrations to access protected resources unlawfully.

Malicious bot traffic can execute serious impacts, including:

- Credential Stuffing: Bots systematically attempt username-password combinations to hijack accounts.

- Web Scraping: Bots voraciously harvest data, which could be utilized or sold for competitive advantage.

- Denial of Service: Bots flood a service with requests, overwhelming it and rendering it inoperable to legitimate users.

- **Cloudflare's Bot Management Architecture**

Cloudflare's bot management framework integrates robust methodologies and intelligent algorithms to identify and handle automated threats. The architecture relies on machine learning models and fingerprinting techniques to discern bot traffic patterns from legitimate requests.

- Challenge-Based Approach: Using challenge-response mechanisms like CAPTCHA, where users must confirm their humanness before accessing resources.

- Behavioral Analysis: Monitoring request patterns, interaction timings, and navigational paths to classify traffic.

- Traffic Fingerprinting: Utilizing device and network configurations to identify unique client signatures.

- **Machine Learning for Bot Detection**

Machine learning (ML) is a cornerstone technology in identifying malicious bots. Cloudflare uses ML to develop models that autonomously classify traffic based on historical and real-time data analysis.

Here is a simplified example illustrating the application of a supervised learning algorithm for bot detection:

```python
from sklearn.ensemble import RandomForestClassifier
import numpy as np

# Sample dataset containing traffic features and labels
features = np.array([[0.2, 1, 35], [0.8, 0, 10], [0.3, 1, 40]])
labels = np.array([0, 1, 0]) # 0 - Legitimate, 1 - Bot

# Train model
classifier = RandomForestClassifier()
classifier.fit(features, labels)

# Predicting new traffic type
new_request = np.array([[0.5, 0, 15]])
prediction = classifier.predict(new_request)
print("Bot detected" if prediction[0] else "Legitimate request")
```

This snippet demonstrates a basic example where Random Forest classification distinguishes between bot and legitimate traffic based on selected attributes.

- **Layered Defense Mechanism**

Cloudflare deploys a layered defense strategy balancing security with user experience, which includes:

- Edge Filtering: Mitigation begins at the network edge, blocking overtly malicious requests before they consume application resources.

65

- Rate Limiting: Implementing thresholds to limit the frequency of requests from a given IP, effectively mitigating account takeovers and scraping attempts.

- JavaScript Challenges: Deploying unobtrusive challenges to track client-side executions, discerning between headless browsers and genuine browsers.

- **Traffic Annotation and Scoring**

Cloudflare provides an annotation system that assigns a "bot score" to incoming requests. This score uses a range scaled from 0 to 100, indicating the likelihood that a request originates from a bot. Scores enable dynamic decision-making, where policies can be configured to take actions based on the assessed risk.

A potential implementation of conditional logic based on a bot score might be:

```
def analyze_request(score):
    if score > 80:
        return "Deny Request"
    elif 40 < score <= 80:
        return "Challenge User"
    else:
        return "Allow Access"

# Example request with a calculated bot score
request_score = 75
action = analyze_request(request_score)
print("Action to perform:", action)
```

This function implements logic to automatically determine access control decisions according to bot risk scores.

- **Real-Time Monitoring and Analytics**

Monitoring and analytics are central to effective bot management. Cloudflare provides real-time dashboards that facilitate the tracking and analysis of traffic flow, behavior anomalies, and bot engagement.

Administrators can leverage these insights to refine policies, enhance model training data quality, and respond promptly to evolving threats.

- **Integration with Existing Security Infrastructure**

Cloudflare's bot management services integrate seamlessly with ongoing security infrastructures, complementing existing WAFs and SIEM systems. This integration permits enriched threat intelligence sharing across platforms, reinforcing security postures.

Here's an example of exporting bot data for integration with external analytics tools:

```
curl -X GET "https://api.cloudflare.com/client/v4/zones/[zone_id]/logs/requests" \
-H "Authorization: Bearer [api_token]" \
-G --data-urlencode "fields=date,requestSource,botscore"
```

The command gathers logs enriched with annotations suitable for downstream analysis and processing.

• Adaptive Countermeasures and User Education

Adaptive countermeasures play a vital role in dynamically responding to bot threats. Cloudflare has instituted various real-time actions contingent on the classification of traffic, from temporary rate limiting to persistent IP banning for repeat offenders.

An often-overlooked element in bot management is the education of end-users and security personnel about the latest bot strategies and responses. By upskilling stakeholders, organizations can foster a more prepared stance against automated threats.

• Ethical Considerations and Privacy

Managing bots also necessitates navigating ethical boundaries. It is crucial to respect user privacy and to differentiate between benign automation and truly malicious activity. Legal compliance with data protection regulations is mandatory when processing vast swaths of internet traffic, ensuring transparency and accountability.

• Future Directions and Innovations

The landscape of bot management is continually transforming, demanding novel solutions to counter complex evolutions in bot behavior. Innovations in machine learning, enhanced identity verification techniques, and blockchain-based certifications provide fertile ground for research and development.

By committing to vendor-agnostic infrastructures and fostering greater cooperation within the industry, stakeholders can enact more potent measures to sustainably mitigate bot threats.

Cloudflare's proactive and adaptive approaches to bot management and mitigation substantially empower organizations to protect their digital estates while maintaining legitimate user engagement. As the landscape of threats continues to evolve, Cloudflare remains vigilant in progressing its suite of defensive mechanisms to address these challenges effectively.

3.5   Rate Limiting and Access Control

In the domain of cybersecurity, rate limiting and access control are fundamental strategies employed to protect web applications from malicious traffic and ensure stability in service delivery. Cloudflare's implementation of these mechanisms is designed to provide robust protection against Distributed Denial of Service (DDoS) attacks, brute-force assaults, and exploit attempts, as well as to enforce policy compliance across diverse use cases. This section explores the intricacies of Cloudflare's rate limiting and access control features, providing technical insights into their configurations, applications, and effectiveness.

Understanding Rate Limiting   Rate limiting is a technique employed to regulate the rate at which requests are allowed to proceed to a web application, based on predefined thresholds. By limiting the number of requests from users or destinations, rate limiting acts to mitigate abuse while ensuring that resources are fairly distributed among legitimate users.

Key goals of rate limiting include:

- Mitigating DDoS Attacks: By curbing excessive requests, rate limiting helps prevent the overloading of servers.

- Preventing Brute-Force Attempts: Limiting authentication attempts stymies attackers trying to exploit login endpoints.

- Controlling API Abuse: Safeguarding API endpoints from being overwhelmed by non-compliant client activities.

Configuring Rate Limiting with Cloudflare Cloudflare allows for precise configuration of rate limiting rules through its web interface and API, making the creation of customized limits straightforward. Administrators can establish criteria based on the number of requests over a specified period from unique client IP addresses.

Example Python script to create and apply a rate limit rule using Cloudflare's API:

```python
import requests

# Configuration details
API_TOKEN = 'exampleToken'
ZONE_ID = 'exampleZoneId'
headers = {
    "Authorization": f"Bearer {API_TOKEN}",
    "Content-Type": "application/json"
}

rate_limit_rule = {
    "disabled": False,
    "description": "Rate limit for login endpoint",
    "threshold": 10,
    "period": 60,
    "action": {
        "mode": "simulate",
        "timeout": 0
    },
    "match": {
        "request": {
            "methods": ["POST"],
            "url": "https://example.com/login"
        }
    }
}

url = f"https://api.cloudflare.com/client/v4/zones/{ZONE_ID}/rate_limits"
response = requests.post(url, json=rate_limit_rule, headers=headers)

print(response.json())
```

This script creates a rate limit rule that simulates limiting requests to 10 per minute for the login endpoint, assisting administrators in fine-tuning limits before implementation.

Advanced Threshold Logic and Granularity Granular control over rate limiting is paramount for tuning performance and security. Cloudflare offers the capability to apply rate limits with various levels of granularity, including IP addresses, subnets, and more.

Advanced logic may also employ dynamic thresholds adjusted in response to prevailing threat levels, converting static policies into adaptive defenses. This is achieved through integration with monitoring systems that collect and process traffic pattern data, systematically adjusting limits in real-time.

Access Control Mechanisms Access control is the selective restriction of access to a system or resource, often governed through policies outlining who, how, and when data can be accessed. While rate limiting provides quantitative control, access control enforces qualitative restrictions, ensuring that only authorized entities can interact with sensitive application interfaces.

Core elements of access control strategies include:

- Role-Based Access Control (RBAC): Assigns permissions based on user roles, thereby minimizing exposure.

- Discretionary Access Control (DAC): Empowers users to determine the sharing of their resources.

- Mandatory Access Control (MAC): Enforces strict rules set by an administrator, critical for environments with stringent security requirements.

Implementing Access Control with Cloudflare Through Cloudflare's firewall and access control features, organizations can define and enforce policies that regulate traffic based on various attributes such as geographical location, threat reputation, and the presence of specific request headers or cookies.

Example of firewall rules configured to restrict access based on GeoIP:

```
firewall_rule = {
    "action": "block",
    "description": "Block access from specific countries",
    "filter": {
```

```
        "expression": "(ip.geoip.country in {'CN', 'RU'})"
    }
}

url = f"https://api.cloudflare.com/client/v4/zones/{ZONE_ID}/firewall/rules"
response = requests.post(url, json=firewall_rule, headers=headers)

print(response.json())
```

The rule effectively blocks incoming requests originating from China or Russia while allowing traffic from other regions, thus enhancing security posture based on geographical considerations.

Integration with Identity and Access Management (IAM) Integration between Cloudflare and existing IAM systems is critical for enforcing access control policies comprehensively. By leveraging identity providers (IdP) such as Okta, Azure Active Directory, or other SAML-compliant solutions, organizations can harmonize access controls across all facets of their infrastructure.

Integrations typically include:

- Single Sign-On (SSO): Centralizes authentication, simplifies user management, and improves integration security.

- Multi-Factor Authentication (MFA): Bolsters security by requiring additional verification methods.

Monitoring and Analytics in Rate Limiting and Access Control Monitoring tools are indispensable for tracking the effectiveness of rate limiting and access control measures. Cloudflare provides real-time analytics and log exports that allow for extensive data analysis, which aids in adjusting controls and enhancing strategic response capabilities.

Log analysis example filtering blocked requests:

```
grep "blocked by firewall" /var/log/cloudflare/access.log
```

This command examines log files to single out entries concerning blocked requests, offering insights into the nature and frequency of unauthorized access attempts.

71

Challenges and Best Practices   The implementation of rate limiting and access controls does not come without its challenges, including the risk of incorrectly configured policies that can inadvertently disrupt legitimate traffic. Therefore, adopting best practices is paramount:

- Continuous Testing: Simulate attacks to validate and refine rule effectiveness without locking out authorized users.

- Incremental Deployment: Implement policies gradually, allowing time to monitor their impact on traffic.

- Visibility and Auditing: Maintain rigorous logging and audit trails to track access and adjust policies accordingly.

- User Education: Educate stakeholders on the importance and operation of security measures, fostering security-aware cultures.

Future Directions in Access Control Innovations   Emergent technologies forecast a profound evolution in access control paradigms. Beyond traditional methods, adaptive and context-aware access controls are gaining traction, using contextual data to adjust policies dynamically as risk conditions change. Self-sovereign identity models grounded in blockchain technologies promise to shift data ownership back to users, heralding increased privacy and control.

By advancing integration with AI-driven insights and incorporating Zero Trust architectures, Cloudflare is positioned to remain at the vanguard of rate limiting and access control solution development. This commitment ensures protection against a continuously evolving threat landscape while supporting the dynamic scalability needs of digital enterprises.

Cloudflare's strategic outlook and technical robustness in rate limiting and access control provide organizations with finely-tuned tools to maintain optimal security postures that safeguard web applications against existential threats.

3.6 Security Settings and Best Practices

The effectiveness of web application security highly depends on the optimal configuration and ongoing management of security settings. Cloudflare provides a comprehensive suite of security settings that can be tailored to protect web environments from an array of threats. This section delves into the strategic configuration of Cloudflare's security settings, emphasizing best practices that enhance the security posture of web properties while ensuring operational integrity and user experience.

Configuring Firewall Rules Effective firewall management is pivotal in precluding unauthorized access and mitigating prevailing threats. Cloudflare simplifies firewall rule configuration through an intuitive interface and powerful API, enabling policies fine-tuned to the requirements and risk profiles of individual web assets.

Example of granular firewall rule configuration utilizing the Cloudflare API:

```
import requests

# API and zone details
API_TOKEN = 'exampleToken'
ZONE_ID = 'exampleZoneId'
headers = {
    "Authorization": f"Bearer {API_TOKEN}",
    "Content-Type": "application/json"
}

# Example firewall rule to block suspicious user-agents
firewall_rule = {
    "action": "block",
    "description": "Block bad bots based on User-Agent",
    "filter": {
        "expression": "(http.user_agent contains 'BadBot')"
    }
}

# Create firewall rule
url = f"https://api.cloudflare.com/client/v4/zones/{ZONE_ID}/firewall/rules"
response = requests.post(url, json=firewall_rule, headers=headers)
print(response.json())
```

This rule showcases blocking requests with specific user-agent strings, a common characteristic of non-compliant bots.

Harnessing Rate Limiting for Security Rate limiting serves as a frontline defense against volumetric attacks alongside protecting sensitive endpoints from brute force and credential-stuffing attempts. Cloudflare's rate limiting is versatile, extendable to specific HTTP methods and user-defined thresholds.

Illustration of setting up a rate limit rule using Cloudflare API:

```
rate_limit_rule = {
    "disabled": False,
    "description": "Protect API endpoint",
    "threshold": 100,
    "period": 3600,
    "action": {
        "mode": "ban",
        "timeout": 3600
    },
    "match": {
        "request": {
            "methods": ["POST", "GET"],
            "url": "https://example.com/api"
        }
    }
}

url = f"https://api.cloudflare.com/client/v4/zones/{ZONE_ID}/rate_limits"
response = requests.post(url, json=rate_limit_rule, headers=headers)
print(response.json())
```

Here, requests beyond a defined threshold to a sensitive API endpoint trigger a temporary ban, dissuading abusive behaviors.

Optimal Use of SSL/TLS Settings SSL/TLS plays a fundamental role in encrypting data in transit. Configuring SSL/TLS settings for maximum security includes enabling protocols and ciphers that ensure robust encryption, complemented by automated certificate management through Cloudflare's interface.

Best practices involve:

- Enforcing TLS 1.2+: Disable legacy protocols (e.g., SSLv3, TLS 1.0) to guard against vulnerabilities tied to protocols obsolescence.

- Configuring Strong Cipher Suites: Prioritize ciphers supporting forward secrecy, such as ECDHE, to thwart decryption efforts even if session keys are compromised.

74

Example for configuring SSL settings via Cloudflare API:

```
ssl_settings = {
    "ssl": {
        "value": "full",
        "min_tls_version": "1.2"
    }
}

url = f"https://api.cloudflare.com/client/v4/zones/{ZONE_ID}/settings/ssl"
response = requests.patch(url, json=ssl_settings, headers=headers)
print(response.json())
```

This modifies SSL configurations to establish secure connections while enforcing TLS 1.2 or higher protocol compliance.

Leveraging Bot Protection   Malicious bots pose significant challenges to web environments. Cloudflare's Bot Management services utilize a blend of heuristic analysis and AI technologies to precisely identify and mitigate bot activities.

Integrated workflows with security stacks augment bot protection. An example configuration through Cloudflare's API could include:

```
bot_management_rule = {
    "action": "challenge",
    "description": "Challenge suspected bots",
    "filter": {
        "expression": "(cf.bot_management.score lt 30)"
    }
}

url = f"https://api.cloudflare.com/client/v4/zones/{ZONE_ID}/firewall/rules"
response = requests.post(url, json=bot_management_rule, headers=headers)
print(response.json())
```

This rule challenges requests scoring below a predefined threshold, assigning intense scrutiny to potentially harmful bots.

Maintaining Security Settings Through Automation and Monitoring   Automation is crucial for adapting to evolving security landscapes effectively. Cloudflare's robust API facilitates seamless integration with Infrastructure as Code (IaC) practices and Continuous Integration/Continuous Deployment (CI/CD) pipelines, ensuring that configuration management is consistent and reproducible.

75

Real-time monitoring coupled with comprehensive analytics allows immediate detection of anomalies and validation that security controls are performing as expected.

Security Enhancements with Content Security Policy (CSP) and HTTP Headers   CSP and security-focused HTTP headers such as X-Content-Type-Options and X-Frame-Options serve as valuable countermeasures against content injection and clickjacking.

Key settings include:

- CSP Directives: These dictate permissible content sources, preventing content injection attacks through stricter controlled resource loading.

- Frame Options and Other Headers: These protect against UI redressing attacks by disallowing untrusted framing and asserting MIME-type consistency.

Example CSP directive configuration:

```
Content-Security-Policy: default-src 'self'; script-src 'self' https://trusted.cdn.com;
```

Security Through Identity and Authentication   Security settings are not solely technologic but intersect with effective identity and access management, governed by privileged access policies. By fortifying authentication and leveraging principles such as least privilege, organizations substantially diminish exploitable vectors.

Policy facets may include:

- Multi-Factor Authentication (MFA): Augmenting passwords with OTPs or hardware tokens as primary safeguards.

- Assessing IAM Frameworks: Integrating robust IAM solutions like Azure AD, Okta, or Google Workspace as partners in security.

76

Challenges and Recommendations Despite high-end automation and security tools, challenges persist in misconfigurations and complacency in settings oversight. Ensuring robust security entails:

- Regular Audits and Penetration Testing: Detect vulnerabilities through continuous assessment and fortify configurations.

- Keeping Security Controls Up-to-Date: Reflect on technological evolutions, and prioritize updates and protocols that align with current security paradigms.

- Training Stakeholders: Near-constant changes in threat vectors necessitate ongoing security awareness programs.

Convergence of Zero Trust Principles Zero Trust frameworks add layers to existing defensive systems by adhering to the concept of "never trust, always verify". Adapting Cloudflare's architecture comprises employing zero trust solutions encompassing strict identity verification, endpoint security, and comprehensive security telemetry to enforce least-privilege access controls.

Employing context-aware perimeter security and challenging every suspicious entity with fine-grained control aids in the holistic security of digital assets.

Cloudflare's security settings and best practices are precisely designed to reinforce defenses, leveraging strategic configurations and innovations to address both present and emerging threats, supporting the fortification of web environments in a complex digital age. By coupling these configurations with proactive monitoring and continuous education, organizations can sustain their security postures robustly and resiliently.

3.7 Security Event Logging and Analysis

Security event logging and analysis are foundational components of robust cybersecurity strategies, providing critical insights into the operational status and security posture of web applications. Cloudflare offers extensive logging and analytical capabilities that facilitate in-depth evaluation of security events, empowering organizations to identify, respond to, and mitigate threats proactively. This section explores the details and best practices for leveraging Cloudflare's security event logging and analytics features to enhance web application security.

The Importance of Security Event Logging   Effective security event logging serves multiple crucial functions:

- **Incident Detection and Response**: Enables rapid identification of unauthorized access attempts and anomalies.

- **Forensic Analysis**: Provides a comprehensive audit trail for post-incident investigation and legal compliance.

- **Threat Intelligence Enrichment**: Feeds threat intelligence systems with data to adapt to new attack vectors.

- **Compliance and Reporting**: Assists in meeting regulatory requirements by maintaining detailed logs of system activities.

Cloudflare's Logging Infrastructure   Cloudflare's logging infrastructure is designed to provide high-fidelity, real-time data capture, encompassing a broad array of security events. This includes logs for Web Application Firewall (WAF) actions, DDoS attack mitigations, firewall rule matches, access attempts, bot management interventions, and more.

Example structure of an entry in a typical Cloudflare log:

```
{
    "timestamp": "2023-11-01T15:30:45Z",
    "zone_id": "exampleZoneId",
    "event_type": "firewall_match",
    "action": "block",
    "source_ip": "192.168.1.100",
    "user_agent": "BadBot/1.2",
    "rule_id": "1001",
    "request_uri": "/login"
}
```

Each log entry captures essential details about the event, enabling comprehensive analysis and response strategies.

Log Access and Retrieval Mechanisms   Cloudflare offers multiple interfaces for accessing logs, including:

- **Dashboard**: Provides an intuitive graphical interface for real-time log visualization and exploration.

- **API Access**: Supports programmatic retrieval and processing of logs for automation and integration into existing systems.

- **Logpush Service**: Enables automatic streaming of logs to storage services such as AWS S3, Google Cloud Storage, or a SIEM solution for centralized analysis.

Example API usage to retrieve logs:

```
import requests

API_TOKEN = 'exampleToken'
ZONE_ID = 'exampleZoneId'
payload = {
    "fields": [
        "timestamp", "zone_id", "event_type", "action", "source_ip", "user_agent"
    ],
    "filter": {"event_type": ["firewall_match"]}
}

headers = {
    "Authorization": f"Bearer {API_TOKEN}",
    "Content-Type": "application/json"
}

url = f"https://api.cloudflare.com/client/v4/zones/{ZONE_ID}/logs/requests"
response = requests.get(url, params=payload, headers=headers)

print(response.json())
```

This script demonstrates retrieving logs related to firewall rules, filtering for specific event types using Cloudflare's API.

Integration with Security Information and Event Management (SIEM) Systems   Integrating Cloudflare logs with SIEM solutions enables enhanced real-time monitoring, correlation, and incident response. These integrations facilitate deeper threat analysis and visualization of potential security incidents, contextualizing data across all facets of the network infrastructure.

79

Steps to integrate Cloudflare logs with a SIEM system involve configuring the log push endpoint and parsing strategy to ingest and process logs via JSON, Syslog, or CEF (Common Event Format) standards.

Analyzing Security Event Logs for Threat Detection Log analysis includes thematic and statistical evaluation of events, deploying anomaly detection algorithms and correlation rules to identify threats heretofore unseen. By constructing behavior-based models, Cloudflare logs can power alert systems for deviations indicative of malicious activity.

Example pseudocode for anomaly detection in request frequency:

```
def detect_anomalies(logs):
    threshold = calculate_threshold(logs) # Custom method for dynamic baseline
    anomalies = []

    for log in logs:
        request_count = count_requests(log["source_ip"], time_frame="1m")
        if request_count > threshold:
            anomalies.append(log)

    return anomalies

# Assume 'logs' is a list of log entries fetched from Cloudflare
anomalies_detected = detect_anomalies(logs)
print(f"Anomalies detected: {len(anomalies_detected)}")
```

This algorithm outlines a simplified approach to detecting request frequency anomalies, a common sign of unauthorized access attempts.

Dashboards and Visual Analytics Cloudflare's platform supports visualizations that allow administrators to craft dashboards spanning multiple KPIs. Graphical representations of log data are invaluable for instant situational awareness and trend identification.

By employing tools like Grafana combined with Cloudflare logs, it is possible to create visualizations such as heatmaps and time-series analyses that interpret security trends and potential breaches.

User and Entity Behavior Analytics (UEBA) Integrating UEBA systems with Cloudflare logs assists in understanding behavioral patterns and identifying deviations from established baselines, potentially

80

revealing insider threats, compromised accounts, or sophisticated external attacks.

Example UEBA detection scenarios include:

- **Unusual Access Times**: Identifying logins occurring outside of normal operating hours.

- **Abnormal Data Exfiltration**: Monitoring unusual amounts of outbound traffic indicative of data theft.

Best Practices for Security Event Logging and Analysis
Maintaining the efficacy of security event logging requires adherence to several best practices:

- **Comprehensive Logging Strategy**: Ensure that logs capture all relevant events without overwhelming the system, balancing between verbosity and performance.

- **Protected Log Storage**: Secure the integrity of logs with encryption and access controls, safeguarding against tampering and unauthorized access.

- **Regular Auditing**: Systematically review logs to refine detection methods and identify areas for improving control measures.

- **Automated Alerts**: Configure automated alerting systems to respond immediately to high-risk events without human intervention, reducing manual monitoring overhead.

Compliance Management with Audit Trails Logs play a paramount role in compliance verification by serving as an immutable record of system operations. They provide the necessary transparency to satisfy the demands of regulations such as GDPR, PCI DSS, and HIPAA, ensuring that proper protective measures are documented and auditable.

Cloudflare's audit trails can be directed to generate compliance reports detailing activities, access attempts, and policy compliance over defined periods, fortifying organizations' compliance postures.

Challenges in Security Event Logging and Forward Plans
Challenges in security event logging include managing the volume and velocity of data, ensuring data integrity across distributed systems, and handling false positives in detection models. Future advances in AI and machine learning hold promise for mitigating these issues, providing smarter, context-aware analytics models for better decision-making.

Emerging technologies, like the application of blockchain for immutable log verification, offer opportunities to redefine trust in logging systems. As organizations continue to face increasingly sophisticated adversaries, the evolution of security event logging will remain integral to defense strategy.

By utilizing advanced logging and analysis tools, organizations can bolster their capabilities to predict, detect, and thwart security threats effectively. Cloudflare's comprehensive solutions provide a pivotal resource in this endeavor, equipping enterprises with the insights requisite for building resilient, fortified digital infrastructures.

Chapter 4

Optimizing Website Performance with Cloudflare

This chapter delves into the strategies and tools Cloudflare offers to significantly enhance website performance. It covers the use of caching, image optimization, and minification techniques to reduce load times and improve user experience. Additionally, the chapter examines the role of Cloudflare's global network in minimizing latency through efficient content delivery. Readers will gain practical insights into configuring Cloudflare's performance settings to achieve optimal site speed and reliability, tailored to both desktop and mobile users.

4.1   Understanding Web Performance

Web performance refers to the speed and efficiency with which web content is delivered and rendered in a user's browser. This encompasses various factors, including network latency, server processing time, and client-side rendering efficiency. Effective web performance directly correlates with user satisfaction and retention, as well as the visibility and ranking of a website in search engine results. As users increasingly demand faster and more interactive web experiences, optimizing web performance is paramount.

In the digital landscape, web performance is often quantified by several key metrics. These metrics allow developers and site owners to measure, analyze, and improve the delivery of content. Understanding these metrics is crucial for implementing effective performance enhancements.

1. **Page Load Time:** This is the total time taken from the moment a user requests a page until it is fully loaded in the browser. It encompasses DNS lookup, TCP connection, server processing, and browser rendering.

2. **Time to First Byte (TTFB):** This metric is the duration from the request initiation by a user to the point at which the first byte of data is received from the server. A low TTFB is essential for good performance, indicating efficient server response times.

3. **First Contentful Paint (FCP):** Measures how long it takes for the first piece of content from the DOM to be rendered on the screen. Faster FCP indicates a more responsive feel to users.

4. **Largest Contentful Paint (LCP):** This is the time it takes for the main content of the page to become visible. It is one of the Core Web Vitals and is critical for visual stability.

5. **Cumulative Layout Shift (CLS):** Measures the visual stability of a webpage. It calculates the amount of unexpected layout shifts during the entire lifespan of the page.

6. **First Input Delay (FID):** This metric gauges the responsiveness of a page by measuring the time from when a user first interacts with a site to the time when the browser actually interprets that interaction.

For effective web performance optimization, it is important to focus on improving these metrics through various techniques and tools that streamline content delivery and rendering processes.

A significant aspect of web performance is the optimization of resource loading on a website. This involves strategies like minimizing HTTP requests, optimizing media files, and efficiently using web technologies such as synchronous/asynchronous loading. Consider the following example demonstrating asynchronous JavaScript loading:

```
<script async src="example.js"></script>
```

In this example, the async attribute allows the JavaScript file to load asynchronously with HTML parsing, reducing render-blocking scripts from delaying page load time.

Network Latency and Bandwidth

Network latency is a critical component of web performance, referring to the delay before a transfer of data begins following an instruction for its transfer. High latency can result from physical distance, network congestion, or inefficient routing paths. To mitigate latency issues, the deployment of Content Delivery Networks (CDNs) is a common practice. CDNs cache content across multiple geographic locations, serving user requests from the nearest node, thus reducing latency and improving load times.

Bandwidth, on the other hand, is the capacity of a network to transfer data within a given time. While high bandwidth does not necessarily alleviate high latency, it enables the transfer of more data in a shorter amount of time, contributing to perceived performance improvements.

Server-Side Performance

Server-side performance concerns effective rendering and data processing by a web server. Strategies for improving server-side performance involve optimizing server configurations, employing server-side caching mechanisms, and enabling efficient database queries. Here's a simple example of server-side caching using PHP:

```php
// Check if a recent cache file exists
if (file_exists('cache.html') && (time() - filemtime('cache.html') < 3600)) {
    // Serve cache file if it's less than an hour old
    echo file_get_contents('cache.html');
} else {
    // Perform server processing tasks and generate content
    ob_start();
    echo "<p>This is dynamically generated content.</p>";

    // Write the output to cache file
    $cachedContent = ob_get_contents();
```

85

```
    file_put_contents('cache.html', $cachedContent);
    ob_end_flush();
}
```

In this example, server-side caching allows the system to store dynamically generated content in a cache file, significantly reducing processing time during subsequent requests.

Client-Side Performance

Client-side performance pertains to executing scripts and rendering HTML/CSS updates efficiently in the browser. Techniques for enhancing client-side performance include minimizing the use of heavy scripts, leveraging browser caching, and optimizing CSS delivery.

Code Example:

Suppose a web application requires frequent DOM updates. Inefficient updates can lead to performance bottlenecks. The following JavaScript snippet demonstrates efficient DOM manipulation using the Document Fragment API:

```
// Create a document fragment for batch updates
let fragment = document.createDocumentFragment();

// Simulating adding new elements
for (let i = 0; i < 100; i++) {
    let newDiv = document.createElement('div');
    newDiv.textContent = 'This is element number ${i}';
    fragment.appendChild(newDiv);
}

// Append fragment to the DOM in one operation
document.getElementById('container').appendChild(fragment);
```

By using a document fragment, this example reduces reflow and repaint operations, avoiding potential slowdowns associated with repeatedly updating the DOM.

Impact on User Experience and SEO

Web performance directly influences the user experience, affecting bounce rates, user engagement, and overall satisfaction. Users are likely to abandon a website if it takes too long to load or if interactive elements are unresponsive, negatively impacting retention and conversion rates. Optimizing web performance not only elevates user experience but also plays a significant role in search engine optimization

86

(SEO). Search engines, like Google, consider page speed as a ranking factor, prioritizing fast-loading sites in search results. Thus, performance optimizations have a dual benefit by enhancing user interaction and improving site visibility.

The correlation between web performance and SEO can be illustrated with tools like Google PageSpeed Insights. This tool analyzes web pages and generates suggestions for performance improvements, yielding scores that directly influence search ranking algorithms. One essential approach is reducing render-blocking resources, typically achieved via techniques like inlining critical CSS or using preloading headers:

```
<link rel="preload" href="styles.css" as="style">
```

Preloading resources, as shown above, allows for immediate loading of essential resources, enabling faster rendering and lower perceived load times.

Aligning with a user-centric framework, the Core Web Vitals introduced by Google emphasize key aspects of user experience, including loading performance (LCP), interactivity (FID), and visual stability (CLS). Optimizing these metrics can significantly enhance both SEO and user satisfaction.

Each improvement in web performance involves routing efficiencies, optimizing resources, and leveraging advanced technologies in content distribution. As digital platforms continue to evolve, the significance of understanding and integrating web performance optimization grows exponentially, affecting every aspect of digital interaction and engagement.

4.2 Caching Strategies with Cloudflare

The modern web necessitates rapid and efficient delivery of content, especially as websites grow increasingly complex. Caching is a pivotal strategy employed to accelerate content delivery by storing copies of resources closer to users. Cloudflare, a prominent Content Delivery Network (CDN), excels in providing caching solutions that significantly enhance web performance.

Cloudflare's caching system works by distributing static and dynamic content copies across its global network of data centers, bringing content physically closer to end-users. This reduces the distance data must travel, lowering latency and improving page load times. Understanding and configuring Cloudflare's caching strategies is crucial for optimizing content delivery.

Cache Levels and Page Rules

Cloudflare provides various cache levels, allowing users to tailor caching behavior according to the specific needs of their website. Cache levels determine which resources are cached, ranging from basic to more aggressive settings.

- **No Cache:** This level instructs Cloudflare not to cache any resources. It is rarely used, reserved for pages that must deliver real-time data.

- **Standard:** Caches static resources such as images, CSS, and JavaScript files, leaving dynamic content unaffected. This setting balances immediate data delivery with the need for accuracy on dynamic pages.

- **Aggressive:** Caches all content, including dynamic content. Suitable for largely static sites or when content updates infrequently.

To further refine caching control, Cloudflare offers Page Rules, empowering webmasters with the flexibility to apply specific caching and other behaviors to particular URLs or URL patterns.

Example of Creating a Page Rule:

Consider a scenario where a website admin wants to cache all images under a '/images' directory aggressively. The configuration could be set as follows:

```
URL pattern: *example.com/images/*
Settings: Cache Level: Cache Everything
```

In this example, all requests matching the URL pattern will be cached according to the "Cache Everything" directive, minimizing load times for frequently requested images.

88

Edge Cache TTL

Cloudflare's edge cache Time-to-Live (TTL) setting plays a crucial role in determining how long cached resources are stored at its edge locations before being fetched anew from the origin server. Setting an optimal TTL balances freshness with performance. Common configurations include short TTLs for frequently updated content and longer TTLs for static assets.

Managing edge cache TTL involves resource-specific considerations. For instance, an e-commerce site could configure short TTLs for product pages to accommodate frequent inventory updates, while setting extended TTLs for assets like logos and stylesheet files, which change infrequently.

Caching Dynamic Content

Dynamic content responds to user interactions and database queries, traditionally seen as non-cacheable due to frequent changes and personalized data. Cloudflare alleviates this challenge with technologies like **Cache-Control headers** and **Bypass Cache on Cookie**.

Cache-Control headers instruct browsers and CDNs on resource caching mechanisms. Here is an example of setting cache headers in PHP:

```php
<?php
  header("Cache-Control: max-age=3600, public");
?>
```

This directive sets a max-age of 3600 seconds (1 hour), advising Cloudflare and browsers to cache the output for this duration. Applying strategic Cache-Control configurations ensures that content is cached sensibly, aligning with specific site requirements.

The Bypass Cache on Cookie feature permits caching pages while ignoring specific HTTP cookies. This can be useful for sites where personalization (like a user being logged in) alters content delivery. It ensures Cloudflare caches the unlogged version while serving personalized pages directly from the server.

Cloudflare Workers and Custom Caching Logic

Cloudflare Workers allow developers to write custom JavaScript logic executed at Cloudflare's edge. This capability extends caching strategies beyond pre-defined settings, enabling bespoke solutions for individualized site scenarios.

```
// Example of using Cloudflare Workers for custom caching
addEventListener('fetch', event => {
  event.respondWith(handleRequest(event.request))
})

async function handleRequest(request) {
  let response = await fetch(request)

  // Customize cache logic based on response headers
  if (response.ok && request.method === 'GET') {
    let newResponse = new Response(response.body, response)
    newResponse.headers.set('Cache-Control', 'public, max-age=7200')
    return newResponse
  }

  return response
}
```

This snippet demonstrates a rudimentary Cloudflare Worker script setting custom cache controls, allowing caching decisions to be made dynamically based on request characteristics. Such granular control optimizes how resources are cached and served.

Cache Purging and Control

Occasionally, cached content may need immediate purging due to updates or corrections. Cloudflare facilitates cache purging via its dashboard or REST API, ensuring changes propagate swiftly across its network.

The REST API allows for programmatic purging, a key feature for automated cache management workflows often integrated into Continuous Integration and Continuous Deployment (CI/CD) pipelines. Here's an example of purging a cache via the Cloudflare API using curl:

```
curl -X POST "https://api.cloudflare.com/client/v4/zones/{zone_id}/purge_cache" \
-H "X-Auth-Email: {email}" \
-H "X-Auth-Key: {api_key}" \
-H "Content-Type: application/json" \
--data '{"purge_everything":true}'
```

This command clears all cached files for a specific zone, ideal when substantial site updates occur that necessitate immediate cache invalidation.

Cloudflare provides a balance of automation, precision, and control in caching, allowing content to be delivered with optimal speed and reliability. Through Cloudflare's sophisticated caching mechanisms, web administrators dramatically enhance performance, reduce server load, and ensure a seamless experience for global users. This fusion of network technology and cache optimization constitutes a robust architecture for today's web demands, where efficiency and user satisfaction are paramount. Understanding and implementing these caching strategies is essential for anyone seeking to leverage Cloudflare's capabilities fully.

4.3   Image Optimization Techniques

Images represent a significant component of web content and are often the largest contributors to page weight, affecting page load times, bandwidth consumption, and overall user experience. Image optimization is therefore crucial to enhancing website performance. Cloudflare offers a suite of tools designed to automate and simplify the process of refining images for the web, ensuring they load quickly and efficiently without compromising quality.

The key facets of image optimization include resizing, compression, format selection, and serving the right images based on user-device capabilities. By employing these techniques through Cloudflare, web developers can significantly improve loading speeds, especially on image-heavy sites.

Image Resizing

Resizing is the process of adjusting the image dimensions to match the display requirements. This technique saves bandwidth by ensuring that no unnecessary pixel data is transferred.

In Cloudflare, the Image Resizing feature allows on-demand scaling of images at the CDN level, reducing the need for multiple image versions stored on an origin server. This dynamic approach tailors images to the end-user's device viewport or predefined dimensions in HTML/CSS.

```
<img src="https://example.com/cdn-cgi/image/width=150,height=150/https://
    example.com/image.jpg" alt="Resized Image">
```

The above HTML example demonstrates using Cloudflare's resizing capabilities, adjusting an image to 150x150 pixels, ensuring users receive an optimally sized image.

Image Compression

Compression reduces the overall file size by eliminating redundant data and can be lossy or lossless. Cloudflare's AutoMinify feature, while typically associated with code files, extends to images through its automatic compression protocols.

- **Lossy Compression:** Results in smaller file sizes at the cost of some data loss. Suitable for photographs where a slight quality tradeoff is acceptable.

- **Lossless Compression:** Retains all original data, maintaining image fidelity. Ideal for graphics and images where detail preservation is important.

Cloudflare supports efficient real-time image compression, automatically compressing JPEGs, PNGs, and GIFs, leading to smaller image delivery without manual processes.

Image Format Optimization and WebP Conversion

Selecting modern image formats that offer better compression and quality efficiency than traditional formats is essential. WebP is a leading format, providing superior lossless and lossy compression for images on the web. Cloudflare facilitates the automatic conversion of images to WebP, enabling support for browsers that can decode this format.

```
<img src="https://example.com/cdn-cgi/image/format=auto/https://example.com/
    image.jpg" alt="Optimized Image">
```

In this instance, setting the 'format=auto' parameter tells Cloudflare to serve the best available format based on the request, delivering WebP to supported browsers and falling back to PNG or JPEG for others.

Adaptive Pixel Density

Opting for images that adapt to device pixel density ensures clarity on high-resolution screens without unnecessarily serving large files to users with standard density displays. Cloudflare's image delivery system intelligently assesses a user's device to cater appropriately scaled images, optimizing load times while maintaining high image quality.

Serving Responsive Images

Responsive images adjust according to the user's device screen size, orientation, and resolution. The '<picture>' element in HTML is well-suited for this purpose:

```
<picture>
    <source srcset="image-320w.jpg 320w, image-480w.jpg 480w, image-800w.jpg 800w
        " sizes="(max-width: 320px) 280px,
            (max-width: 480px) 440px, 800px" type="image/jpeg">
    <img src="image-800w.jpg" alt="Responsive Image">
</picture>
```

This code selects the appropriate image version depending on the viewport size, reducing overhead by not downloading unnecessary pixels.

Leveraging Cloudflare's Mirage

Cloudflare Mirage presents another layer of image optimization, designed specifically to enhance performance for mobile and bandwidth-constrained users. It streamlines image loading through techniques like lazy loading and progressive rendering.

Mirage assesses the availability of network resources and defers the loading of off-screen images until necessary, conserving bandwidth and enhancing the perceived load speed. Activation of Mirage is a straightforward toggle in Cloudflare's dashboard, requiring no additional code changes.

Polished Image Delivery with Cloudflare Polish

Cloudflare's Polish feature further optimizes image delivery by compressing images and selectively converting them to WebP. It is configurable either to retain the highest fidelity ('Lossless mode') or prioritize maximal size reduction ('Lossy mode').

```
Zone Settings: Optimized Images > Polish On (Lossy or Lossless)
```

This setting ensures every image request is subjected to cloud-based optimization, automatically enhancing performance at scale.

Coding Integration for Enhanced Image Strategies

Finally, integrating Cloudflare's image optimization services programmatically offers greater control. With Cloudflare Workers, developers can script custom image-serving logic, facilitating unique optimization pathways based on application demands.

```
// Cloudflare Worker for custom image processing
addEventListener('fetch', event => {
    event.respondWith(handleImageRequest(event.request))
})

async function handleImageRequest(request) {
    const url = new URL(request.url)
    if (url.pathname.endsWith('.jpg') || url.pathname.endsWith('.png')) {
        // Custom logic for image processing
        url.searchParams.append('width', '300')
        url.searchParams.append('format', 'webp')
    }
    return fetch(url.toString(), { method: request.method })
}
```

This sample worker script appends parameters to requests targeting image files, utilizing Cloudflare's resizing and format optimization.

By mastering Cloudflare's image optimization features, developers equip themselves with powerful tools to enhance web performance dramatically. This amalgamation of advanced techniques not only reduces latency and page load times but also sustains the visual richness expected in modern web experiences, particularly as the demand for high-quality multimedia content proliferates. Cloudflare's innovations in image optimization exemplify robust solutions tailored to the dynamic needs within the digital ecosystem, empowering web professionals to deliver fast, efficient, and compelling visual content.

4.4   Minification and Compression

In the quest to optimize web performance, minimizing the size of resources such as HTML, CSS, and JavaScript files is a critical strategy. Minification and compression are foundational techniques to achieve smaller file sizes, enhancing download speed and reducing bandwidth usage. These strategies not only contribute to faster page loads but also improve the overall user experience, particularly for users on slower networks or devices.

- **Minification**
  Minification involves removing all unnecessary characters from

source code without changing its functionality. This process includes the elimination of whitespace, comments, and redundant anonymous functions or variables. By reducing the file size, minification decreases the amount of data that needs to be transferred over the network, accelerating loading times.

Cloudflare offers automated minification for JavaScript, CSS, and HTML files, minimizing the effort required by developers to streamline their web resources.

Example of Minified Code:

Consider a simple JavaScript block before and after minification:

```
// Original JavaScript code
function greet() {
  var message = "Hello, World!";
  console.log(message);
}
greet();
```

The same code, minified, becomes:

```
function greet(){console.log("Hello, World!");}greet();
```

Here, unnecessary whitespace and comments are stripped out, and variable declarations are optimized, shrinking the file size while retaining the functional integrity.

- **Compression**
  Compression reduces the size of files by encoding the data more efficiently. The most commonly used method on the web is the Gzip compression algorithm, which can reduce the size of typical web files by 70-90%. Modern browsers support Gzip, making it a practical and widely adopted solution.

  Cloudflare automatically applies Gzip compression to delivered resources that benefit from it, offering better compression ratios without additional setup on the origin server.

```
Accept-Encoding: gzip, deflate
```

This HTTP header informs the server that the client can accept compressed content. Cloudflare, acting as an intermediary, ensures compressed data is issued if this capability is indicated by the client's request.

- **Brotli Compression**
  Cloudflare also supports Brotli, a newer compression algorithm developed by Google, known for its superior compression performance compared to Gzip, especially for text files like HTML, CSS, and JavaScript.

  When enabled, Brotli can further reduce the size of transmitted files, leading to even faster resource delivery. Configuration in Cloudflare's dashboard involves selecting this option alongside existing compression methods.

- **Advanced Configuration and Consideration**
  While Cloudflare automates much of the minification and compression process, understanding advanced configurations can lead to better performance results under complex scenarios.

  For instance, you might want to exclude specific resources from minification or apply custom logic for determining when compression should be utilized, based on network speed or resource type.

Custom Minification and Compression Logic Using Cloudflare Workers

Through Cloudflare Workers, developers can script their own rules for minification and compression, tailoring the site's performance strategy to precise needs.

```
// Example Cloudflare Worker for conditional compression
addEventListener('fetch', event => {
  event.respondWith(handleRequest(event.request))
})

async function handleRequest(request) {
  let acceptEncoding = request.headers.get('Accept-Encoding') || ''
  let response = await fetch(request)
  let newHeaders = new Headers(response.headers)

  // Custom logic for compression
  if (acceptEncoding.includes('br')) {
    newHeaders.set('Content-Encoding', 'br')
  } else if (acceptEncoding.includes('gzip')) {
    newHeaders.set('Content-Encoding', 'gzip')
```

```
}

return new Response(response.body, {
  status: response.status,
  statusText: response.statusText,
  headers: newHeaders,
})
}
```

This example demonstrates a custom logic that adjusts content encoding based on what the client can handle, optimizing both performance and compatibility.

- **Implications for Web Performance**
  Optimizing file size through minification and compression has direct implications on how quickly a site's resources are delivered and rendered. Smaller files result in faster first paint times and reduced time to interact, crucial metrics in today's performance-centric web environment. Enhanced compression capabilities, such as Brotli through Cloudflare, push this optimization a step further, setting a high standard for efficient data delivery.

- **SEO and Best Practices**
  Web performance improvements via minification and compression not only benefit end-user experience but also contribute positively to search engine optimization (SEO). Faster loading sites are more favorably ranked by search engines like Google that prioritize speed in their algorithms.

  Incorporating best practices for resource management ensures that minification and compression are effective. This includes scrutinizing and refining code for inefficiencies, utilizing system tools or IDE plugins like UglifyJS for JavaScript, and testing the impact of applied techniques using PageSpeed Insights or Lighthouse for performance auditing.

- **Challenges and Trade-offs**
  While minification and compression are generally beneficial, potential challenges include the accidental minification of functional code, leading to runtime errors if not properly tested. Furthermore, certain files may be better left uncompressed if they are already in a compressed format, such as JPEG images or

97

other binary formats like videos and PDFs, where additional compression efforts are superfluous and could degrade quality.

Ensuring careful implementation, with proper staging and testing, avoids these pitfalls, leveraging Cloudflare's capabilities to maximize the efficiency of web resource delivery.

4.5 Edge Network and Content Delivery

The rapid delivery of web content is a cornerstone of modern user experience, particularly in a globally interconnected world. Cloudflare's edge network plays a pivotal role in accelerating content delivery by distributing content closer to users around the globe. This strategy minimizes latency, reduces loading times, and enhances the overall reliability and efficiency of web services.

At the heart of Cloudflare's approach is its global edge network, which consists of numerous data centers strategically located across various geographical regions. By caching static content at these distributed locations, the network ensures that users can access resources such as HTML files, images, and scripts from the nearest server, rather than the origin server which may be situated halfway across the world.

- **Geographic Proximity:** Content is stored in data centers closest to the user's physical location, reducing the physical distance data must travel when a request is made. This strategic placement lowers latency substantially, allowing for near-instantaneous content delivery.

- **Caching Efficiency:** The edge network utilizes intelligent caching strategies to store both static and, in some cases, dynamic content. Cached content is readily available for similar requests, reducing server load and speeding up response times.

- **Scalability:** Cloudflare's network is designed to automatically handle variable loads, scaling up resources to accommodate traffic spikes without compromising performance.

- **Security Integration:** In addition to performance benefits, the edge network incorporates robust security measures, protecting against DDoS attacks and malicious activities while filtering out harmful traffic before it reaches the origin server.

Content Delivery Mechanisms

The effectiveness of the Cloudflare edge network in content delivery hinges on several sophisticated mechanisms:

- **Content Caching:** Caching at the edge plays a vital role in reducing data retrieval times. Cloudflare's caching logic allows frequently requested resources to be stored and retrieved at the edge, enhancing access speed.

```
Cache-Control: public, max-age=31536000
```

The HTTP header above indicates that resources are cacheable by any cache (both servers and clients) and should be stored for a period of one year ('31536000' seconds).

- **Dynamic Content Optimization:** While static content can be effortlessly cached, dynamic content is largely generated server-side and poses unique challenges. Cloudflare's edge network employs technology like Argo Smart Routing to optimize the delivery path, expediting transit even for dynamic requests.

- **Content Purge:** When updates are made to content, it's crucial to purge outdated versions from the cache. Cloudflare provides mechanisms for seamless cache invalidation, ensuring users always receive the latest information.

```
curl -X POST "https://api.cloudflare.com/client/v4/zones/{zone_id}/
    purge_cache" \
-H "X-Auth-Email: {email}" \
-H "X-Auth-Key: {api_key}" \
-H "Content-Type: application/json" \
--data '{"purge_everything":true}'
```

This API command purges all cache associated with a given zone, useful when content needs to be refreshed immediately network-wide.

API-Based Content Serving and Edge Logic

The flexibility of Cloudflare's edge is extended through Cloudflare Workers, a serverless execution environment that empowers developers to build and customize logic directly at the edge. This capability transcends traditional content delivery limitations, accommodating custom calculations, decisions, and responsive modifications relative to inbound requests.

```
// Cloudflare Worker to customize content delivery
addEventListener('fetch', event => {
  event.respondWith(handleRequest(event.request))
})

async function handleRequest(request) {
  const cacheKey = new Request(request.url, request)
  let response = await caches.default.match(cacheKey)

  if (!response) {
    response = await fetch(request)
    // Put a copy of the response in the cache
    event.waitUntil(caches.default.put(cacheKey, response.clone()))
  }

  return response
}
```

This Worker script customizes the way content is fetched and cached, offering granular control over how responses are issued directly from the edge.

Network Topology and Optimization

Cloudflare's network topology ensures that data traverses the most efficient path possible, optimizing throughput and reducing latency. Their network employs advanced routing algorithms which not only pick the shortest physical path but also account for congestion, packet loss, and faults in the network to dynamically choose the optimal route.

Moreover, the introduction of technologies like HTTP/3 (based on QUIC) within Cloudflare's network further advances performance. HTTP/3 reduces the time applications need to establish a secure, reliable connection, thereby expediting initial content delivery which is especially beneficial in high-latency environments.

```
Alt-Svc: h3-23=":443"; ma=3600
```

The above HTTP header instructs a browser that an alternate protocol (HTTP/3) is available, poised for swift adoption when compatible.

100

Cost Efficiency and Edge Utilization

By locating content closer to end users, Cloudflare's edge reduces the bandwidth and operational impact on origin servers. This reduction translates to cost savings in terms of data egress fees associated with traditional server colocation at centralized data centers. Businesses can mitigate the escalations associated with scaling origin infrastructure by diverting traffic loads efficiently across Cloudflare's distributed edge nodes.

Future Proofing with Cloudflare

As digital landscapes evolve and content becomes increasingly complex, the role of Cloudflare's edge network will continue to grow in importance. New innovations in content encoding, multicasting over content delivery networks, and further efficiencies in protocol utilization will likely integrate seamlessly with Cloudflare's edge-focused design.

Moreover, the ability for developers to enhance and deploy codes at the edge ensures adaptability amidst emerging standards and web complexities. The Cloudflare edge serves both as an accelerator and firewall, a duality essential for advancing digital services in a rapidly evolving online ecosystem.

Understanding and leveraging Cloudflare's edge network is vital for any web presence that prioritizes speed, reliability, and scalability. It not only optimizes the paths and methods through which content reaches users but ensures that businesses remain competitive and responsive in a world where digital efficacy correlates directly with success. Cloudflare continues to set benchmarks in distributed content delivery, fortifying the global web infrastructure with state-of-the-art edge capabilities.

4.6 Accelerating Mobile Experiences

The mobile landscape has matured into a dominant platform for accessing the web, rendering the optimization of mobile experience a crucial imperative for web developers and businesses alike. Mobile devices face unique challenges, including smaller screen sizes, diverse hardware capabilities, and varied network conditions. These factors necessitate a distinct approach to web performance optimization, with a focus on fast, seamless, and responsive user experiences.

Cloudflare presents an array of strategies and tools specifically designed to enhance mobile web performance. By addressing issues such as responsive design, resource loading, and progressive web enhancement, Cloudflare empowers developers to significantly improve mobile website speed and user engagement.

Responsive Design and its Implications

Responsive design ensures that a website adapts seamlessly to different screen sizes and orientations. It is the cornerstone of modern web design, accommodating desktop, tablet, and mobile interfaces without compromising user experience.

Cloudflare aids in responsive web design through mobile optimization settings that automatically adjust resource delivery based on user device characteristics. Additionally, the integration of Cloudflare's mobile-specific features aids in preserving design fidelity across diverse devices.

Example of a Responsive HTML Structure Utilizing Media Queries:

```
<!DOCTYPE html>
<html lang="en">

<head>
    <meta charset="UTF-8">
    <meta name="viewport" content="width=device-width, initial-scale=1.0">
    <title>Responsive Design Example</title>
    <style>
        body {
            font-size: 16px;
        }

        @media (max-width: 600px) {
            body {
                font-size: 12px;
            }
        }
    </style>
</head>

<body>
    <h1>Welcome to a Responsive World</h1>
    <p>This text adjusts based on screen size.</p>
</body>
```

```
</html>
```

This example involves scaling font size based on the device width, ensuring content is legible at smaller resolutions, a fundamental practice in responsive design methodology.

Reducing Mobile Load Times

Reducing load times is critical on mobile devices where network speeds are generally slower and less stable compared to wired connections. Cloudflare provides several mechanisms to mitigate these challenges:

- **Image Optimization for Mobile:** Images are a major facet of page weight. Cloudflare's mobile optimization automates image compression and resizing, including converting images to modern formats like WebP that consume less bandwidth without degrading quality.

```
<img src="https://example.com/cdn-cgi/image/width=300/optimize.webp"
     alt="Optimized Image">
```

Here, images are dynamically resized to width based on device specifications and served in an optimized format.

- **Script and Resource Minimization:** JavaScript files and CSS can be minified, reducing the size and number of requests required. Cloudflare's AutoMinify feature strips unnecessary characters from these files automatically.

- **Efficient Caching of Mobile Resources:** Mobile devices benefit significantly from caching strategies that reduce redundant network requests, taking advantage of Cloudflare's edge caching facilities to store frequently accessed content nearby.

```
Cache-Control: public, max-age=86400
```

This directive allows caching of static resources for a specified period, reducing load upon repeat visits.

- **Lazy Loading for Efficient Resource Use:** Through lazy loading, off-screen images and resources are loaded only as they enter the viewport, conserving bandwidth. This is particularly useful for image-rich content on mobile devices, implemented with attributes like loading="lazy" in HTML5.

Accelerated Mobile Pages (AMP) and Cloudflare

Accelerated Mobile Pages (AMP) is an open-source initiative that optimizes pages for mobile performance. It strips down HTML and JavaScript, relying on AMP-specific markup to ensure rapid load times.

Cloudflare AMP integration enhances delivery by pre-rendering AMP content in the edge network. This ensures instant content availability and instantaneous rendering akin to native applications.

```
<!doctype html>
<html >
<head>
<meta charset="utf-8">
<title>AMP Page Example</title>
<link rel="canonical" href="/example">
<meta name="viewport" content="width=device-width,minimum-scale=1,initial-scale
    =1">
<style amp-custom>
  /* Custom AMP specific styling */
  body { font-family: Arial, sans-serif; }
</style>
<script async src="https://cdn.ampproject.org/v0.js"></script>
</head>
<body>
  <h1>Welcome to AMP</h1>
  <p>This is an Accelerated Mobile Page.</p>
</body>
</html>
```

Through this AMP HTML structure, Cloudflare can deliver the page efficiently in a mobile-friendly format, expediting load times via simplified markup and optimized delivery.

Mobile-specific Debugging and Analytics

Enhanced debugging tools tailored for mobile are integral to identifying and rectifying performance issues. Cloudflare provides analytics tools that focus on mobile metrics, facilitating in-depth insights into load times, bounce rates, and user interactions specific to mobile.

This data guides strategic optimization, validates changes, and measures improvement baselines fostering continuous enhancement in the mobile experience lifecycle.

Example Analysis Dashboard Information:

- **Load Time Breakdown:** Visualizes time spent on DNS lookups, TCP connections, and resource rendering to identify bottlenecks.

- **User Interaction Heatmaps:** Showcases most interacted elements, informing design refinement.

The Role of Progressive Web Apps (PWA)

Progressive Web Apps (PWAs) blend web and native app capabilities, delivering fast, reliable user experiences akin to native applications. Utilization of service workers ensures smooth offline experiences, caching resources for use when network connectivity is intermittent or absent.

Cloudflare Workers aid significantly, executing code at the network edge to further streamline PWA services.

```
// Service Worker with basic caching logic
self.addEventListener('install', (event) => {
  event.waitUntil(
    caches.open('v1').then((cache) => {
      return cache.addAll([
        '/',
        '/index.html',
        '/styles.css',
        '/script.js'
      ]);
    })
  );
});

self.addEventListener('fetch', (event) => {
  event.respondWith(
    caches.match(event.request).then((response) => {
      return response || fetch(event.request);
    })
  );
});
```

PWAs configured with proper caching allow sites to operate with offline capabilities, crucial for maintaining performance due to unreliable mobile connections.

Future Directions and Continued Innovation in Mobile Experience

As technology progresses, mobile web performance will continuously evolve, reflecting advancements in network technologies, device capabilities, and user expectations. Cloudflare remains at the forefront, iterating on features and capacities to accommodate innovations such as 5G, augmented reality, and sophisticated mobile applications.

Through ongoing research and development, Cloudflare seeks to integrate cutting-edge algorithms, further compressing resources, and unlocking higher levels of efficiency in mobile web delivery. The inclusion of AI-driven optimizations offers the potential for automatically adjusted performance enhancements, tailored to the nuances of individual user environments.

Accelerating mobile experiences is a multifaceted objective, demanding efficient resource management, adaptive technology use, and embracing emerging standards like AMP and PWAs. Cloudflare equips developers with powerful tools to achieve these aims, delivering responsive, fast, and engaging mobile websites that not only meet but exceed user expectations, ensuring robust engagement in an ever-mobile-centric digital future.

4.7 Performance Tracking and Analysis

Performance tracking and analysis are critical components of maintaining an optimized website, providing insights into how well a site delivers content and interacts with users. Identifying performance bottlenecks and understanding user interaction patterns enable developers to make informed decisions in enhancing web performance and user experience. Cloudflare offers a suite of analytic tools and monitoring services that aid in comprehensive performance tracking, allowing for nuanced analysis, troubleshooting, and optimization of website operations.

- **The Importance of Performance Metrics**

Performance metrics serve as benchmarks for evaluating the efficiency and responsiveness of a website. Core Web Vitals, introduced by Google, have become pivotal metrics that encompass several aspects

106

of user experience, including loading performance, interactivity, and visual stability.

- **Largest Contentful Paint (LCP):** Measures how long it takes for the largest visible content element to load and become visible within the viewport.

- **First Input Delay (FID):** Captures the time from when a user first interacts with a page to the time when the browser is able to begin processing event handlers in response to that interaction.

- **Cumulative Layout Shift (CLS):** Tracks the sum total of all unexpected layout shifts that occur during the lifespan of the page.

These key performance indicators (KPIs) provide a holistic view of the user's experience, directly influencing search engine rankings and user engagement. Cloudflare's analytic tools integrate these metrics, offering real-time data and historical perspectives for in-depth performance evaluations.

- **Cloudflare Analytics Dashboard**

Cloudflare's analytics dashboard offers a centralized view of site performance, featuring both real-time and historical data on traffic, security threats, and performance metrics. Key components include:

- **Traffic Trends:** Analyze traffic by examining patterns of incoming and outgoing data, identifying peaks, geographical distribution, and user demographics.

- **Performance Summaries:** Visualize speed-related metrics, including time to first byte (TTFB), download time, and interaction metrics such as LCP, FID, and CLS. These insights facilitate the identification of areas needing optimization.

- **Security Insights:** Monitoring attempts of unauthorized access or attacks provide insights into potential vulnerabilities, enabling proactive security enhancements.

107

• Real-Time Monitoring and Alerts

Real-time monitoring allows for the immediate identification of unexpected changes in website behavior. Cloudflare's services can be configured to send alerts when performance thresholds are crossed, ensuring rapid response times to evolving conditions. These notifications ensure that teams are informed of critical events, permitting timely intervention.

• Sample Code for Setting Up Performance Alerts Using Webhooks:

Cloudflare supports webhook integration, facilitating automated alert systems for performance metrics.

```python
import requests
import json

def send_webhook_alert(message):
    url = "https://hooks.example.com/services/T00000000/B00000000/
        XXXXXXXXXXXXXXXXXXXXXXXX"
    payload = {
        "text": message
    }
    headers = {
        "Content-Type": "application/json"
    }
    response = requests.post(url, data=json.dumps(payload), headers=headers)
    if response.status_code == 200:
        print("Alert sent successfully!")

# Usage
performance_issue_detected = True
if performance_issue_detected:
    send_webhook_alert("Performance issue detected: High LCP recorded")
```

This script demonstrates triggering a webhook when a specified performance issue is detected, ensuring immediate team notifications.

• Advanced Performance Analysis with Cloudflare Workers

Cloudflare Workers enable the customization of content delivery and tracking, offering the flexibility to adjust responses based on request characteristics dynamically.

108

```
// Cloudflare Worker example to log request and response parameters
addEventListener('fetch', (event) => {
  event.respondWith(logAndFetch(event.request))
})

async function logAndFetch(request) {
  console.log('Request URL:', request.url)
  const init = {
    method: request.method,
    headers: request.headers
  }
  const response = await fetch(request.url, init)
  console.log('Response Status:', response.status)

  return response
}
```

This worker script logs request and response properties, enabling deep analytical insight into the performance of the content delivery process. By customizing response logic, developers gain the ability to conduct specific performance experiments or troubleshoot operational issues.

- **Integrating with Third-party Analytics**

While Cloudflare provides robust analytic tools, integrating with third-party analytics like Google Analytics or New Relic can further enhance visibility across performance dimensions.

```
<!-- Google Analytics Global site tag (gtag.js) -->
<script async src="https://www.googletagmanager.com/gtag/js?id=UA-XXXXXX
    "></script>
<script>
  window.dataLayer = window.dataLayer || [];
  function gtag(){dataLayer.push(arguments);}
  gtag('js', new Date());

  gtag('config', 'UA-XXXXXX');
</script>
```

This integration script demonstrates the incorporation of Google Analytics for in-depth tracking and insight collaboration.

- **Actionable Insights and Performance Optimization**

The data obtained through Cloudflare's analysis tools offer guidance for practical optimization actions. By evaluating lagging performance metrics, developers can prioritize efforts on specific elements such as reducing resource sizes, optimizing server response times, or refining cache strategies.

- **Example Analysis and Recommendations:**

- **High Time to First Byte (TTFB):** Improve server response times by optimizing server-side processing, reducing DNS lookup durations, or scaling hosting infrastructure.

- **Excessive Cumulative Layout Shift (CLS):** Assign explicit size attributes to all images and referenced media to avoid layout shifts, and avoid inserting content above existing content except in response to user interaction.

- **Large LCP Times:** Prioritize the loading of above-the-fold content by deferring non-critical JavaScript and employing lazy loading for images.

- **Visualizing Performance Trends Over Time**

Cloudflare's historical data archival ensures that performance trends can be visualized over time, enabling the evaluation of ongoing improvement initiatives and the validation of applied optimizations.

- **Predictive Analytics and Automation**

As advancements in machine learning algorithms progress, predictive analytics becomes attainable, potentially automating performance optimizations by predicting future traffic patterns and pre-emptively adjusting configurations and resources.

Chapter 5

Leveraging Cloudflare for DDoS Protection

This chapter focuses on the mechanisms Cloudflare employs to defend against Distributed Denial of Service (DDoS) attacks, ensuring uninterrupted service availability. It outlines Cloudflare's multilayered approach, combining automated threat detection and intelligent traffic filtering. Readers will learn how to configure DDoS protection settings, analyze case studies of effective defense strategies, and implement best practices for maintaining robust security postures. The chapter provides a framework for understanding the intricacies of DDoS attacks and the proactive steps Cloudflare facilitates to counteract these threats.

5.1   Understanding DDoS Attacks

Distributed Denial of Service (DDoS) attacks represent a significant challenge in the realm of cybersecurity, exploiting the distributed nature of computing resources to interrupt services, degrade performance, or bring down entire systems. In this section, we delve into the mechanics of DDoS attacks, exploring how they function, their underlying structures, and the potential impact on online services.

DDoS attacks are executed by overwhelming a targeted system with a flood of traffic from multiple sources. These attacks harness a network of compromised computers, often referred to as a botnet, which are infected through various means, including malware and phishing attacks. Each computer within the botnet acts as a participant in the attack, sending an overwhelming volume of requests or data packets to the target system. By exceeding the capacity of the network or server, a DDoS attack can render the service unavailable to legitimate users.

Types of DDoS Attacks

DDoS attacks can be categorized into several types, each targeting different components of the network infrastructure:

- *Volumetric Attacks*: Also known as flood attacks, these aim to saturate the bandwidth of the targeted site. Common methods include UDP floods, ICMP floods, and DNS amplification attacks. These attacks typically generate a large volume of traffic intended to consume the available bandwidth, effectively clogging the network.

- *Protocol Attacks*: These attacks exploit weaknesses in network protocols to exhaust server resources. Examples include SYN floods, which abuse the TCP handshake process, and Ping of Death, which involves sending malformed or oversized packets.

- *Application Layer Attacks*: These target specific applications or services, aiming to exhaust resources by mimicking legitimate user traffic. HTTP floods and Slowloris attacks fall into this category, both of which can disrupt web servers by overwhelming application resources rather than the underlying network infrastructure.

```
import socket

host = 'target-server.com'
port = 80
requests_number = 1000

try:
    for i in range(requests_number):
        s = socket.socket(socket.AF_INET, socket.SOCK_STREAM)
```

```
        s.connect((host, port))
        request = f"GET / HTTP/1.1\r\nHost: {host}\r\n\r\n"
        s.send(request.encode())
        s.close()
        print(f"Request {i+1} sent")
except Exception as e:
    print(f"Error occurred: {e}")
# A simple script to demonstrate how incessant requests could contribute to an
    application layer DDoS attack.
```

The script above illustrates how an HTTP flood attack might execute. It repeatedly sends HTTP GET requests to a target server, aiming to exhaust its resources. Although rudimentary, this example highlights the potential threat posed by even simple scripts when leveraged across a distributed network of bots.

Botnets and Their Role in DDoS Attacks

One of the defining characteristics of DDoS attacks is their use of botnets. A botnet is a collection of internet-connected devices, which may include PCs, servers, mobile devices, and IoT gadgets, that are infected and controlled by malware. Attackers distribute this malware across the internet to conscript these devices into their botnet, often unbeknownst to the device's legitimate user.

Botnets enable attackers to generate the massive scale of requests necessary for a DDoS attack. They allow for the distribution of attack loads, making it challenging to pinpoint and block a single source. Over time, botnets have evolved in complexity, incorporating advanced evasion techniques and employing algorithms that make attribution and mitigation more difficult.

In recent years, the proliferation of IoT devices has exacerbated the threat posed by DDoS attacks. Many IoT devices lack robust security measures, making them easy targets for malware. Once compromised, these devices can contribute substantial bandwidth to an attack, as seen in the case of the Mirai botnet, which co-opted IoT devices around the world to execute some of the most significant DDoS attacks on record.

Impact of DDoS Attacks

The impacts of a successful DDoS attack can be extensive, affecting business operations, revenue, and reputation. Immediate consequences include:

- *Downtime*: The most direct impact, where services become inaccessible to users. This can be particularly damaging for e-commerce, banking, and online services that rely on consistent availability.

- *Financial Losses*: Direct revenue losses from service disruptions, alongside potential cost implications from the need for incident response and mitigation.

- *Reputational Damage*: Prolonged outages can erode customer trust, negatively affecting brand reputation and customer retention.

- *Operational Disruption*: Internal operations can be derailed, affecting employee productivity and resource allocation as IT staff are redirected to address the attack.

Service Disruption	Financial Impact
XYZ E-commerce site experienced 6 hours of downtime during a Holiday Sale event.	Estimated loss of sales: $500,000
Incident response and system recovery costs: $80,000	

The example above illustrates hypothetical financial data from a DDoS incident to highlight the potential economic repercussions.

Current Trends in DDoS Attacks

A significant trend in DDoS attacks is the increasing scale and sophistication of threats. Advances in technology and changing internet trends contribute to evolving attack vectors. Some notable trends include:

- *IoT-driven Attacks*: The expanding IoT landscape broadens the attack surface, and the vast number of connected devices presents new opportunities for attackers. IoT devices often come with less stringent security measures, making them ideal candidates for botnet assimilation.

- *Application-level Complexity*: As understanding of lower-level DDoS techniques increases, attackers are shifting to more complex application-layer attacks, which can be harder to detect and mitigate. These attacks may involve authentic-looking HTTP requests or layer 7 protocols that simulate legitimate traffic.

- *Ransom DDoS (RDoS)*: Attackers threaten an imminent DDoS attack unless a ransom is paid. This not only endangers system availability but also coerces victims into financial transactions under duress.

- *Multi-vector Attacks*: Increasingly, attacks employ multiple vectors simultaneously, combining volumetric, protocol, and application layer tactics to exploit a broader range of system vulnerabilities.

Detection and Mitigation Challenges

DDoS attack detection and mitigation present unique challenges due to the diversity of vectors and the distributed nature of attack sources. Early detection is crucial for effective mitigation. Organizations employ a range of strategies, including:

- *Traffic Analysis*: Monitoring network traffic to identify unusual patterns or spikes indicative of an attack. Algorithms analyze traffic in real-time, considering deviations from normal behavior.

- *Anomaly Detection Systems*: Use machine learning to differentiate between legitimate and malicious traffic, adapting over time to new threat landscapes.

- *Rate Limiting and Filtering*: Controls the number of requests that users can issue within a specific time frame, useful for mitigating volumetric attacks.

- *Redundancy and Elasticity*: Designing infrastructure to withstand surges in traffic, utilizing cloud-based resources to absorb volumetric attacks.

The dynamic nature of attack techniques requires continuous adaptation of detection and mitigation measures, often combining automated systems with human oversight to refine responses.

```
from scapy.all import *
from collections import Counter

traffic = rdpcap('network_traffic.pcap')
```

```
ip_counter = Counter(pkt[IP].src for pkt in traffic if IP in pkt)

print("Top 5 IP addresses by packet count:")
for ip, count in ip_counter.most_common(5):
    print(f"{ip}: {count} packets")
# This snippet showcases basic traffic analysis, helping identify IPs involved in
    potential DDoS activities.
```

This Python script utilizes the Scapy library to analyze packet captures, demonstrating how traffic patterns can be monitored to determine potential DDoS sources.

Understanding DDoS attacks in depth empowers organizations to better prepare and respond. As technologies evolve and attack methodologies become more sophisticated, the importance of awareness, comprehensive defense strategies, and proactive planning cannot be overstated. Adopting a multilayered approach to cybersecurity, encompassing technological measures, process improvements, and strategic planning, is essential for mitigating the risks associated with DDoS attacks.

5.2 Cloudflare's DDoS Mitigation Techniques

Cloudflare employs a comprehensive suite of strategies to protect against Distributed Denial of Service (DDoS) attacks, leveraging advanced technology and extensive global infrastructure. This section provides an in-depth analysis of the various techniques Cloudflare utilizes to safeguard network resources and ensure uninterrupted service availability.

Cloudflare's approach to DDoS mitigation is multifaceted, integrating automatic threat detection, intelligent traffic filtering, and real-time adaptive learning. These techniques encompass both the prevention and mitigation phases, aiming to detect potential threats early and neutralize them effectively.

Infrastructure and Network Capacity

At the core of Cloudflare's DDoS mitigation strategies lies its global anycast network, designed to disperse incoming traffic across numerous data centers strategically located worldwide. This infrastructure ensures not only redundancy and load balancing but also minimizes latency, distributing the impact of incoming DDoS traffic and absorbing large-scale volumetric attacks.

Key features include:

- *Anycast Network*: Routes requests to the nearest data center, distributing traffic efficiently and preventing any single location from becoming overwhelmed. Anycast networking reduces latency while enhancing the capability to withstand large DDoS attacks by spreading them across the entire network.

- *Global Load Balancing*: Employs robust load balancing mechanisms to allocate network traffic based on real-time conditions. In the event of abnormal traffic surges, overloads are managed by distributing requests across an array of data centers, thereby alleviating pressure on specific nodes.

- *Elastic Scalability*: Automatically adjusts resource allocation in response to changing traffic patterns, essential for absorbing sudden spikes associated with DDoS attacks.

Through an extensive and resilient architecture, Cloudflare manages to handle vast magnitudes of traffic, turning the edge of its network into a powerful DDoS mitigation tool.

Traffic Analysis and Anomaly Detection

Cloudflare utilizes sophisticated traffic analysis mechanisms to distinguish between legitimate and malicious traffic. This involves analyzing data at both packet and protocol levels, leveraging machine learning algorithms that adapt to ever-evolving attack tactics.

- *Real-time Traffic Monitoring*: Ongoing surveillance of incoming traffic allows for instantaneous detection of anomalies that may indicate a DDoS attack. Features such as flow analysis and deep packet inspection facilitate the rapid recognition of suspicious patterns.

- *Anomaly Filtering*: Leveraging statistical models and machine learning, Cloudflare enhances filtering capabilities, automatically identifying atypical flow patterns indicative of DDoS attempts. Machine learning models are continuously trained on vast datasets, ensuring they maintain high precision in differentiating legitimate from malicious activities.

- *Behavioral Analysis*: User behavior patterns are scrutinized to identify anomalies. Typical behaviors, such as connection time, frequency of requests, and source-IP reputation, are monitored over time, automatically adapting models to discern shifts that could signify a DDoS attempt.

```
from scapy.all import *
from collections import defaultdict

def find_anomalies(packets):
    packet_counts = defaultdict(int)

    for packet in packets:
        if IP in packet and TCP in packet:
            packet_counts[packet[IP].src] += 1

    threshold = 1000
    for ip, count in packet_counts.items():
        if count > threshold:
            print(f"Anomalous activity detected from IP: {ip} with {count} requests")

capture = rdpcap('http_traffic.pcap')
find_anomalies(capture)
# This script processes packet data to identify IPs exceeding predefined request
    thresholds, simplifying anomaly detection.
```

This example illustrates the concept of detecting anomalous HTTP traffic volumes using Python. By monitoring activity, such scripts help identify suspicious traffic patterns likely linked to DDoS activities.

Rate Limiting and Filtering Techniques

To combat application layer attacks and mitigate volumetric attacks, Cloudflare applies rigorous rate limiting and filtering rules. These mechanisms ensure that legitimate traffic is prioritized and malicious requests are blocked or throttled.

- *Rate Limiting*: Controls the number of requests a user or device can issue over a given timeframe. This is particularly effec-

118

tive against low-rate, high-volume attacks targeting web applications.

- *IP Reputation and Blacklisting*: Maintains an extensive list of known malicious IP addresses compiled through collaborative threat intelligence. Suspicious IPs are automatically blocked from accessing network resources.

- *Protocol and Resource Scrubbing*: Scrubs incoming traffic based on protocol standards. Any deviations from standard protocol operations are flagged and periodically blocked, reducing the risk of protocol-based DDoS attacks.

Rate limiting is implemented in conjunction with algorithms that dynamically adjust limits based on current network conditions, increasing flexibility and reducing the chances of accidental false positives that could affect legitimate user access.

Web Application Firewall (WAF)

Cloudflare's Web Application Firewall (WAF) forms a critical component of its DDoS mitigation strategy, providing a specialized barrier that filters, monitors, and blocks HTTP/HTTPS traffic to and from a web service.

- *Customizable Rulesets*: Users can configure specific rulesets to tailor protection to their unique use cases. These rules might include URL blocking, SQL injection prevention, and cross-site scripting (XSS) safeguard mechanisms.

- *Automatically Updated Threat Intelligence*: WAF leverages global threat intelligence to keep its database up-to-date. Thus, the system proactively updates its defense mechanisms with new threat signatures.

- *Zero-day Exploit Protection*: By integrating with threat intelligence services that identify zero-day vulnerabilities, Cloudflare's WAF can rapidly adapt, providing provisional shielding even before official patches are issued.

The WAF operates synergistically with other mitigation tools, providing layered defenses against both DDoS and application-level attacks, thus ensuring comprehensive security.

```
from flask import Flask, request, abort

app = Flask(__name__)

BLACKLISTED_IPS = {'192.168.1.100', '172.16.0.3'}

@app.before_request
def limit_remote_addr():
    if request.remote_addr in BLACKLISTED_IPS:
        abort(403) # Forbidden

@app.route('/')
def index():
    return "Welcome to the site!"

if __name__ == '__main__':
    app.run()
# Simulated application leveraging IP blacklisting to prevent known malicious traffic.
```

This script exemplifies a simple Flask web application implementing IP blacklisting, a fundamental concept within broader DDoS mitigation practices.

Adaptive Mitigation Strategies

Beyond the technical implementations, Cloudflare employs adaptive strategies to fine-tune and enhance mitigation efforts. These strategies combine automated processes with human insights to ensure security measures respond to evolving threat landscapes.

- *Continuous Learning Systems*: These systems aggregate and analyze vast quantities of data to refine detection algorithms continuously, embracing an ongoing cycle of learning and improvement.

- *Manual Review and Intervention*: In scenarios where automated tools require additional accuracy or specificity, experts conduct manual traffic pattern reviews to adjust configurations and develop customized response strategies.

- *Community-driven Insights*: Cloudflare benefits from a vast constituency of global clients. Interaction with this user base contributes diverse security insights, allowing for the identification of emerging threats and collaborative innovation in defensive countermeasures.

The combination of advanced automation and expert analysis ensures that Cloudflare not only defends against current DDoS attack methodologies but also anticipates potential future threats, adapting plans accordingly.

Cloudflare's multifaceted DDoS mitigation framework exemplifies a modern, integrated approach to cybersecurity, addressing threats with a blend of technological innovation, expansive infrastructure, and adaptive strategies. Through these measures, Cloudflare successfully maintains service availability and performance, establishing itself as a leader in the provision of internet security solutions against the persistent threat of DDoS attacks.

5.3 Configuring DDoS Protection in Cloudflare

Configuring Distributed Denial of Service (DDoS) protection in Cloudflare involves a comprehensive set of actions aimed at optimizing both automatic and manual defense mechanisms available via the Cloudflare dashboard. This section provides a detailed guide on setting up DDoS protection, including step-by-step instructions and insights into leveraging Cloudflare's robust suite of security features.

The configuration process starts with understanding the various protection levels and mechanisms Cloudflare provides. These include essential settings for traffic analysis, rate limiting, and customized rules that combine to offer a seamless shield against a spectrum of DDoS attacks.

Initial Setup and Dashboard Overview

Upon registering a domain with Cloudflare, the first step is to navigate the Cloudflare dashboard, a centralized interface providing access to all security settings and features. Users gain insights into traffic statistics, performance metrics, and security alerts, which are pivotal for managing DDoS protection.

- *Domain Integration*: The initial setup involves updating DNS records so that traffic routes through Cloudflare's network. This process essentially entails changing your domain's name servers to Cloudflare's specified values.

- *Dashboard Navigation*: Familiarize with the main dashboard sections: Overview, Analytics, Security, Firewall, and Speed. Each section provides specific tools and data relevant to different aspects of website management and protection.

- *Security Center*: The Security tab is critical for DDoS protection configuration. It hosts tools like firewall rules, IP access rules, and security settings, including DDoS mitigation configurations.

Automatic DDoS Protection

Cloudflare offers automated DDoS protection features designed to respond swiftly to DDoS events. These automatic settings adapt to network traffic dynamics, maintaining the availability of sites under attack.

- *Always On DDoS Protection*: Automatically detects and mitigates DDoS attacks. This feature continuously monitors traffic patterns, deploying automatic countermeasures as soon as abnormal activities are detected.

- *Traffic Threshold Configuration*: Within the settings, users can adjust traffic thresholds that dictate when DDoS protection triggers. Customizing these thresholds ensures they align closely with individual usage patterns and potential vulnerabilities.

- *Severity Levels*: Cloudflare provides settings for varying DDoS protection severity levels. Users can calibrate these levels based on perceived threat levels — Low, Medium, High — dictating how aggressively the system responds to potential threats.

Fine-tuning Firewall and Rate Limiting Rules

A critical aspect of Cloudflare's configurable features includes setting precise firewall rules and rate limits to mitigate DDoS and application layer attacks.

- *Firewall Rules*: Devise rules that govern access based on IP addresses, geographical locations, and even specific request headers. Firewall rules can be customized to allow, challenge, or completely block traffic meeting specified conditions.

```
{
    "id": "1d2f3b4a5c6d",
    "expression": "(http.request.uri.path contains \"login\" and ip.geoip.
        country ne \"US\")",
    "action": "block",
    "description": "Block all non-US requests to the login page"
}
```

The above JSON snippet displays a hypothetical firewall rule in Cloudflare, restricting access to a login page for requests emerging from beyond the United States, thus diminishing exposure to unauthorized access attempts.

- *Advanced Rate Limiting*: Configure rate limitations to manage the number of requests clients can make over specified durations. Rate limiting acts as a deterrent against application layer attacks aiming to overwhelm system resources slowly.

In the configuration panel, administrators can specify request URLs, set threshold counts, and define response actions once thresholds are crossed, such as logging, challenge prompts, or outright blocking.

Customizing Security Events with Page Rules

Cloudflare's page rules offer opportunities to fine-tune security configurations even further by applying specific settings based on URL patterns. This flexibility allows for more granular control over visitor interactions and security postures.

- *Creating Page Rules*: Navigate to the 'Page Rules' section within the dashboard. Page rules facilitate application of settings like caching behaviors, redirect operations, or security configurations according to URL matching patterns.

- *URL Pattern Matching*: Specify URL patterns to which particular rule sets should apply. These may involve including hostnames, paths, and query parameters, ensuring tailored responses against DDoS attempts targeting specific website areas.

- *Rule Prioritization*: Page rules function based on priorities. Cloudflare evaluates rules in a top-down sequence; hence, proper ordering is crucial for ensuring expected rule applications without unintended conflicts.

```python
import requests

api_token = 'your_api_token'
zone_id = 'your_zone_id'
url = 'https://api.cloudflare.com/client/v4/zones/{}/pagerules'.format(
    zone_id)

headers = {
    'Authorization': 'Bearer {}'.format(api_token),
    'Content-Type': 'application/json'
}

page_rule = {
    "targets": [
        {
            "target": "url",
            "constraint": {
                "operator": "matches",
                "value": "example.com/api/*"
            }
        }
    ],
    "actions": [
        {
            "id": "disable_security"
        }
    ],
    "priority": 1,
    "status": "active"
}

response = requests.post(url, json=page_rule, headers=headers)

print(response.json())
# Automating the creation of a page rule via Cloudflare's API,
    demonstrating how security settings could be configured
    programmatically.
```

This Python script communicates with Cloudflare's API to create a page rule, highlighting the capability of automating security configurations programmatically for specific URL paths.

Security Logging and Monitoring

An integral part of any DDoS protection strategy includes regular monitoring and logging for auditing, compliance, and continuous improvement.

- *Security Logs Access*: Cloudflare provides detailed logs on firewall executions, security events, and traffic statistics. These logs are accessible through the dashboard and integrations with services such as SIEM platforms, offering comprehensive insights into attempted attacks.

- *Analytics and Reporting*: The Analytics section allows users to visualize traffic trends and security events over time. Graphical representation aids in understanding traffic origins, successful mitigations, and potential weaknesses for future refinement.

- *Event Alerts and Notifications*: Set up notifications to alert when defined traffic patterns, anomalies, or potential DDoS activities are detected. Alerts can be configured to communicate through various channels, enhancing response readiness.

```
Log Example:
Time: 2023-11-01 14:23:12
Action: Blocked
Rule: country_block
Source IP: 203.0.113.76
Country: CN
Description: Non-US IP attempting access blocked by rule.

# Sample log entry illustrating security actions taken based on configured
  rules and detected patterns.
```

By maintaining comprehensive logs, organizations can engage in detailed post-event analyses, informing ongoing mitigation strategy development and proactive threat anticipation.

Comprehending and configuring Cloudflare's DDoS protection settings ensures robust defense postures against evolving cyber threats, facilitating optimal resource availability while enhancing resilience. Adjusting configurations regularly and tailoring settings to meet specific demands enable administrators to harness Cloudflare's capabilities fully, securing their networks effectively against potential disruptions.

5.4   Case Studies of DDoS Defense

This section examines real-world scenarios where Cloudflare's DDoS defense mechanisms were pivotal in mitigating large-scale attacks. Through these case studies, we gain insights into practical applications of Cloudflare's strategies and learn valuable lessons in adapting methods to emerging threats.

Case Study 1:   Mitigating a Volumetric Attack on E-Commerce Platforms

An international e-commerce platform experienced an unexpected influx of traffic, severely impairing its operations. The attack was identified as a volumetric DDoS attempt, overwhelmingly consuming bandwidth through a barrage of UDP and ICMP packets.

- *Challenge*: The primary challenge lay in maintaining availability for legitimate users amidst a continuous high-volume attack. Immediate identification and response were necessary to prevent revenue loss during a peak shopping season.

- *Solution*: Cloudflare rapidly deployed its global anycast network to absorb the traffic. The deployment leveraged automatic threat detection leveraging their extensive data center network, distributing the attack load and isolating malicious traffic patterns.

- *Outcome*: Within minutes, the platform's availability was restored, and normal operations continued without significant disruption. The ability to maintain bandwidth and resource integrity protected both the site's reputation and financial interests during a critical period.

```
from scapy.all import *
from collections import Counter

def udp_flood_detect(packet):
    if packet.haslayer(UDP) and packet[IP].dst == "target-ip":
        return packet[IP].src

packets = sniff(offline='traffic_dump.pcap')
potential_attackers = Counter([udp_flood_detect(pkt) for pkt in packets if
    udp_flood_detect(pkt)])
for attacker, count in potential_attackers.items():
    print(f"Potential attacker: {attacker} sent {count} UDP packets")
# This code processes packet data to pinpoint IPs responsible for a large number of
    UDP packets, indicating potential flood attempts.
```

This script exemplifies UDP flood detection, an initial step in identifying and dealing with volumetric DDoS attacks, similar to the case at hand.

Case Study 2: Application Layer Attack on Financial Services

A prominent financial services company fell victim to an elaborate application-layer attack, targeting its login credentials authentication system. This low-rate but highly effective onslaught aimed to exhaust system resources by simulating realistic user behavior through slow HTTP requests.

- *Challenge*: The insidious nature of the attack made it difficult to distinguish malicious actions from legitimate user transactions. The attack effectively stretched backend resources, risking both security and user experience.

- *Solution*: Cloudflare's application firewall (WAF) and rate limiting capabilities were critical. Applying specific rate limiting rules curtailed excessive requests per minute, and a configured WAF rule blocked requests identified as part of the slow HTTP attack pattern, such as incomplete headers or unusually long response times.

- *Outcome*: Resource usage gradually normalized, user accessibility was restored, and critical financial services continued operating without further disruption. By refining detection algorithms, the system became better equipped to recognize similar threats in the future.

```
from scapy.all import *
from time import time

def slow_http_detect(packet):
    if packet.haslayer(TCP) and packet[TCP].dport == 80:
        start_time = time()
        payload = packet[TCP].payload
        if payload and len(payload) < 50: # Arbitrary small payload indicating
                potential slow-read
            elapsed_time = time() - start_time
            return packet[IP].src, elapsed_time

packets = sniff(offline='slow_http_traffic.pcap')
for pkt in packets:
    result = slow_http_detect(pkt)
    if result:
        print(f"Slow HTTP attack suspected from {result[0]} with elapsed time {result
            [1]:.2f}s")
```

This Python example scrutinizes HTTP request patterns, aiding in identifying slow HTTP attacks akin to those experienced by the company.

Case Study 3: Multi-vector Attack on a Content Delivery Network

A large content delivery network (CDN) faced a sophisticated multi-
vector DDoS attack aggregating volumetric, protocol, and application
layer tactics. Attack vectors included SYN Flood for protocol exploitation, DNS amplification for volumetric overload, and HTTP GET/-
POST floods targeting application layers.

- *Challenge*: The multi-pronged nature of the attack required si-
  multaneous mitigation across different network layers, involving
  multiple attack signatures and techniques within a single timeframe.

- *Solution*: Comprehensive defense involved the coordinated application of Cloudflare's DDoS defense arsenal: from rate limiting and WAF at application layers to packet analysis and filtering at network and transport layers. Automated threat detection
  countered each vector with tailored strategies, while manual intervention by expert analysts optimized firewall configurations.

- *Outcome*: The CDN succeeded in both mitigating the attack and
  minimizing user experience impact. The integrated response

showcased Cloudflare's capacity to manage multi-vector threats effectively while maintaining high availability.

Analysis and Lessons Learned

These case studies furnish valuable lessons in DDoS defense, underscoring the importance of a holistic, adaptable approach. Lessons include:

- *Proactive Configuration*: Proactive settings and a broad range of pre-configured rules enhance the speed of effective response during actual attack scenarios.

- *Automated Versus Manual Intervention*: While automation substantiates initial mitigation, human expertise is vital in adapting and customizing defenses amidst evolving attack chains, affecting network layers concurrently.

- *Leveraging Machine Learning*: The continuation of adaptive learning processes through machine learning is paramount, allowing systems to identify diverse attack vectors, enhancing recognition capabilities across volumetric, protocol, and application layers.

- *Resilience and Redundancy*: Building resilience into network architectures, backed by extensive redundancy, remains critical. It contributes to attack impact diffusion, providing extra layers of security and continuity.

Building a Future-proof DDoS Strategy

Evident from these case studies is the necessity for an overarching, future-proofed DDoS mitigation strategy that evolves alongside technological and threat landscapes.

Key considerations for an enduring mitigation strategy include:

- *Regular Assessments and Updates*: Deploying frequent security audits, reviewing configuration settings, and updating rulesets based on recent threat intelligence and vulnerability assessments.

- *Collaboration and Information Sharing*: Proactively engaging in information sharing with cybersecurity communities and leveraging threat intelligence feeds to enhance visibility and preparedness.

- *Comprehensive Training Programs*: Ensuring personnel receive ongoing education and training tailored toward new attack methodologies and tools, empowering them to respond capably to dynamic threat vectors.

- *Strategic Research and Development Investments*: Investing in research and innovation ensures organizations remain at the forefront of technology, continually advancing defenses against increasingly sophisticated DDoS methods.

Successfully addressing future DDoS challenges requires a dynamic and integrative approach, capable of neutralizing both anticipated and innovative attack formats. By embracing a versatile strategic mindset, organizations can sustain optimal service availability and operational resilience amidst the complexities of evolving cyber threats.

5.5   Testing and Validating DDoS Readiness

Ensuring system robustness and resilience against Distributed Denial of Service (DDoS) attacks necessitates meticulous testing and validation of readiness measures. This section examines comprehensive strategies and methodologies for testing and validating DDoS defenses, thus equipping organizations to optimize response times and fortify their networks effectively.

Testing DDoS readiness requires an orchestrated approach that includes simulating potential attack vectors, evaluating performance under stress conditions, and calibrating defense mechanisms to align with evolving threat landscapes.

Understanding the Scope and Objectives of DDoS Testing

The primary goal of DDoS testing is to ascertain the ability of networks, applications, and infrastructure to withstand and efficiently mitigate attack impacts. Key objectives involve:

- Identifying Vulnerabilities: Discover weaknesses within the current security posture, covering network, application, and infrastructure layers.

- Measuring Defense Effectiveness: Validate existing defenses and mitigation mechanisms in handling simulated attack patterns in real-world scenarios.

- Optimizing Response Strategies: Enhance incident response plans by practicing the deployment of mitigation measures in a controlled setting.

- Evaluating Alert Systems and Reporting: Assess the performance of monitoring, logging, and alert systems, ensuring accurate, timely notifications and reporting during attack simulations.

Simulating DDoS Attacks

Conducting controlled DDoS simulations facilitates an authentic assessment of system response capabilities. Techniques and tools for simulating attacks include:

- Traffic Generation Tools: Utilize tools like LOIC (Low Orbit Ion Cannon), Hping3, or Tsunami UDP to simulate volumetric attacks. Ensure testing occurs within isolated environments to prevent unintended network disruption.

- Application Layer Simulation: Tools such as Slowloris or OWASP HTTP POST simulate slow-rate attacks, targeting specific application vulnerabilities.

- Custom Script Development: Develop scripts to emulate targeted attacks, customizing packet structures, request behaviors, or protocol anomalies.

```
import requests
from concurrent.futures import ThreadPoolExecutor

target_url = "http://target-server.com"
num_requests = 1000
concurrent = 100

def send_request():
    try:
        response = requests.get(target_url)
        print(f"Response Code: {response.status_code}")
    except Exception as e:
        print(f"Request failed: {e}")

with ThreadPoolExecutor(max_workers=concurrent) as executor:
    for _ in range(num_requests):
        executor.submit(send_request)
# Simulates an HTTP flood by generating multiple concurrent requests targeting a
    specified URL.
```

This Python script demonstrates how an HTTP flood could be programmatically simulated to assess web application resilience against volumetric attacks.

Performance Evaluation and Stress Testing

Through rigorous performance evaluation, organizations assess the impact of simulated attacks on system architecture, pinpointing stress points and bottlenecks.

- Load Testing with Tools: Employ dedicated tools like Apache JMeter or Gatling to load test applications, mimicking heavy user traffic.

- Key Metrics Assessment: Monitor network latency, server CPU and memory utilization, bandwidth consumption, and packet loss rates during simulations.

- Infrastructure Review: Analyze data center capacity, redundancy deployment, and edge server efficiency to evaluate readiness for absorbing attack traffic without degradation of service.

Performance Test Sample Metrics	
CPU Utilization	Pre-test: 35%, During test: 95%
Network Latency	Pre-test: 20ms, During test: 150ms
Bandwidth Usage	Pre-test: 500MB/s, During test: 3000MB/s

Such simulated metrics offer a clear snapshot of network and server performance under DDoS conditions, directing improvement efforts where most needed.

Validating Defense Mechanisms

Validation tasks center on testing the effectiveness of defense configurations, rate limits, and rule-based protection protocols.

- Firewall and Rate Limit Checks: Validate Cloudflare firewall rules and rate limits, ensuring response actions are correctly triggered by attack simulations.

- Dynamic Filtering Evaluation: Test the accuracy of anomaly detection and dynamic filtering algorithms in identifying malicious traffic.

- Redundancy and Failover Testing: Simulate failover scenarios to assess the robustness of redundancy mechanisms and backup resources during prolonged DDoS events.

Adapting Defense Strategies Based on Test Results

Post-testing analyses involve dissecting simulation data to refine defense strategies, thus improving resilience against future threats.

- Reporting and Review: Generate detailed reports of testing outcomes, documenting observed vulnerabilities, defense successes, and areas requiring improvement.

- Continual Configuration Refinement: Adjust firewall rules, update threat intelligence, and modify thresholds based on thorough analysis of test encounters and outcomes.

- Incident Response Plan Updates: Reinforce incident response workflows to incorporate insights gained from real-world simulations, emphasizing enhancements to response efficiency and communication channels.

Integrating Regular DDoS Readiness Drills

Routine inclusion of DDoS readiness drills within an enterprise's security program reinforces resilience through readiness verification exercises.

- Scheduled Simulations: Establish regular intervals for executing attack simulations aligning with internal security review cycles and new infrastructure deployments.

- Cross-team Collaboration: Engage diverse teams — IT, Network Security, Incident Response, and Business Continuity — to facilitate comprehensive readiness evaluations, incorporating multifaceted expertise.

- Scenario Diversity: Vary attack simulation scenarios to include emerging tactics and exploit vectors, preparing defenses for a wide spectrum of potential threats.

- Comprehensive Feedback Loops: Develop channels for collecting feedback from all participating teams post-simulation, supporting continuous improvement.

Integrating these methods within a continuous posture of readiness amplifies organizational capacity to withstand DDoS attacks efficiently, minimizing disruption while safeguarding business functions.

Leveraging Cloudflare Tools and Services for Testing

Leverage Cloudflare's tools and integrated services to enrich DDoS readiness testing efforts, providing organizations with critical capabilities needed for comprehensive assessments.

- Cloudflare Radar and Analytics: Use these tools to track global threat landscapes, customize threat watches, and analyze traffic patterns, aligning more precisely with observed attack trends.

- API Integrations: Utilize Cloudflare's robust API to programmatically test and manipulate firewall settings, page rules, and alerts, paralleling actual attack scenarios for more insightful evaluations.

- Monitoring and Logging Services: Configure Cloudflare Alerts and logging integrations for cross-platform visibility, ensuring actionable data access from test executions.

```
import requests

api_token = 'your_api_token'
zone_id = 'your_zone_id'
url = 'https://api.cloudflare.com/client/v4/zones/{}/firewall/rules'.format(zone_id)

headers = {
    'Authorization': 'Bearer {}'.format(api_token),
    'Content-Type': 'application/json'
}

firewall_rule = {
    "mode": "challenge",
    "configuration": {
        "target": "ip",
        "value": "203.0.113.0/24"
    },
    "notes": "Simulated test addition"
}

response = requests.post(url, json=firewall_rule, headers=headers)

print(response.json())
# Automates creating a test firewall rule using Cloudflare's API for DDoS simulation
    purposes.
```

This Python script demonstrates the execution of automated test tasks through Cloudflare's API, vital for streamlining configuration adjustments during DDoS simulations.

Through methodical testing and validation of DDoS readiness, organizations create a fortified, adaptive posture against myriad DDoS threats. Such readiness reinforces trust and ensures operational continuity, aligning defenses with the strategic imperatives of maintaining resilience and service availability in the face of escalating cyber challenges.

5.6 Incident Response and Post-Attack Analysis

In the contemporary digital landscape, the ability to respond effectively to a Distributed Denial of Service (DDoS) attack is crucial for main-

135

taining service continuity and minimizing disruptions. This section details comprehensive strategies for incident response during a DDoS onslaught and the invaluable practices of post-attack analysis. Such a structured approach ensures immediate threat neutralization, thorough understanding of attack dynamics, and fortification of defenses against future incidents.

Incident Response Planning

A robust incident response plan tailored to DDoS attacks is foundational to any cybersecurity strategy. It comprises predefined steps aligned with best practices for identifying, containing, and mitigating attacks.

- *Preparation and Resource Allocation*: Start by assembling a response team with defined roles, including network engineers, security analysts, and communication officers. Equip them with the necessary tools and authority to act promptly.

- *Activation Criteria*: Specify criteria and conditions that will trigger the incident response protocol. This could involve defined thresholds for unusual traffic behavior or alerts from monitoring systems indicating possible attack vectors.

- *Communication Protocols*: Ensure clear and efficient communication lines, both internally and externally, to disseminate critical information rapidly. Establish predefined communication templates for notifying stakeholders, both technical and non-technical.

Real-time Monitoring and Attack Detection

Modern DDoS response relies heavily on real-time monitoring to detect anomalies and verify incidents rapidly. Cloudflare and similar services offer comprehensive monitoring and alert capabilities essential for timely detection.

- *Traffic Anomaly Detection*: Implement advanced monitoring tools that assess traffic patterns in real-time, identifying anomalies in volume, source IP addresses, or irregular access patterns.

- *Automated Alerts*: Deploy automated alert systems that provide immediate notifications of detected threats. Alerts can be configured based on traffic spikes, failed access attempts, or an escalation of error rates.

- *Integration with SIEM Systems*: Integrate monitoring solutions with Security Information and Event Management (SIEM) systems to enhance data analysis and facilitate automated response actions.

```
from smtplib import SMTP
from email.mime.text import MIMEText

def send_alert(subject, message, recipient):
    alert_msg = MIMEText(message)
    alert_msg['Subject'] = subject
    alert_msg['From'] = 'alert@yourdomain.com'
    alert_msg['To'] = recipient

    with SMTP('smtp.yourdomain.com') as server:
        server.starttls()
        server.login('user', 'password')
        server.send_message(alert_msg)

monitor_data = {
    'traffic_spike': True,
    'source_ips': ['203.0.113.1', '203.0.113.2'],
    'threshold_exceeded': 10000
}

if monitor_data['traffic_spike']:
    message = f"Traffic spike detected. Source IPs: {monitor_data['source_ips']}. "
    message += f"Threshold: {monitor_data['threshold_exceeded']}"
    send_alert("DDoS Alert - Traffic Spike", message, "admin@yourdomain.com")
# This code demonstrates the setup of an email alert for a detected DDoS threat
    scenario.
```

This practical example illustrates activating an automated alert via email when specific criteria are met during traffic monitoring.

Attack Mitigation Techniques

Once detection is affirmed, immediate mitigation actions should follow to limit attack impacts:

- *Rate Limiting and Traffic Shaping*: Apply rate limits to incoming request surges. Utilize traffic shaping techniques to prioritize legitimate service traffic and degrade attack traffic impact.

- *IP Blacklisting and Geo-blocking*: In cases where threat sources are identifiable by IP address or geographical location, implement IP blacklisting and geo-blocking to mitigate incoming attack traffic.

- *Failover Procedures*: Activate failover systems that redirect traffic to backup servers or data centers, ensuring persistent service availability even under high incoming traffic loads.

- *Engagement with Service Providers*: If DDoS attacks surpass internal mitigation capabilities, engage third-party DDoS protection providers who specialize in large-scale traffic analysis and neutralization.

```
ip_blacklist = {'203.0.113.15', '198.51.100.23', '192.0.2.0'}

def is_ip_blocked(ip):
    return ip in ip_blacklist

incoming_traffic = ['203.0.113.15', '203.0.113.30', '198.51.100.23']

for ip in incoming_traffic:
    if is_ip_blocked(ip):
        print(f"Blocked IP: {ip}")
    else:
        print(f"Allowed IP: {ip}")
# Example Python script to demonstrate an IP blacklist implementation during a
    DDoS attack.
```

This script serves as a simple yet effective mechanism to instantly respond to identified attack sources by blocking known malicious IPs.

Post-Attack Analysis and Review

After immediate threats are mitigated, conducting a post-attack analysis is essential. This phase involves a comprehensive examination of the attack, aimed at understanding the dynamics, improving defense mechanisms, and preventing future incidents.

- *Data Collection and Artifacts Analysis*: Gather detailed logs and artifacts from the incident, including traffic patterns, alerts, response actions, and impacted services, for in-depth analysis.

- *Root Cause Determination*: Identify the root causes of vulnerabilities exploited during the attack. This may involve reviewing firewall configurations, application layer defenses, or network entry points.

- *Impact Assessment*: Evaluate the operational, financial, and reputational impacts of the attack. This includes assessing downtime duration, revenue losses, and potential customer trust erosion.

- *Defense and Policy Refinement*: Use insights gathered from the attack assessment to refine defense policies, update security measures, and enhance incident response plans.

Continuous Improvement and Learning

Converting attack occurrences into learning opportunities ensures continual improvement in DDoS defense strategies. Incorporate feedback loops and regular training efforts to reinforce readiness:

- *Case Study Development*: Document completed incidents as case studies, contributing to institutional knowledge and training resources, improving awareness across teams.

- *Cross-functional Feedback*: Organize post-mortem meetings across departments such as IT, security, and business units to share findings and integrate diverse insights into refined incident response protocols.

- *Training and Drills*: Conduct regular training for incident response teams and execute drills based on recent attack patterns to better prepare for future scenarios.

By proactively engaging in these activities, organizations can significantly enhance their defensive posture against DDoS threats in a rapidly evolving digital landscape.

Attack Analysis Summary (Sample)	
Attack Date	2023-11-02
Attack Duration	3 hours
Attack Types	UDP flood, HTTP GET flood
Mitigation Actions	Rate limiting, IP blocking, provider escalation
Impact Assessment	Minimal service downtime, no data breach confirmed
Improvements	Enhancements to rate limit configurations and geo-blocking policies

Summarizing attack incidents and mitigation outcomes through structured documentation provides an explicit post-attack reference framework to support ongoing defense enhancements.

Through the execution of well-defined incident response plans and structured post-attack analyses, organizations bolster their capacity to respond to DDoS threats effectively and refine their defenses consistently. Such endeavors contribute to maintaining robust service delivery and protecting organizational integrity within an increasingly challenging cyber landscape.

5.7   Legal and Ethical Considerations

When deliberating the complexities of Distributed Denial of Service (DDoS) attacks, it is vital to consider the legal and ethical dimensions surrounding the prevention, response, and recovery processes. This section explores the multifaceted legal frameworks governing DDoS activities, the ethical responsibilities of stakeholders, and the balance between security initiatives and civil liberties.

The proliferation of DDoS attacks has precipitated an urgent need for comprehensive legal structures at national and international levels, aiming to mitigate risks while instituting protocols for liability, deterrence, and jurisdictional coordination.

Legal Frameworks and International Cooperation

Legal measures addressing DDoS attacks vary worldwide, but they collectively focus on criminalizing unauthorized access and interference with computer systems and networks.

- *Country-specific Legislation*: Countries enact distinct laws such as the Computer Fraud and Abuse Act in the United States and the Computer Misuse Act in the United Kingdom. These regulations outline penalties for illegal access and damage to computer systems.

- *International Directives and Standards*: International cooperation, through conventions like the Budapest Convention, aims to harmonize legislation, promote cross-border assistance, and facilitate the adoption of procedural laws necessary for investigating and prosecuting cybercrimes, including DDoS attacks.

- *Role of Cybersecurity Policies*: Regional policies such as the European Union's NIS Directive enhance security across critical infrastructures, necessitating member states to adopt stringent cybersecurity measures, including safeguards against DDoS attacks.

Legal frameworks are integral, ensuring that perpetrators face consequences while enabling victim organizations to seek redress and assistance.

Liability and Accountability

Understanding liability in the event of a DDoS attack involves analyzing both perpetrators and the roles of intermediaries, including Internet Service Providers (ISPs) and content delivery networks.

- *Perpetrator Liability*: Actors orchestrating DDoS attacks are subject to criminal prosecution under varying degrees of statutory penalties, which may include fines, imprisonment, or both, contingent on jurisdiction and the magnitude of the offense.

- *Intermediary Liability*: ISPs and third-party providers like Cloudflare may face scrutiny regarding their efforts to mitigate DDoS threats. Legal considerations determine the extent to which they are accountable for failing to prevent or alleviate coordinated attack impacts.

- *Organizational Responsibility*: Entities must ensure robust cybersecurity measures, as negligence in fortifying defenses might result in diminished legal protection and increased exposure to secondary liabilities, such as data breach consequences ensuing from a successful DDoS attack.

```
import logging

# Setup logging for compliance records
logging.basicConfig(filename='security_compliance.log', level=logging.INFO)
```

```
def log_security_event(event_description):
    logging.info(f"Security Event: {event_description}")

# Sample log entries for incidents
log_security_event("Initiated DDoS mitigation protocol at 14:23 UTC")
log_security_event("Alerted legal team about potential breach implications")
log_security_event("Reviewed defense logs for unauthorized access attempts")

# Demonstrates tracking security measures to establish compliance with legal
    obligations.
```

The coding example illustrates logging of security procedures to maintain a document trail that supports compliance with legal obligations and standards during post-attack introspections.

Ethical Considerations

Beyond legal obligations, the ethical landscape of DDoS defenses includes evaluating the broader implications of protective actions on privacy, civil liberties, and the principle of fairness.

- *Balancing Security and Privacy*: Organizations must balance augmenting their defense mechanisms with respecting user privacy rights. Extensive data collection for threat analysis must adhere to privacy laws such as GDPR, ensuring transparency and data minimization.

- *Ethics of Active Defense*: Implementing active defense measures such as IP traceback or 'hack-back' tactics raises ethical queries. While protecting assets against DDoS attacks is vital, overstepping such measures may infringe on rights or lead to collateral damage.

- *Responsibility Toward Stakeholders*: Institutions bear an ethical duty towards stakeholders, encompassing customers, employees, vendors, and the public. Providing clear communication and maintaining trust throughout an attack underscores organizational ethics.

- *Community Cooperation*: Sharing threat intelligence transparently within industry circles and public bodies fosters collective protection, strengthening community defense postures ethically and collaboratively.

Embedding ethical frameworks within DDoS mitigation strategies assures stakeholders of the organization's intent to operate transparently, respecting societal values.

Policy Formulation and Governance

Effective governance frameworks are pivotal to steering cybersecurity measures in an ethically and legally compliant direction.

- *Internal Policy Development*: Organizations must develop comprehensive internal policies detailing incident response protocols, data handling practices, and employee training plans to sustain a secure environment.

- *Governance and Oversight*: Appointment of a dedicated data protection officer (DPO) or cybersecurity governance team facilitates continuing oversight, policy enforcement, and conformance with applicable legal standards.

- *Regular Audits and Assessments*: Implement periodic security audits and risk assessments to identify and rectify vulnerabilities, ensuring compliance with evolving legislative and ethical standards.

Policy Checklist Sample
Disseminate incident response protocols to all departments
Train employees in identifying and reporting security threats
Conduct quarterly data protection impact assessments (DPIA)
Ensure third-party compliance with security and privacy standards

Such policy checklists demonstrate a structured approach to formalizing governance practices, paving the way for sustainable cybersecurity compliance and ethics.

Future Directions and Evolving Challenges

As digital ecosystems grow more intricate, legal and ethical challenges posed by DDoS attacks will continue to evolve. Future focus areas may include:

- *Dynamic Legal Revisions*: Cyber laws require periodic updates to address new vectors and more advanced attack techniques, ensuring that statutory provisions remain robust and verifiable.

143

- *International Harmonization and Collaboration*: Greater international collaboration facilitates consistent legislation and the sharing of best practices, harnessing collective efforts to tackle global DDoS threats.

- *Privacy-conserving Defensive Techniques*: Encouragement of research and development in privacy-preserving cybersecurity technologies will help balance security and privacy imperatives.

- *Comprehensive Ethical Guidelines*: As technology advances, establishing ingrained ethical guidelines for technology use and security practices will remain imperative, navigating gray areas constructively.

Addressing these directions and challenges involves unlocking opportunities for constructive dialogue and innovation, ultimately reflecting a commitment to a principled approach while combating DDoS attacks.

By committing to robust legal frameworks and ethical practices, organizations position themselves favorably in their battle against DDoS threats. This holistic perspective safeguards not just digital assets but also the trust and goodwill of the communities they serve, reinforcing resilience, accountability, and integrity in an increasingly networked world.

Chapter 6

Content Delivery Networks (CDN) and Cloudflare

This chapter examines the role of Content Delivery Networks (CDN) in optimizing web content distribution, focusing on Cloudflare's extensive CDN architecture. It explains how CDNs improve user experience by reducing load times through strategically located servers that deliver content closer to end-users. The chapter details the configuration of Cloudflare's CDN features and highlights the security measures incorporated within this framework. Additionally, it presents case studies to illustrate successful CDN implementations and discusses troubleshooting methods for common CDN-related challenges.

6.1 Concept of Content Delivery Networks

Content Delivery Networks (CDNs) represent a crucial architectural strategy within the realm of web technology, designed to alleviate latency and enhance the overall distribution of web content. The core principle underlying CDNs is the geographic dispersion of content through a network of strategically located servers, thereby ensuring that digital content is delivered to the end user with increased speed and reliability.

CDNs primarily aim to ameliorate the challenges associated with delivering internet-based content over large distances, which can include increased load times and connectivity issues. By caching content at multiple, globally-distributed data centers, CDNs seek to bring content physically closer to users, reducing the latency that arises from network distance. This architecture not only serves to improve load times and user experience but also enhances content availability and reduces bandwidth consumption on origin servers.

- **Origin Server:** This is where the original version of the content resides. It can be a web server, database server, or any other infrastructure that hosts web content.

- **Edge Servers:** These are intermediary servers located in various locations worldwide. Edge servers cache content from the origin server and deliver it to users based on proximity.

- **Distribution Nodes:** In more complex CDN architectures, intermediary distribution nodes may exist to redistribute and manage content between the origin and edge servers.

- **Network Layer:** A robust network layer that includes routing, switching, and other networking services necessary for the transmission of data between nodes.

The general operation of a CDN involves a user request being routed to the nearest edge server, which reduces the wait time required to access a webpage or piece of content. This process begins when the DNS (Domain Name System) redirects the request to the optimal server, using

146

algorithms that determine proximity and load conditions. Upon receiving the request, the edge server quickly delivers cached content. If the content is not present in the cache, the edge server fetches it from the origin, caches it for future requests, and forwards it to the requester.

- **Caching Mechanisms in CDNs:** The efficiency of content delivery is significantly bolstered by caching mechanisms employed by CDNs. Caching is implemented using various strategies, such as Least Recently Used (LRU), Most Frequently Used (MFU), and Time-to-Live (TTL) policies. These strategies determine how and when content is stored and purged from cache.

```python
class LRUCache:
    def __init__(self, capacity: int):
        self.cache = {}
        self.capacity = capacity
        self.order = []

    def get(self, key: int) -> int:
        if key in self.cache:
            self.order.remove(key)
            self.order.append(key)
            return self.cache[key]
        return -1

    def put(self, key: int, value: int) -> None:
        if key in self.cache:
            self.order.remove(key)
        elif len(self.cache) >= self.capacity:
            oldest = self.order.pop(0)
            del self.cache[oldest]
        self.cache[key] = value
        self.order.append(key)
```

The above Python code illustrates a rudimentary implementation of an LRU (Least Recently Used) Cache. This algorithm maintains a fixed-size cache that stores frequently accessed content and discards the least recently accessed data to make space for new entries. Such caching algorithms are integral to CDNs in ensuring rapid data retrieval without overwhelming storage resources.

- **CDN Performance and Optimization:** Performance optimization is central to the operations of a CDN. Factors influencing CDN efficiency include bandwidth allocation, content compression, and protocol optimizations. Bandwidth allocation is optimized through dynamic load balancing, which distributes requests across servers based on current load and geographic location. Content compression, such as gzip for HTML pages, reduces the size of the data transmitted over the network.

HTTP/2 protocol optimizations in CDNs also contribute significantly by allowing multiplexed request-response streams over a single TCP connection. This reduces the overhead associated with establishing multiple connections and improves the efficiency of data transfer.

- **Security Features in CDNs:** Beyond performance, security is an integral part of CDN offerings. CDNs include several layers of security to protect content and maintain the integrity of delivered data. Secure Sockets Layer (SSL) and Transport Layer Security (TLS) encrypt content delivered via edge servers, ensuring data privacy during transmission.

CDNs also employ Web Application Firewalls (WAFs) to monitor and block malicious traffic, providing protection against Distributed Denial of Service (DDoS) attacks, data breaches, and other vulnerabilities. Furthermore, CDNs can implement token-based authentication mechanisms to ensure that only authorized users can access specific content.

- **Illustrative Example: DNS Redirection in CDNs:** For a practical example, consider the process of DNS redirection in a CDN setup. The Domain Name System is fundamentally responsible for directing user requests to the CDN's servers. This redirection is essential for directing traffic to the most appropriate edge server.

```
def resolve_dns(hostname):
    dns_records = {
        "example.com": "192.0.2.1",
        "cdn.example.com": "203.0.113.1",
    }
    return dns_records.get(hostname, None)

hostname = "cdn.example.com"
ip_address = resolve_dns(hostname)
if ip_address:
    print(f"DNS Resolution: {hostname} -> {ip_address}")
```

```
else:
    print("DNS Resolution failed.")
```

DNS Resolution: cdn.example.com -> 203.0.113.1

In this code example, we simulate a simple DNS resolution process where the hostname "cdn.example.com" resolves to an IP address. This redirection allows the CDN to determine the closest or least-loaded edge server for delivering the requested content.

- **Economic Benefits of CDNs:** In addition to technical advantages, CDNs offer significant economic benefits. By optimizing bandwidth usage and reducing server load, CDNs decrease the operational cost for content providers. They also reduce the necessity for infrastructure investment by leveraging the distributed caching and processing capabilities of the CDN provider.

These advantages are particularly pronounced for businesses operating on a global scale where reaching a multiregional audience efficiently is imperative. CDNs facilitate content localization, allowing enterprises to tailor content for specific audiences without the need for maintaining separate infrastructure in each geographic location.

CDNs have thus revolutionized the way content is delivered over the internet, capitalizing on distributed networking principles to serve a growing demand for faster, more reliable online experiences. The ongoing evolution and increasing adoption of CDNs mark a significant stride toward optimizing web performance and accessibility.

6.2 Cloudflare's Global CDN Architecture

Cloudflare's Content Delivery Network (CDN) architecture is a robust framework designed to improve the performance, security, and reliability of web applications across the globe. By leveraging a globally distributed network of servers, Cloudflare optimizes the content delivery process, ensuring that digital content is served with minimal latency and maximum speed to end users regardless of their location.

- **Overview of Cloudflare's CDN Infrastructure.** Cloudflare's CDN consists of a vast array of data centers strategically positioned around the world. These data centers, known as edge locations, are responsible for caching content close to users and form the backbone of Cloudflare's infrastructure. As of the most recent updates, Cloudflare operates over 200 data centers in more than 100 countries. This expansive reach allows Cloudflare to serve requests from proximate edge servers, thus reducing the round-trip time associated with fetching content from far-reaching origin servers.

- Cloudflare's network architecture is built on software-defined networking (SDN) principles, which enable dynamic and automated network management. This capability supports rapid scaling, resilience to network anomalies, and seamless integration with other internet services.

- **Edge and PoP Architecture.** At the core of Cloudflare's CDN are the Edge Servers and Points of Presence (PoPs). Each PoP is a collection of Cloudflare's servers located in a specific geographical region. These Edge servers are instrumental in providing various CDN functionalities, including caching, load balancing, and traffic management.

  Caching is executed at the edge servers to store frequently accessed content, reducing the load on the origin server and decreasing content retrieval time for users. Cloudflare employs a Pull CDN method, where content is pulled from the origin server to the edge on the first request and then cached for subsequent user requests.

- **Request Routing and DNS Resolution.** Central to the operation of Cloudflare's CDN is the intelligent routing of user requests. When a user attempts to access a webpage hosted on Cloudflare's CDN, the request is first handled by Cloudflare's DNS service. This DNS service resolves the user's request to identify the closest and most optimal edge server for serving the content.

  Cloudflare employs Anycast routing for directing traffic to the nearest available data center. With Anycast, the same IP address is advertised from multiple locations. The benefit of this setup is that traffic is automatically routed to the closest or least congested location based on real-time network conditions. This setup enhances load balancing and ensures high availability.

```
class AnycastRouting:
    def __init__(self, locations):
        self.locations = locations

    def get_best_route(self, user_location):
        # Simplified logic to select the nearest data center
        selected_location = min(
            self.locations,
            key=lambda loc: self.calculate_distance(user_location, loc)
        )
        return selected_location

    def calculate_distance(self, loc1, loc2):
        # Dummy function to calculate distance
        return abs(loc1 - loc2)

anycast = AnycastRouting(locations=[100, 200, 300, 400])
user_location = 150
print(f"Best route for user at {user_location}: {anycast.get_best_route(user_location)
    }")
```

Best route for user at 150: 100

The example above demonstrates a simple mechanism by which a user request is routed to the closest data center based on calculated distances, a principle similar to real-world Anycast routing.

- **Security Features Integrated into Cloudflare's CDN.** In addition to performance improvements, Cloudflare's CDN architecture incorporates comprehensive security features. One of the primary security mechanisms is the Cloudflare Web Application Firewall (WAF) which secures web applications by filtering and monitoring HTTP traffic between a web application and the Internet.

  Another key feature is the DDoS protection, where Cloudflare absorbs and dissects potentially harmful traffic close to the attack sources, thereby protecting the original server. Additionally, Cloudflare implements SSL/TLS encryption, ensuring secure transmission of data between users and the CDN's edge servers.

- **Traffic Optimization and Protocol Support.** Cloudflare enhances traffic optimization through advanced protocol support and optimization techniques. The network supports HTTP/2, a protocol that speeds up web page loading by parallelizing requests over a single TCP connection, reducing latency of resource fetching.

  Moreover, Cloudflare offers additional protocol enhancements like QUIC (Quick UDP Internet Connections) and HTTP/3. QUIC, developed by Google, reduces latency compared to traditional TCP by omitting round trips to establish a connection. This is particularly impactful in environments with high packet loss or latency.

```
class QUICConnection:
    def __init__(self, initial_packet):
        self.connection_established = False
        self.packet_queue = [initial_packet]

    def establish_connection(self):
        if len(self.packet_queue) > 0:
            self.connection_established = True
            self.packet_queue.pop(0)
        return self.connection_established

quic_conn = QUICConnection(initial_packet="syn")
print(f"Connection Established: {quic_conn.establish_connection()}")
```

Connection Established: True

The code snippet illustrates a simplified concept of setting up a connection using principles akin to QUIC, where the initial packet setup reduces the time to establish a connection compared to traditional TCP setup.

- **Real-Time Traffic Analysis and Adaptive Load Balancing.** Cloudflare's CDN is empowered with real-time traffic analysis and adaptive load balancing, ensuring the efficient distribution of network traffic across its vast network of servers. This involves monitoring traffic loads and dynamically adjusting the distribution of traffic to prevent any one server or data center from becoming overwhelmed.

Adaptive load balancing employs algorithms that consider server health, data center conditions, and network performance metrics to guide traffic flow strategically.

- **Economic and Operational Advantages.** Deploying Cloudflare's CDN architecture brings tangible benefits. Financially, businesses can reduce costs associated with maintaining individual data centers and server infrastructure. Operational efficiency is heightened as businesses can leverage Cloudflare's extensive network without heavy capital expenditures.

  Cloudflare's CDN also enables companies to serve global markets without the latency and performance issues traditionally associated with international data exchange. This global reach without performance trade-offs translates to increased user satisfaction and potentially higher conversion rates for online businesses.

- **Use Cases and Real-World Implementations.** Cloudflare's architecture is applied across various industries, serving content-rich media companies, e-commerce platforms, SaaS providers, and enterprise businesses. A prime example is its service to media companies where large video files are rapidly distributed to audiences worldwide, providing seamless playback experiences without buffering.

  Additionally, e-commerce platforms utilize Cloudflare's CDN to ensure rapid page load times, improving user experience and potentially reducing cart abandonment rates. These are enhanced further by Cloudflare's ability to handle surges in traffic, such as during flash sales or peak shopping seasons.

  The architectural design and network capabilities of Cloudflare's CDN continue to evolve in response to technological advancements and changing user demands. By prioritizing speed, security, and adaptability, Cloudflare maintains its position as a leading provider in the content delivery domain, enabling robust, scalable, and secure online experiences across the globe.

153

6.3 Benefits of Using a CDN with Cloudflare

Leveraging a Content Delivery Network (CDN) such as Cloudflare offers numerous advantages to enhance the delivery and management of web content. Cloudflare's CDN provides a comprehensive set of benefits that range from improved performance to heightened security, which can be pivotal for businesses striving to maintain a competitive edge. This section elucidates these benefits in detail, providing insights into how Cloudflare's CDN can sustainably optimize web services.

- **Reduced Latency and Improved Load Times.** One of the most significant advantages of utilizing Cloudflare's CDN is the reduction in latency. Web latency refers to the delay before a transfer of data begins following an instruction for its transfer. Cloudflare achieves latency reduction by serving content from edge locations that are geographically closer to users, minimizing the distance data must travel across the network. This proximity facilitates quicker data retrieval, substantially improving page load times.

  Faster load times lead to enhanced user experience, as users can access websites and applications more swiftly, potentially reducing bounce rates. For e-commerce platforms, improved page speeds can result in higher conversion rates, turning visitors into paying customers more effectively.

- **Scalability and Load Handling.** Cloudflare's CDN provides massive scalability, allowing businesses to accommodate traffic spikes without degradation in performance. Scalability is critical during periods of high demand, such as marketing promotions or major product launches, where sudden influxes of user requests can overwhelm origin servers.

  Cloudflare manages scalability through its extensive network of edge servers, distributing user requests and balancing loads effectively. This load balancing is automatic and adaptive, ensuring that no single server bears more load than it can handle, thus maintaining consistent service levels irrespective of traffic volume.

154

- **Enhanced Content Availability and Redundancy.** Availability is crucial for any online platform, as downtime can lead to loss of revenue and damage to reputation. Cloudflare's vast network contributes to increased availability through redundancy, which ensures that content remains accessible even if some servers or data centers experience issues.

  Redundancy is achieved by replicating data across multiple edge servers, allowing the CDN to serve content from alternative locations if a specific PoP faces connectivity problems. This capability also extends to disaster recovery scenarios where Cloudflare can re-route traffic to unaffected regions, providing an additional layer of reliability.

- **Bandwidth Optimization and Cost Efficiency.** Another compelling benefit of Cloudflare's CDN is bandwidth optimization. By caching content at edge servers, Cloudflare significantly reduces the load on origin servers, leading to decreased bandwidth consumption. This reduction in data transfer requirements results in noteworthy cost savings for businesses, particularly those with high traffic volumes.

  Additionally, Cloudflare's adaptive image and video delivery can compress media content, further optimizing bandwidth usage without compromising quality. These optimizations contribute to lower operational costs associated with data usage and improve overall resource management.

- **Security Enhancements and DDoS Protection.** Security is a cornerstone feature of Cloudflare's CDN, providing robust protection against various threat vectors without needing additional infrastructure. Cloudflare's CDN includes sophisticated DDoS protection, capable of mitigating massive attacks that aim to disrupt services by overwhelming them with traffic.

  This is complemented by Cloudflare's Web Application Firewall (WAF), which filters and blocks malicious traffic based on predefined rules. The CDN also supports advanced security features such as bot management, which identifies and mitigates automatic programs that could compromise security or degrade performance.

- **SSL/TLS Encryption and Data Integrity.** Security is further intensified through SSL/TLS encryption, which ensures that data transmitted between user devices and Cloudflare's edge servers is secure from interception. This encryption is paramount in protecting sensitive information such as user credentials and payment details, aligning with both user expectations and regulatory compliance standards.

```
import OpenSSL

# Generate Key
key = OpenSSL.crypto.PKey()
key.generate_key(OpenSSL.crypto.TYPE_RSA, 2048)

# Create a self-signed certificate
cert = OpenSSL.crypto.X509()
cert.get_subject().CN = "www.example.com"
cert.set_serial_number(1000)
cert.gmtime_adj_notBefore(0)
cert.gmtime_adj_notAfter(365*24*60*60) # Valid for one year
cert.set_issuer(cert.get_subject())
cert.set_pubkey(key)
cert.sign(key, 'sha256')

with open("selfsigned.cert", "wt") as cert_file:
    cert_file.write(OpenSSL.crypto.dump_certificate(OpenSSL.crypto.
        FILETYPE_PEM, cert).decode("utf-8"))

with open("private.key", "wt") as key_file:
    key_file.write(OpenSSL.crypto.dump_privatekey(OpenSSL.crypto.
        FILETYPE_PEM, key).decode("utf-8"))
```

The example code provides a straightforward method to generate a self-signed certificate using Python's OpenSSL library, facilitating secure communications by encrypting data flows.

- **SEO Improvements.** Implementing Cloudflare's CDN can positively impact Search Engine Optimization (SEO). Search engines favor websites that load quickly, which directly affects ranking on search results. By improving site performance through reduced latency and faster load times, Cloudflare's CDN can indirectly enhance a site's search engine visibility.

  Moreover, by maintaining high availability and security standards, Cloudflare ensures fewer downtimes, which is another critical factor for maintaining SEO rankings as search engine crawlers rate constant uptime and stable service very favorably.

- **Global Reach with Local Performance.** Cloudflare's CDN extends your application's reach to a global audience while ensuring local performance excellence. By serving content from nearby servers, Cloudflare aligns with the increasing expectations for rapid load times, regardless of where users are connecting from globally. This capability is crucial in fulfilling the demands of a distributed user base without needing region-specific infrastructure investments.

- **Automatic Content Optimization and Compression.** Cloudflare's CDN provides automatic content optimization features, such as JavaScript and CSS minification. Minification removes unnecessary characters from code without altering functionality, reducing the size and accelerating the delivery of resources to users.

  Additionally, the CDN's Brotli compression further enhances performance by compressing web traffic more efficiently than the traditional gzip. These optimizations occur seamlessly and require minimal configuration from the user, alleviating manual performance enhancement efforts.

- **Flexibility and Customizability.** Cloudflare's CDN is highly flexible and customizable, providing options to tailor caching behavior, security settings, and optimization features to align with specific business requirements. Cloudflare's CDN includes custom cache-control headers, page rules for setting behavior per URL, and configuration settings for tailoring security measures.

```python
from flask import Flask, make_response

app = Flask(__name__)

@app.route('/')
def index():
    response = make_response("Hello, world!")
    response.headers['Cache-Control'] = 'public, max-age=3600'
    return response

if __name__ == '__main__':
    app.run()
```

The Python Flask web application example above demonstrates how to set custom cache-control headers, instructing the CDN on how to cache responses for a given timeframe, contributing towards effective bandwidth management and performance.

- **Customer Support and Developer Tools.** Cloudflare provides extensive support and a suite of developer tools to ease integration and management of CDN services. Through an intuitive dashboard, users can configure CDN settings, monitor traffic statistics, and access real-time analytics. The detailed logs and insights help in understanding traffic patterns and optimizing performance further.

  Cloudflare's network diagnostic tools enable easy troubleshooting to ensure uninterrupted service, offering responsive customer support that addresses technical challenges efficiently.

The advantages of integrating a CDN such as Cloudflare's into web architectures are substantial. By reducing latency, optimizing resource usage, and strengthening security, Cloudflare enhances the delivery and experience of digital content on a global scale. The capacity to achieve these benefits with minimal overhead or modifications to existing infrastructure makes Cloudflare's CDN an essential component for modern web applications and services.

6.4   Configuring and Customizing Cloudflare CDN

Efficiently configuring and customizing Cloudflare's CDN is vital to fully leverage its capabilities for enhancing web performance and security. This section delves into the necessary steps and various customization options available within Cloudflare's CDN, illustrating how to configure these to align with specific organizational needs. Understanding the configuration mechanics ensures that web applications perform optimally and securely in any environment.

Setting Up Cloudflare CDN.   Initial configuration of Cloudflare's CDN requires the integration of Cloudflare with your domain. This process entails adding your website to the Cloudflare platform and updating DNS records to route your traffic through Cloudflare's network. Here is a step-by-step guide on how to set up Cloudflare for your website:

1. Registering with Cloudflare: Begin by creating a Cloudflare account, through which you can manage all your DNS settings and server configurations.

2. Adding Your Domain: Once logged in, go to the Cloudflare dashboard and input your domain name. Cloudflare will scan your domain's existing DNS records, which you'll need to confirm or adjust as required.

3. Updating Name Servers: Cloudflare provides specific name servers that need to be set at your domain registrar. This step is crucial to directing traffic through Cloudflare's network.

4. Configuration Confirmation: After name server updates, revisit your Cloudflare dashboard to verify that your configuration is complete and active.

Customizing Cache Settings.   Cloudflare offers advanced options to manage how content is cached on their CDN. Properly configuring cache settings is essential for improving load speeds and reducing server load while ensuring that users receive up-to-date content.

- Cache-Control Headers: These HTTP headers instruct Cloudflare on the rules for caching specific resources. Configuring these headers can be done through server-side configurations or directly via Cloudflare Page Rules.

```python
# Example of setting HTTP cache-control headers using Flask
from flask import Flask, make_response

app = Flask(__name__)

@app.route('/data')
def data():
    response = make_response('Resource Data')
    response.headers['Cache-Control'] = 'public, max-age=86400' # Cache for 1 day
    return response
```

159

```
if __name__ == '__main__':
    app.run()
```

- Edge Cache TTL: Control the duration that resources are cached at Cloudflare's edge servers. This is particularly beneficial for static resources like images and stylesheets.

Using Page Rules for Customization. Cloudflare's Page Rules provide a powerful mechanism to customize performance and security settings on a per-URL basis. Each Cloudflare plan supports a specific number of page rules, which can be tuned to meet various requirements.

For example, you can:

- Redirect HTTP to HTTPS: Ensure secure connections by automatically redirecting all HTTP traffic to HTTPS.

- Modify Cache Level: Override default cache settings to ensure specific resources are cached according to defined parameters.

- Enhance Performance: Enable features like Rocket Loader, which improves site performance by asynchronous loading of JavaScript.

Page Rules can be configured in Cloudflare's dashboard under the "Page Rules" section where conditions and actions for each URL can be specified.

SSL/TLS Configuration. Secure data transmission is facilitated through the effective configuration of SSL/TLS settings within Cloudflare. It's essential to choose the appropriate SSL/TLS option based on the existing setup of your web infrastructure.

Cloudflare offers several SSL settings:

- Flexible SSL: Encrypts traffic between your users and Cloudflare, though it does not encrypt communication between Cloudflare and your origin server.

- Full SSL: Requires an SSL certificate on the origin server, encrypting data in both directions.

- Full (Strict) SSL: Demands a valid SSL certificate from a trusted Certificate Authority on the origin server.

Customizing Security Settings. Security configuration is crucial to protect data and maintain the integrity of web applications. Cloudflare's CDN offers numerous security settings that can be tailored to specific threats and vulnerabilities that a website might face.

- Access Control: Set IP address restrictions and create whitelists or blacklists to control who can access your site.

- Rate Limiting: Protects websites from being overwhelmed by excessive client requests through rate limit rules that can be adjusted based on inbound traffic patterns.

- Bot Management: Helps mitigate automated traffic from bots that might be harmful, providing insights and controls over bot-driven activity.

Performance Optimization Through Workers and Apps. Cloudflare Workers and Apps are valuable tools that allow further customization of how requests are processed through Cloudflare's network.

- Cloudflare Workers: These are JavaScript functions that execute on Cloudflare's edge, enabling real-time customization of request and response handling. For instance, rewriting HTTP headers for a particular route can be done using Workers.

```
// Example Worker script to modify headers
addEventListener('fetch', event => {
  event.respondWith(handleRequest(event.request))
})

async function handleRequest(request) {
  let response = await fetch(request)
  response = new Response(response.body, response)
  response.headers.set('X-Custom-Header', 'MyValue')
  return response
}
```

- Cloudflare Apps: Offer plug-and-play functionality enhancements without modifying the web application codebase, such as integrating analytics or content management solutions.

DNS Management and CNAME Flattening. Cloudflare simplifies DNS management with a user-friendly interface that supports advanced DNS practices. CNAME Flattening is one of the unique features offered by Cloudflare, addressing issues where the root domain ('example.com') encounters CNAME restrictions traditionally resolved with an IP address.

Cloudflare's CNAME Flattening allows root domain CNAME compatibility without the usual DNS restrictions, optimizing DNS resolution and enhancing the overall responsiveness of the domain hosting setup.

Monitoring, Analytics, and Alerts. Comprehensive monitoring is vital for maintaining performance standards and security integrity. Cloudflare offers robust analytics that provide real-time insights into site traffic, threat metrics, and performance data.

- Traffic Analytics: Analyze visitor data, request response times, and geographical sources of web traffic.

- Security Threat Logs: Detail potential threats mitigated by Cloudflare's security protocols, including blocked access attempts and DDoS event logs.

- Custom Alerts: Set up notifications for various network events, deviations in traffic patterns, or security incidents, ensuring prompt responses to emerging concerns.

APIs for Automation and Advanced Management. Cloudflare's API enables advanced configurations, management automation, and integration with third-party systems, streamlining operations and reducing reliance on manual processes.

APIs can be used to automate configuration changes, manage DNS records, purge cache at scale, and retrieve analytic data programmatically. This capability enhances operational efficiency and integrates well with CI/CD pipelines for continuous deployment scenarios.

Considerations for Global Optimization. Configuring Cloudflare's CDN for global optimization involves tailoring settings that cater specifically to international traffic. This includes enabling Argo Smart Routing for enhanced traffic routing, providing faster and more reliable connections by using real-time network conditions to route traffic along the fastest paths available.

By taking advantage of Cloudflare's broad feature set, businesses can configure their CDN settings to maximize performance, security, and cost-efficiency. Effective configurations and customizations ensure that Cloudflare's CDN delivers its full potential, providing a comprehensive, agile, and scalable solution for modern web ecosystems.

6.5 Securing Content with Cloudflare CDN

In the contemporary digital landscape, securing web content is paramount. Cloudflare's CDN is engineered to offer enhanced security measures, ensuring that data transmission is safeguarded against numerous threats. Leveraging Cloudflare's CDN for content delivery not only optimizes performance but also fortifies security, providing a multilayered defense strategy for digital assets. This section examines the mechanisms by which Cloudflare secures content, outlining best practices and advanced configurations for comprehensive protection.

- **Transport Layer Security (TLS) and SSL Configuration.** Cloudflare employs advanced Transport Layer Security (TLS) protocols to encrypt data between end users and edge servers. This encryption is crucial for protecting sensitive information such as credentials and personal data transmitted over the Internet. The configuration of Secure Sockets Layer (SSL) and TLS involves selecting from various security modes that fit your existing web infrastructure:

  - **Flexible SSL Mode:** Encrypts traffic between the user's browser and Cloudflare but leaves the connection between Cloudflare and the origin server unencrypted. This mode is useful for setups where the origin server does not support SSL.

- **Full SSL Mode:** Provides encryption between both the user and Cloudflare and Cloudflare to the origin server. This mode requires a self-signed or Cloudflare-originated certificate at the server instead of a public certificate.

- **Full (Strict) SSL Mode:** Demands a publicly recognized SSL certificate installed on the origin server, ensuring a chain of trust that confirms identity and authenticity.

Enhancing data integrity and trust is also facilitated through the use of modern encryption algorithms such as Elliptic Curve cryptography and secure ciphers, which Cloudflare automatically prioritizes.

- **Content Protection Through Web Application Firewall (WAF).** Cloudflare's Web Application Firewall offers critical protection for web applications by filtering and monitoring HTTP traffic between a web application and the Internet. This feature blocks attacks often targeting applications, such as SQL injection, cross-site scripting (XSS), and application layer DDoS attacks.

```
import re

def is_sql_safe(query):
    # Basic pattern checking for common SQL injection patterns
    if re.search(r"(INSERT|DROP|UPDATE|DELETE|SELECT|--|\')", query,
        re.IGNORECASE):
        return False
    return True

user_input = "SELECT data FROM users WHERE id='1' --"
if is_sql_safe(user_input):
    print("Query seems safe.")
else:
    print("Potential SQL injection detected.")
```

In this example, rudimentary SQL injection detection is demonstrated, underscoring the necessity for employing comprehensive protection mechanisms like WAF to safeguard dynamic content access points systematically.

- **Mitigating Distributed Denial of Service (DDoS) Attacks.** Distributed Denial of Service attacks, which aim to overwhelm services and render them unusable, pose significant threats to web infrastructure. Cloudflare provides robust DDoS protection to absorb and neutralize massive spikes in malicious traffic. This protection extends to both network-layer and application-layer attacks, with capabilities designed to detect and respond to threats in real-time, ensuring service continuity.

Cloudflare achieves this by using rate limiting, which controls the number and rate of requests that a server will accept during a given period. Furthermore, Cloudflare employs real-time traffic analysis to identify and block unusual patterns characteristic of DDoS activity promptly.

- **Secure Token and Access Management.** Cloudflare offers token-based security measures whereby access tokens authenticate requests, confirming that only authorized users can access specific resources. This is particularly useful for applications requiring stringent user verification.

```
import jwt
import datetime

def generate_token(secret_key, user_id, expiration=3600):
    payload = {
        'user_id': user_id,
        'exp': datetime.datetime.utcnow() + datetime.timedelta(seconds=
            expiration)
    }
    token = jwt.encode(payload, secret_key, algorithm='HS256')
    return token

secret = 'your_secret_key'
token = generate_token(secret, user_id=12345)
print(f"Generated Token: {token}")
```

In the above example, a JSON Web Token (JWT) is generated to authenticate API requests. Implementing such tokens helps in maintaining secure and manageable access across distributed network resources.

- **Bot Management and Threat Prevention.** Bots play varied roles on the Internet, with some contributing to site analytics while others may note hostile interactions. Cloudflare's Bot Management tools distinguish between beneficial and malicious bots, applying tailored policies to handle each category. Machine learning models are used to analyze traffic patterns and behaviors continuously, refining rule sets that dictate permitted activities for bots.

Users can configure threat levels and automate responses to bot interactions, from merely logging activities to blocking and challenging unwanted traffic. The granularity of these controls ensures that only genuine interactions are processed, conserving resources and maintaining security integrity.

- **Content Security Policy (CSP) Implementation.** Content Security Policy (CSP) is a W3C standard enforced by Cloudflare that helps mitigate cross-site scripting (XSS) attacks by specifying domains that browsers should consider valid sources of executable scripts. Implementing CSP within your Cloudflare setup reinforces your security posture by dramatically reducing exposure to XSS and related vulnerabilities.

```
<!DOCTYPE html>
<html>
<head>
    <meta http-equiv="Content-Security-Policy" content="default-src 'self';
        script-src 'self';">
    <title>Secure Web Page</title>
</head>
<body>
    <p>Web page with CSP implemented</p>
    <script>
        // Inline scripts disallowed unless explicitly permitted
    </script>
</body>
</html>
```

This example shows how CSP can be applied to allow resources strictly from authorized domains, establishing a strong security boundary that restricts rogue scripts.

- **Security Analytics and Threat Intelligence.** Cloudflare delivers comprehensive security analytics, enabling organizations to monitor potential vulnerabilities and attacks with real-time insights into security events. By providing detailed logs and reports, Cloudflare assists in identifying trend anomalies and taking preemptive actions.

  - **Insightful Dashboards:** Present aggregated security metrics, threat types, and attack vectors, facilitating data-driven decisions for security enhancement.

166

- **Automated Alerts:** Trigger notifications based on pre-defined security incident thresholds, allowing for rapid response to emerging threats.

- **Zero Trust Security Model.** Cloudflare's Zero Trust framework ensures that no device, user, or request is inherently trusted without continuous verification across the network. Leveraging Cloudflare Access, a part of the Zero Trust suite, organizations can secure access to internal applications, ensuring that only authenticated users can interact with sensitive resources without relying on a traditional corporate perimeter.

Configuring secure content delivery is pivotal in safeguarding user data and ensuring the reliability of web services. Cloudflare's CDN integrates advanced security features that not only protect against current threats but also adapt to emerging vulnerabilities. By implementing these mechanisms within a unified platform, organizations can resist multifaceted attacks, thereby securing the digital experience comprehensively.

6.6 Case Studies: CDN Implementation with Cloudflare

Exploring real-world applications of Cloudflare's CDN offers valuable insights into its capabilities and effectiveness. Various organizations have integrated Cloudflare's CDN into their infrastructure to solve specific challenges, enhancing performance, security, and global reach. This section presents detailed case studies demonstrating successful CDN implementations with Cloudflare, showcasing both the technical processes involved and the subsequent benefits.

- **Case Study 1: Enhancing E-Commerce Performance.** A leading global e-commerce platform faced significant challenges in maintaining high performance during peak sales events. These sales triggered massive influxes of user traffic, resulting in increased load times and server strain. The platform sought solutions that could effectively handle this traffic while ensuring secure transactions and fast content delivery.

167

Solution: Cloudflare's CDN was leveraged to decentralize content delivery, providing several key advantages:

- **Load Distribution:** Cloudflare's global network of edge servers enabled efficient load distribution. By caching static assets such as images, CSS, and JavaScript libraries near users, the CDN reduced server load and accelerated load times.

- **Secure Transactions:** The platform implemented Cloudflare's Full SSL configuration to securely transmit sensitive customer data, maintaining trust and compliance with industry standards.

- **DDoS Protection:** Cloudflare's advanced security features shielded the platform from volumetric DDoS attacks, ensuring uninterrupted access and service availability even during high-demand periods.

Results: Post-implementation, the e-commerce platform experienced a dramatic reduction in load times, with pages loading 30-40% faster. Their infrastructure also reported decreased bandwidth usage on origin servers, translating to cost savings on server maintenance and operation.

- **Case Study 2: Safeguarding a Media Streaming Service.** A popular media streaming service aimed to expand its reach globally while maintaining high-quality streaming experiences and safeguarding content from piracy.

Solution: Cloudflare's CDN was utilized to enhance global content delivery and protect media assets from unauthorized access:

- **Global Edge Distribution:** The CDN cached media content across Cloudflare's distributed edge locations, reducing buffering and latency for international audiences.

- **Token-Based Secure Access:** By implementing secure tokens for media URLs, the service controlled access to streaming content, ensuring that only authenticated subscribers could access videos.

– **CSP and Firewall:** Cloudflare's Content Security Policy (CSP) and WAF were configured to prevent content theft and protect against vulnerability exploits.

Results: With Cloudflare's intervention, the streaming service achieved a 50% growth in international subscriber base due to enhanced content accessibility and performance. Moreover, piracy incidents declined significantly, preserving revenue from legitimate views.

- **Case Study 3: Accelerating SaaS Platform Delivery.** A software-as-a-service provider faced challenges in delivering applications to multi-regional clients without delays. Latency and connection drop-offs were fretting user experience, necessitating an agile solution.

Solution: Cloudflare's service was integrated to optimize application delivery and improve connectivity:

– **Argo Smart Routing:** The SaaS provider employed Cloudflare's Argo Smart Routing to optimize data path routing dynamically. By using real-time performance data, Argo identified the fastest paths across Cloudflare's network, decreasing latency substantially.

– **Automated SSL/TLS:** For establishing secure connections, SSL/TLS was automatically deployed, offering peace of mind and compliance with client security requirements.

– **Cache Optimization:** Through nuanced control of caching rules, the SaaS provider ensured repeat application data requests were served more quickly from edge caches.

Results: The platform observed a notable reduction in latency by up to 35%, with client applications reporting increased responsiveness. These improvements led to higher client satisfaction, stronger retention rates, and a competitive advantage in the SaaS market.

- **Case Study 4: Content Delivery for a News Organization.** A digital-first news publication required a robust solution to handle surges in web traffic, which occur during breaking news events without compromising performance.

Solution: Cloudflare's CDN was implemented to efficiently manage dynamic traffic patterns:

- **Dynamic Content Caching:** Through Cloudflare's Workers, the publication cached dynamic content descriptions based on user locations, reducing the load and speeding up content delivery.

- **Rate Limiting:** Rate limiting was configured to prevent bots from overwhelming services, ensuring human users retained upfront access to breaking content.

- **Real-Time Analytics:** The organization leveraged Cloudflare's analytics to gauge article interaction metrics in real-time, enabling editorial and logistical adjustments as needed.

Results: The news organization was able to handle traffic spikes efficiently, offering steady access and performance even during high peak events. Enhanced analytics supported strategic content decision-making to captivate large audiences effectively.

- **Case Study 5: Improving Security for a Financial Institution.** A financial services company engaged in online transactions needed to bolster its defenses against emerging cyber threats to protect client data and ensure regulatory compliance.

Solution: Cloudflare offered comprehensive security reinforcements:

- **Web Application Firewall:** Cloudflare's WAF was deployed to filter malicious requests and shield web applications from attack vectors such as SQL injections and cross-site scripting.

- **Zero Trust Security:** By implementing Cloudflare's Zero Trust model, the institution ensured no resource requests from users or devices were trusted implicitly, enhancing the cybersecurity framework.

- **DDoS Mitigation:** Real-time DDoS protection neutralized massive attack attempts before they could distress banking services, preserving uptime and reliability.

Results: The financial institution reported increased trust from clients due to reinforced security posture, while also meeting strict industry regulatory obligations. Incident response times were halved, supported by proactive threat intelligence and analytics.

These case studies affirm Cloudflare's CDN as a versatile, powerful solution for businesses across multiple sectors. The benefits of reduced latency, enhanced security, effective scalability, and global accessibility are manifested in real-world scenarios, demonstrating how tailored implementations can yield strategic advantages for organizations in a competitive digital economy.

6.7 Troubleshooting Common CDN Issues

Content Delivery Networks (CDNs) like Cloudflare enhance performance and security, yet complexities in configuration and myriad external variables can occasionally result in issues. Solving these issues promptly ensures that the CDN continues to deliver the intended benefits. This section delves into common CDN-related problems and provides detailed troubleshooting techniques to resolve these issues effectively.

Identifying Caching Issues. Caching improves performance by storing copies of content at edge locations. However, misconfigurations or misunderstandings of cache behavior can result in outdated or incorrect content delivery.

- **Outdated Content Issues:** When cached content does not update as expected, users may receive stale content. This commonly occurs due to improper cache expiration settings or failure to invalidate cache when updates occur.

  Solution:

  – Review and configure appropriate cache-control headers in the origin server response to dictate specific cache expiration rules.

- Use the Cloudflare dashboard's purge cache feature to remove outdated content manually.

```
from flask import Flask, make_response

app = Flask(__name__)

@app.route('/update')
def update_content():
    response = make_response('Latest Update')
    response.headers['Cache-Control'] = 'no-cache, no-store, must-revalidate'
    return response

if __name__ == '__main__':
    app.run()
```

- **Unexpectedly High Cache Misses:** A high rate of cache misses can degrade performance as requests repeatedly fetch data from the origin server.

  Solution:

  - Ensure the correct configuration of cache levels in Cloudflare. The default cache level might be conservative for certain dynamic resources.
  - Analyze cached asset URLs to confirm they remain consistent and are not impacted by query strings or URL changes.

Addressing SSL/TLS Configuration Problems. Secure Sockets Layer (SSL) configurations provide encrypted connections, but misconfigurations can lead to security warnings, broken pages, or inaccessibility.

- **SSL Handshake Failures:** These are often manifested as SSL handshake errors during the establishment of a secure connection between Cloudflare and the origin server.

  Solution:

  - Confirm that the SSL certificate on the origin server is not expired and is correctly implemented.
  - Ensure that Cloudflare's SSL settings align with the origin server's supported configurations (e.g., Full or Full (Strict) mode).

- **Mixed Content Warnings:** Occur when secure pages attempt to load insecure (HTTP) resources.

  Solution:

  - Perform a comprehensive review of page source code to reference HTTPS URLs for all resources.
  - Use Cloudflare's "Automatic HTTPS Rewrites" feature to resolve content issues programmatically.

Mitigating DNS-Related Issues. DNS resolution is integral to routing visitors through Cloudflare's CDN. Misconfigurations here could lead to site unavailability or misrouting.

- **Propagation Delays:** A common DNS challenge, where changes to DNS records do not immediately reflect globally due to caching across the internet.

  Solution:

  - Allow a time buffer (typically up to 24-48 hours) for DNS changes to propagate, while configuring low TTL (Time-To-Live) settings temporarily if rapid updates are expected.
  - Verify that Cloudflare's DNS settings match the correct and current A, CNAME, and MX records as listed in your domain registrar.

Rectifying Performance Bottlenecks. Performance issues may arise from improper configuration, network issues, or server-side processing delays.

- **High Latency:** Users experience delays in accessing content due to network latency or overloaded servers.

  Solution:

  - Enable Cloudflare's Argo Smart Routing, which optimizes the paths taken by requests across the network using the fastest available routes.
  - Monitor and scale origin server resources where bottlenecks consistently recur under high traffic conditions.

173

- **Asset Minification Problems:** Minification can result in broken scripts or unexpected behaviors if not correctly implemented.

  Solution:

  - Disable Cloudflare's minification feature temporarily to identify if it's the cause of issues, and verify script compatibility before re-enabling smartly.

Dealing with Security Challenges. Ensuring robust security requires careful oversight of most of the server configurations, Cloudflare settings, and access controls.

- **False Positives in Security Rules:** Legitimate traffic may be misclassified as malicious, leading to blocks or challenges for genuine users.

  Solution:

  - Review Web Application Firewall (WAF) logs to identify repeat false positives and amend relevant security policies.
  - Set appropriate sensitivity for security features to balance protection against user experience.

- **Bot-Driven Incidents:** Automatic bots might inadvertently get through or be blocked, impacting KPI metrics.

  Solution:

  - Employ Cloudflare's Bot Management services to distinguish between helpful and harmful bots and configure responses accordingly.

Utilizing Diagnostic Tools and Support. Effectively troubleshooting is predicated on accurate diagnostics.

- **Diagnostic Tools:** Cloudflare provides a suite of diagnostic tools and real-time analytics. From evaluating DNS settings to checking HTTP response headers, these tools pinpoint the misconfigurations reliably.

174

- **Support Engagement:** Leverage Cloudflare's support community, developer forums, and official customer service channels for complex issues that require detailed technical support.

By proactively identifying potential problem areas and understanding how to address each issue, organizations can maintain a high-performance, secure, and reliable web environment powered by Cloudflare's CDN. Making full use of the diagnostic capabilities and configuration flexibility provided by Cloudflare empowers administrators to not only resolve existing issues but also safeguard against future occurrences.

Chapter 7

Cloudflare Workers and Edge Computing

This chapter explores the capabilities of Cloudflare Workers and their integration with edge computing, enhancing the flexibility and speed of web applications. It discusses how Workers allow for the execution of JavaScript directly at the edge, minimizing latency and personalizing user interactions. Readers will learn about setting up Cloudflare Workers, their applications in dynamic content delivery, and security considerations to ensure efficient operation. Additionally, the chapter provides insights into testing strategies and cost management, optimizing resource use within Cloudflare's serverless environment.

7.1 Understanding Edge Computing

Edge computing represents a paradigm shift where the processing of data occurs at or near the source of data generation, rather than relying solely on centralized data centers. This method reduces latency and optimizes bandwidth usage by decreasing the amount of data that needs to be sent to a central repository for processing and storage. The evolution of edge computing can be traced back to the need for faster data processing, which is increasingly critical in applications such as autonomous vehicles, the Internet of Things (IoT), and real-time analytics.

The driving motivation behind edge computing is to bring computing power closer to the location where it is needed. By minimizing the distance that data must travel, edge computing reduces the time it takes for data to be processed and delivers results rapidly to users or applications. This section will explore the architecture, benefits, and differences of edge computing compared to traditional cloud computing, along with illustrative examples and coding demonstrations relevant to edge scenarios.

Edge computing architecture typically consists of a client device, an edge device or server, and the overarching cloud infrastructure. The client device could be any end-device such as a smartphone, sensor, or Internet of Things (IoT) device, which generates data. The edge device, which is situated geographically closer to the client device, collects this data and processes it either partially or completely before relaying it to the cloud. The cloud remains responsible for tasks that require higher computational power or for activities involving longer-term storage and more extensive analytics.

Understanding these components is essential to grasping the function of edge computing within the larger context of data processing infrastructures. Among the critical components in edge computing are:

- **Edge Gateways**: These serve as a bridge for transmitting data between IoT devices and the cloud, converting data into formats used for cloud processing.

- **Edge Servers**: Placed closer to end users and handle some, if not all, data processing, such as filtering and aggregation, locally to optimize computing workloads.

Consider the following Python example within an edge computing context. Suppose we need to preprocess data on an edge device before further analysis:

```
import numpy as np
```

```
def preprocess_data(sensor_data):
    # Remove outliers using a basic Z-score analysis
    threshold = 3
    mean = np.mean(sensor_data)
    std_dev = np.std(sensor_data)
    filtered_data = [x for x in sensor_data if (x - mean) / std_dev < threshold]

    return filtered_data

# Example sensor data
data = [50, 56, 48, 49, 1000, 54, 51, 49, 55, 50] # 1000 is an outlier
processed_data = preprocess_data(data)

print("Processed Sensor Data:", processed_data)
```

The script above demonstrates an elementary form of data preprocessing often executed at the edge. This step is crucial for reducing the data volume since outliers or irrelevant points are removed before the data is transmitted to the cloud for more intensive analytics.

Edge computing differs from cloud computing primarily in where data computation occurs. In traditional cloud computing, computation is centralized in remote data centers, leading to potential issues such as latency due to data transmission times and network bandwidth constraints. These issues can be mitigated by edge computing, which places computation at locations closer to where data is generated, thereby achieving faster processing times and more efficient bandwidth utilization.

Let's delve deeper into the core differences and benefits:

- **Latency Reduction**: By processing information locally or in nearby edge networks, latency significantly decreases, making real-time data interactions feasible. For instance, a factory using edge computing to monitor equipment can detect anomalies in virtually real-time.

- **Bandwidth Optimization**: Since data is processed or filtered locally, only necessary information or insights are sent to the cloud. This reduces the data that traverses the network, which is particularly important in IoT scenarios where bandwidth may be limited or costly.

- **Scalability and Reliability**: Decentralized processing enhances scalability as bottlenecks at central data repositories

179

are reduced. Furthermore, it improves reliability because local processing can continue during connectivity outages, ensuring uninterrupted operation of critical applications.

- **Data Security and Compliance**: Processing and storing data locally addresses compliance regulations and enhances privacy concerns, as sensitive information may not need to leave its origin or cross through multiple routing points.

Such advantages manifest well in modern applications, where the necessity for rapid processing meets exponentially growing data quantities. Consider the use case in intelligent traffic systems, where sensor data is processed in part at the edge to inform real-time traffic light adjustments and congestion monitoring.

Another beneficial use is within augmented reality (AR) applications, which require swift processing to overlay digital content onto the real world precisely and timely. Edge computing's reduced latency helps maintain high-quality user experiences essential for AR functionality.

Conceptually examining these benefits, a crucial consideration in deploying edge computing solutions is determining when and where to execute computations locally versus in the cloud. Balancing this decision involves analyzing workload characteristics, data sensitivity, the necessity for real-time processing, and the available network infrastructure.

Finally, the synergy between edge and cloud computing rather than an exclusive relationship often leads to hybrid models. Here, edge computing handles latency-sensitive tasks, while the cloud supports long-term data analysis tasks and storage.

Implementing such hybrid architectures incorporates the advantages of both models while addressing their respective weaknesses, presenting an optimal solution for complex computing environments. A representative coding example on a hybrid setup might involve streamlining certain precomputed analytics at the edge and sending summarised results for advanced processing in the cloud.

Edge computing signifies a fundamental enhancement in data processing methodologies driven by the necessity for speed, efficiency, and adaptability. It addresses the inherent limitations of centralized computing models, accommodating the pervasive data influx from modern connective technologies. The subsequent sections will further explore how specific technologies and approaches, such as Cloudflare Workers, integrate seamlessly within this architectural framework to enhance edge computing's efficacy in practical applications.

7.2 Cloudflare Workers: An Overview

Cloudflare Workers provide a powerful platform for deploying serverless applications directly at the edge, thereby allowing for the execution of JavaScript applications in response to inbound HTTP requests. Unlike traditional applications that rely on centralized servers, Cloudflare Workers operate within Cloudflare's global network, enhancing performance by executing scripts in close proximity to the end users. This architectural design optimizes latency and provides a robust scalability framework, empowering developers to create highly responsive applications.

With Cloudflare Workers, developers have the capability to build, test, and deploy serverless functions that manipulate HTTP requests and responses. At its core, the service removes the limitations often associated with centralizing computing resources, facilitating real-time data processing with minimal delay. This section delves into the architecture, functionalities, and benefits of Cloudflare Workers, presenting coding examples to illustrate how they enhance application performance at the edge.

Cloudflare Workers are built upon the Service Workers API provided by modern web browsers; however, they extend the scope of these APIs by running in a Cloudflare-controlled JavaScript V8 engine across the globe. The unique design of Cloudflare Workers provides several advantages that will be explored below.

- **Architecture and Execution Model**: Cloudflare Workers operate within a request-driven model where scripts are executed in response to events such as HTTP requests. This non-blocking execution model allows many requests to be handled simultaneously, taking advantage of the isolated environments created for each worker. The execution of Cloudflare Workers occurs in edge

181

computing locations distributed around the world, thereby decreasing response times by processing data closer to users.

The high-level architecture of Cloudflare Workers is defined by:

- **Event-Driven Execution**: Workers are triggered by events, typically HTTP requests, enabling a powerful mechanism similar to event listeners in traditional web development. - **Isolated Environments**: Each worker runs in an isolated environment within Cloudflare's V8 engine. This ensures that each execution is securely partitioned, enhancing both security and fault tolerance. - **Edge Network Integration**: Workers are executed across Cloudflare's vast edge network, optimizing connectivity by routing traffic to the nearest node for processing.

A simple example of a Cloudflare Worker script is shown below. This worker returns a static HTML response every time it is invoked:

```
addEventListener('fetch', event => {
  event.respondWith(handleRequest(event.request))
})

async function handleRequest(request) {
  return new Response('<h1>Hello from Cloudflare Workers!</h1>', {
    headers: { 'content-type': 'text/html' },
  })
}
```

This code defines an event listener that calls 'handleRequest' whenever a fetch event occurs. The function then sends back a simple HTML response. Executed at the edge, such scripts drastically reduce latency for static content delivery.

- **Benefits of Cloudflare Workers**: The deployment of serverless applications through Cloudflare Workers introduces numerous benefits that enhance both the developer and user experience. Among the most notable benefits:

1. **Reduced Latency**: The proximity of executing Workers to end users minimizes the round-trip time (RTT), thus accelerating the delivery of data. 2. **Scalability**: Since Workers run within Cloudflare's globally distributed network, they automatically scale according to traffic demands without explicit configuration or orchestration. 3. **Continuous Deployment**:

182

Cloudflare Workers support CI/CD pipelines, enabling rapid deployment of updates with minimal interruption. 4. **Security**: Workers offer built-in DDoS protection and execute within secure sandboxed environments, minimizing vulnerability risks. 5. **Cost Efficiency**: The pay-as-you-go pricing model avoids unnecessary server costs, charging only for requests and execution time.

- **Handling and Transforming HTTP Requests**: Beyond serving static content, one of the compelling capabilities of Cloudflare Workers is their ability to intercept and manipulate HTTP requests before reaching the origin server. For instance, a worker could be configured to add custom headers for all outgoing responses, providing additional metadata or controlling client cache behavior.

  Consider the following code snippet, where a Cloudflare Worker adds a 'Cache-Control' header to enhance browser caching mechanisms:

```
addEventListener('fetch', event => {
  event.respondWith(handleRequest(event.request))
})

async function handleRequest(request) {
  const response = await fetch(request)
  const newHeaders = new Headers(response.headers)

  newHeaders.set('Cache-Control', 'max-age=3600')

  return new Response(response.body, {
    ...response,
    headers: newHeaders
  })
}
```

  The worker intercepts the original request, fetches the response from the origin server, and then modifies the response object by adding a 'Cache-Control' header. Leveraging such techniques, developers can enforce caching policies, manage authentication tokens, or any other critical transformations required by business logic.

- **Use Cases and Practical Applications**: Cloudflare Workers are indispensable in myriad scenarios spanning multiple indus-

183

tries. Their versatility and design make them well-suited for:

- **API Shielding**: Edge functions can act as a protective layer for backend APIs, adding an authentication layer or throttling requests to prevent abuse. - **Dynamic Content Personalization**: Workers can tailor web page content dynamically based on user data or geographic location. - **Performance Optimizations**: As browser requests pass through workers, developers can selectively apply optimizations like minifying HTML or fingerprinting assets. - **Edge Routing**: Route traffic efficiently between microservices or failover nodes in multi-region architectures based on specific criteria like path, hostname, or headers.

With the described use cases, Cloudflare Workers pivot towards maximizing edge computing advantages, cementing the importance of positioning logic nearer end users to ensure responsiveness and reliability.

Integrating these Workers into a developer's toolkit offers unseen possibilities in terms of both backend processing and user-facing interactions. An illustrative application showcasing how a Cloudflare Worker manages a simple API gateway might target the personalization of experiences contingent on user segmentation:

```
addEventListener('fetch', event => {
  event.respondWith(handleRequest(event.request))
})

async function handleRequest(request) {
  const country = request.headers.get('cf-ipcountry') || 'US';

  let contentUrl;
  switch (country) {
    case 'US':
      contentUrl = 'https://example.com/us-content';
      break;
    case 'FR':
      contentUrl = 'https://example.com/fr-content';
      break;
    default:
      contentUrl = 'https://example.com/global-content';
      break;
  }

  return fetch(contentUrl);
}
```

In this example, the worker bases content delivery paths on the user's IP-derived country code provided by Cloudflare's 'cf-ipcountry' header. Such design paradigms enable developers to deliver highly personalized content, transforming generic experiences into contexts aware of user locations or preferences.

By incorporating these detailed examples and applications, the overarching grasp of Cloudflare Workers can extend beyond mere theoretical concepts into tangible, day-to-day development operations. As a stepping-stone to continued exploration and implementation, the subsequent sections will navigate through setting up such edge solutions while mitigating common challenges encountered during deployment.

7.3   Setting Up Cloudflare Workers

Setting up Cloudflare Workers involves several steps that transform a development idea into an operational edge service. As a serverless platform, the process of establishing a Cloudflare Worker is streamlined, requiring minimal configuration compared to traditional server setups. This section offers a comprehensive exploration of the steps involved in creating, deploying, and testing Cloudflare Workers, alongside coding demonstrations that emphasize core concepts and operational nuances. Through a meticulous walkthrough, developers can gain the insights necessary to effectively harness the serverless potential at the network edge.

Before creating a Cloudflare Worker, certain prerequisites must be satisfied. Foremost, a valid Cloudflare account is necessary. Interested developers would visit the Cloudflare sign-up page to register, or log in if already established.

The recommended approach for developing Cloudflare Workers is through Wrangler, the official CLI tool provided by Cloudflare. This tool facilitates local development, deployment, and management. To install Wrangler, Node.js and npm should be pre-installed, as they form the backbone for obtaining and executing the CLI.

To install Wrangler, execute the following command in a node-supported terminal:

```
npm install -g wrangler
```

185

This command installs Wrangler globally, equipping the command line interface with necessary commands for Worker development.

Ensure installation validity by executing:

```
wrangler --version
```

If installed correctly, this will display the currently installed version of Wrangler on your system.

With Wrangler installed, developers can create a new Worker project. Navigate to a desired directory and initialize a worker script using:

```
wrangler init my-worker
```

This command generates a new project directory my-worker, which contains critical files, notably worker.js and a configuration file wrangler.toml. The wrangler.toml file stores configuration settings such as account IDs, zone IDs, and worker specifications.

A crucial aspect of Worker projects involves configuring the wrangler.toml file, providing essential metadata that governs deployment attributes. Here's a sample configuration structure, where key-value pairs are defined:

```
name = "my-worker"
type = "javascript"
account_id = "your_account_id"
zone_id = "your_zone_id"
route = "https://example.com/*"
```

In this configuration, several attributes are defined:

- name: The canonical name for the worker project.

- type: Specifies the programming language; options include javascript, rust, or webpack.

- account_id and zone_id: Unique identifiers intrinsic to a Cloudflare account, substitutable by those accessible from Cloudflare Dashboard under account settings.

- route: Dictates the domain path arrangement affected by the worker script, using wildcards such as https://example.com/* to manage all subpaths.

186

Once initialized and configured, begin developing the worker logic within worker.js. Utilize IDE tools supporting JavaScript for robust development experiences.

The following is a basic worker script enabling redirection to another URL when triggered:

```
addEventListener('fetch', event => {
  event.respondWith(handleRequest(event.request))
})

async function handleRequest(request) {
  return Response.redirect('https://new-destination.com', 301)
}
```

This script listens for fetch events, issuing a 301 Moved Permanently HTTP status, effectively redirecting incoming requests to https://new-destination.com. It manifests an uncomplicated logic sample characteristic of edge computing tasks ideal for Cloudflare Workers.

To test scripts locally, Wrangler CLI offers inbuilt command capabilities which enable previewing:

```
wrangler dev
```

This command deploys a test server that allows for checking scripts in real-time. The changes and behaviors can be validated locally, significantly condensing the traditional edit-deploy-debug cycle intrinsic to legacy systems.

After locally testing and refining, the worker is ready for deployment to Cloudflare's global edge network. Ensure that network infrastructure such as DNS settings point appropriately to targeted domains.

Deploy the worker using:

```
wrangler publish
```

Upon execution, Wrangler fetches project configurations from wrangler.toml and executes deployment. Successfully published workers are active through the configured domain paths, feasibly reconfigured at any time by updating wrangler.toml and redeploying.

Post-deployment, continuous monitoring and debugging are pivotal to maintaining operational efficacy and spotting anomalies. Cloudflare offers tools such as Workers KV (Key Value store) integration in scripts

187

for persistent storage needs, enhancing utility and data management options.

Assuming a scenario where request logging is crucial for audits, implement a logging worker:

```
addEventListener('fetch', event => {
  console.log('Incoming request: ${event.request.url}')
  event.respondWith(handleRequest(event.request))
})

async function handleRequest(request) {
  return new Response('Logged', {status: 200})
}
```

This script logs URL information for each incoming request, viewable via the Cloudflare dashboard or CLI logs output method, effectuating comprehensive auditing.

```
wrangler tail
```

Furthermore, integrating error boundaries lends protective layers and user reassurance against operational failures:

```
addEventListener('fetch', event => {
  event.respondWith(handleRequest(event.request).catch(handleError))
})

async function handleRequest(request) {
  if (Math.random() < 0.5) {
    throw new Error('Simulated Error')
  }
  return new Response('Hello World', { status: 200 })
}

function handleError(error) {
  console.error('Error encountered:', error)
  return new Response('Something went wrong!', { status: 500 })
}
```

This pattern introduces a robust way of capturing exceptions, along with informing remote debugging and swift incident response endeavors, fortifying application reliability across the board.

Application of Cloudflare Workers extends beyond theoretical constructs into substantive real-world deployments seeing tangible benefits. Examples include:

- E-commerce Platforms: Augmenting content delivery networks

188

(CDNs) by prefetching popular product recommendations or updates directly at the edge.

- IoT Data Aggregation: Rapid network interfacing to process continuous streams of sensor data, reaching conclusions without requiring central processing delays.

- Dynamic Edge Authentication: Customizable rule-driven security policies, ensuring that only authorized and verified endpoints ever entrust access to critical resources.

Ultimately, setting up Cloudflare Workers entails more than simple deployment; the practice surrounds understanding the service benefit spectrum. Each step from initialization through handling production requests is instrumentalized by the corresponding framework, encompassing both containers for innovation and means to diligently manage challenges emerging in production settings.

7.4   Using Workers for Dynamic Content

Cloudflare Workers stand out as a pivotal technology for the generation and management of dynamic content at the edge. This capability is crucial in the modern web development landscape, enabling developers to offer personalized, context-sensitive experiences to users with reduced latency. By leveraging edge computing, applications can respond to user interactions and data input in real time, circumventing the bandwidth and delay constraints typical of traditional server-heavy architectures. This section delves into methodologies for using Cloudflare Workers to deliver dynamic content, supported by extensive code examples and a discussion of key considerations for development and deployment.

Dynamic content generation involves producing web page elements that adjust based on user input, preferences, or environmental factors, such as geographical location or device type. Traditionally, dynamic content workflows relied significantly on backend servers to process requests and return customized responses. Cloudflare Workers upend this model by enabling modifications directly at the network edge, leading to performance gains and enhanced scalability.

At the core of dynamic content handling with Cloudflare Workers is the script's ability to intercept, analyze, and modify HTTP requests and responses. This interception facilitates real-time decision-making without returning to a centralized server. With Cloudflare's global network, the execution of Workers happens close to the end users, enabling swift tailoring of content.

Key principles underpinning the use of Workers for producing dynamic content include:

- **Proximity and Latency Reduction**: By executing scripts at edge nodes, Workers reduce the geographic distance between users and server logic, translating to swift response times for dynamic page loads.

- **Real-Time Processing**: Dynamic data can be processed at the edge with minimal delay, making real-time content updates feasible for applications such as news feeds or stock tickers.

- **Scalability and Maintenance**: Workers facilitate the easy scaling of dynamic content delivery without altering backend infrastructure, supported by a serverless paradigm that abstracts hardware concerns from developers.

Consider practical scenarios where Cloudflare Workers enhance dynamic content handling. A potent example is the transformation of conventional API requests into edge-optimized interactions. Suppose a user interface needs to present different data fields based on a user's locale; Workers can intercept these requests to modify behavior or responses dynamically.

```
addEventListener('fetch', event => {
  event.respondWith(handleRequest(event.request))
})

async function handleRequest(request) {
  const url = new URL(request.url)
  let userLocale = request.headers.get('Accept-Language')

  userLocale = userLocale ? userLocale.split(',')[0] : 'en'

  const response = await fetch(url.toString())
  const html = await response.text()

  const alteredHtml = modifyContentForLocale(html, userLocale)
```

190

```
  return new Response(alteredHtml, {
    status: response.status,
    headers: { 'content-type': 'text/html' }
  })
}

function modifyContentForLocale(html, locale) {
  // Basic implementation to simulate content alteration
  return html.replace(/default-string/gi, 'Localized content for ${locale}')
}
```

In this script, the Cloudflare Worker inspects the 'Accept-Language' request header to determine the user's locale. It customizes the HTML content fetched from the origin by replacing locale-sensitive strings prior to final delivery. This approach is useful for localizing user interfaces without bloating the base HTML delivered by the origin servers.

Dynamic content is invaluable for A/B testing strategies where user experience variations are tested to determine optimal design or functionality. Cloudflare Workers can dynamically allocate test variations at the edge, directing users to specific versions of a webpage based on weighted probabilities or segment characteristics.

Consider the following worker script designed for A/B testing:

```
addEventListener('fetch', event => {
  event.respondWith(handleRequest(event.request))
})

async function handleRequest(request) {
  const testRatio = 0.5 // 50% chance for each

  const group = Math.random() < testRatio ? 'A' : 'B'
  const url = group === 'A' ? 'https://example.com/test-A' : 'https://example.com/
      test-B'

  return fetch(url)
}
```

This script splits incoming traffic into two cohorts—A and B—by leveraging probabilistic logic managed at the edge, redirecting users seamlessly to appropriate test versions of the site. Conducting variation testing ensures that server-side analytics and interaction insights lead to data-driven design improvements.

In addition to content transformations, Workers can play a central role in aggregating and preprocessing dynamic data from multiple sources. This is particularly beneficial in environments where data streams from various sensors or input adapters converge. Edge processing minimizes the data transfer requirements back to the central server, allowing real-time updates and analytics.

```
addEventListener('fetch', event => {
  event.respondWith(handleRequest(event.request))
})

async function handleRequest(request) {
  const urls = [
    'https://api.example.com/data1',
    'https://api.example.com/data2',
    'https://api.example.com/data3'
  ]

  const responses = await Promise.all(urls.map(url => fetch(url)))
  const dataFragments = await Promise.all(responses.map(resp => resp.json()))

  const aggregatedData = aggregateData(dataFragments)

  return new Response(JSON.stringify(aggregatedData, null, 2), {
    headers: { 'content-type': 'application/json' }
  })
}

function aggregateData(dataFragments) {
  // Naive aggregation assuming array of objects with similar structures
  return dataFragments.reduce((agg, curr) => {
    for (let key in curr) {
      agg[key] = (agg[key] || 0) + curr[key]
    }
    return agg
  }, {})
}
```

Here, the Cloudflare Worker collects JSON data from multiple APIs and aggregates it at the edge. By doing so, a singular response encapsulating all relevant insights can be delivered to the client with reduced response time and network load. This presents a scalable approach to handling data-rich applications, such as dashboards or IoT monitoring systems.

Perhaps the most transformative use of Workers for dynamic content is personalization. By inspecting cookies or session variables in real time, Workers can adjust HTML, CSS, and JavaScript content for uniquely personalized experiences.

```
addEventListener('fetch', event => {
  event.respondWith(handleRequest(event.request))
})

async function handleRequest(request) {
```

192

```
  const url = new URL(request.url)
  const cookies = request.headers.get('cookie') || "

  const userPreferences = getUserPreferences(cookies)

  const response = await fetch(url.toString())
  const html = await response.text()

  const personalizedHtml = applyUserPreferences(html, userPreferences)

  return new Response(personalizedHtml, {
    status: response.status,
    headers: { 'content-type': 'text/html' }
  })
}
function getUserPreferences(cookies) {
  return {
    theme: cookies.includes('theme=dark') ? 'dark' : 'light',
    language: cookies.includes('language=fr') ? 'fr' : 'en'
  }
}
function applyUserPreferences(html, preferences) {
  let modifiedHtml = html
  // Adjust theme
  modifiedHtml = preferences.theme === 'dark' ?
    modifiedHtml.replace(/light-theme/gi, 'dark-theme') : modifiedHtml.replace(/dark-
      theme/gi, 'light-theme')
  // Adjust language
  modifiedHtml = preferences.language === 'fr' ?
    modifiedHtml.replace(/Hello/gi, 'Bonjour') : modifiedHtml.replace(/Bonjour/gi, '
      Hello')

  return modifiedHtml
}
```

In this script, user session details from cookies inform alterations at the edge, effectively customizing the appearance and language of an HTML document before reaching the browser. Personalized content deepens user engagement and satisfaction by creating interfaces that align with user preferences and contexts.

Leveraging Cloudflare Workers for these dynamic content applications unfolds a spectrum of new possibilities. Whether it's localization, testing, aggregation, or personalization, the seamless integration of computational tasks at the edge advances efficiency and user satisfaction. Such an approach aligns with modern demands for responsive, scalable web experiences delivered swiftly and consistently.

Developers are encouraged to envision Workers not as peripheral add-ons but as critical components in a holistic system architecture that excels in delivering adaptable, high-performance applications. Subsequent sections consider additional resource management strategies and security practices that synergize with Cloudflare's serverless offerings, ensuring robust, efficient edge deployments.

7.5   Security and Resource Management

In managing versatile deployments through Cloudflare Workers, ensuring robust security alongside effective resource management is crucial. As serverless platforms operating at edge nodes, Cloudflare Workers present unique advantages and challenges in maintaining security integrity and optimal performance. This section examines best practices for securing workers, managing resources, and providing resilient and efficient applications through comprehensive technical strategies and coding insights.

Isolation and Sandboxing   The architecture of Cloudflare Workers inherently leverages isolation. Each worker runs in a separate and secure V8 runtime environment. This sandboxed setup limits potential cross-script invasions, ensuring individual scripts maintain distinct operational boundaries. This design is essential in preventing scenarios where a compromised worker would otherwise affect a broader system (a feature often exploited in monolithic server architectures).

Secure Communication and Data Handling   Implementing secure data transmission protocols such as HTTPS is non-negotiable for ensuring private and tamper-proof interactions between clients and edge nodes.

Let's consider an illustrative example of a worker script securely handling sensitive headers:

```
addEventListener('fetch', event => {
  event.respondWith(handleRequest(event.request))
})

async function handleRequest(request) {
  if (!request.headers.get('Authorization')) {
    return new Response('Unauthorized', { status: 401 })
  }
```

194

```
const token = request.headers.get('Authorization').replace('Bearer ', '')
if (!isValidToken(token)) {
  return new Response('Forbidden', { status: 403 })
}

// Proceed with authorized actions
const response = await fetch(request)
return new Response(response.body, {
  ...response,
  headers: new Headers({
    'Content-Security-Policy': "default-src 'self'",
    ...response.headers
  })
})
}

function isValidToken(token) {
  // Validate JWT token or equivalent
  return Boolean(token)
}
```

In this example, a simple validation of the Bearer token ensures that only authorized requests proceed further. The worker script appends a stringent 'Content-Security-Policy' header in responses to fortify browser content security, minimizing injection risks.

Data Minimization and Caching Strategies Extracting only necessary elements from requests or responses is central to reducing exposure risk. Furthermore, utilizing Cloudflare's built-in cache control strategies can aid in leveraging content caching at appropriate junctures, improving performance while minimizing sensitive data retention.

Consider implementing caching mechanisms rigorously, exemplified as follows:

```
addEventListener('fetch', event => {
  event.respondWith(handleRequest(event.request))
})

async function handleRequest(request) {
  const cacheUrl = new URL(request.url)
  const cacheKey = new Request(cacheUrl.toString(), request)

  const cache = caches.default
  // Check if response exists in cache
  let response = await cache.match(cacheKey)
  if (!response) {
    // Fetch from origin if not cached
    response = await fetch(request)
```

```
  // Cache only non-sensitive resources
  if (!response.headers.get('Set-Cookie')) {
    event.waitUntil(cache.put(cacheKey, response.clone()))
  }
}

return response
}
```

Through this approach, caching is optimized to prevent storage of re-
quests/options that include sensitive elements such as session cookies
while still reaping performance benefits offered by edge caching capabilities.

Resource Management in Cloudflare Workers   Resource management within Cloudflare Workers revolves around efficiently utilizing compute time, managing in-process memory, and striking a balance between performance, cost, and workload distribution.

Understanding Limits and Quotas   Cloudflare imposes quotas
to ensure fair resource utilization and to avoid abuse. Workers must
operate within constraints of CPU time, memory usage, and in-built
API request limitations. Awareness of these restrictions is vital to ar-
chitect performant and cost-effective solutions.

Specifically:

- CPU Time: Workers have a soft execution time limit that offers
  users equitable time slices, generally capped around 10 ms per
  execution cycle to maintain consistent performance and prevent
  resource monopolization.

- Memory: Workers are provided a lightweight runtime, typically
  constrained around 128 MB. Efficient memory usage is necessary
  to prevent exceeding usage limits leading to forced termination
  or errors.

Optimizing Script Performance   Crafting performant scripts involves minimizing blocking operations, optimizing algorithmic efficiency, and using Worker KV appropriately to store state across requests where necessary.

In tackling an example of efficient memory usage, consider the use of typed arrays over standard arrays for intensive computation tasks:

```
addEventListener('fetch', event => {
  event.respondWith(handleRequest(event.request))
})

async function handleRequest(request) {
  const buffer = new ArrayBuffer(1024)
  const view = new Uint8Array(buffer)
  for (let i = 0; i < view.length; i++) {
    view[i] = i % 255 // Dummy computation
  }
  return new Response(JSON.stringify(view), {
    headers: { 'content-type': 'application/json' }
  })
}
```

This example demonstrates replacing standard arrays with typed arrays for predictable memory footprints and lower overhead in computational tasks.

Best Practices for Scalable Management Beyond internal optimization, consider implementing strategies such as:

- Load Balancing: Configure multiple worker instances across edge nodes to handle high-volume requests, allowing redundant entry points to reduce congestion.

- Batch Processing: Where context allows, handle requests in batches rather than single transactions to improve throughput performance.

- Throttling and Queuing: Introduce rate limits for API requests at worker level to align processing capabilities without overwhelming backend services in service-heavy applications.

Integration with External Analytics For comprehensive management, integrating logging and monitoring tools provides insightful performance and usage data, guiding optimization efforts and identifying bottlenecks or anomalies.

```
addEventListener('fetch', event => {
  event.respondWith(logRequest(event.request))
})
```

```
async function logRequest(request) {
  const response = await fetch(request)
  return new Response(response.body, {
    ...response,
    headers: response.headers,
  }, logToAnalytics(request, response))
}

function logToAnalytics(request, response) {
  console.log('Request URL: ${request.url}')
  console.log('Response Status: ${response.status}')
  // Further integration with external logging systems
}
```

Integration of external logging systems helps capture essential metrics such as latency, request processing time, and response statuses. Tailored analytics guide iterative adjustments and resource planning for workload fluctuations, aligning project needs to performance outcomes.

Proficiently managing security and resource allocation within Cloudflare Workers mandates understanding both internal structural efficiencies and external threat landscapes. These endeavors assure system resilience, reduced operational risks, and sustainable application deployments. Ensuing sections tackle diverse case studies and delve into the specific architectures lending themselves to edge-deployed solutions, further enhancing understanding and strategy adaptation.

7.6   Use Cases and Applications

The deployment of Cloudflare Workers has unlocked a multitude of possibilities across various industries, enhancing application performance by leveraging edge computing. Their versatility enables them to be employed for a range of services such as enhancing API performance, personalizing content, and optimizing web performance through real-time computations performed closer to the end-user. In this section, we'll delve into detailed use cases and applications of Cloudflare Workers, illustrating their pragmatic benefits with related code demonstrations to provide deeper insights into building robust and responsive solutions.

- **API Endpoints and Edge Functionality**

One of the most compelling use cases for Cloudflare Workers is acting as an intermediary for API endpoints. Unlike traditional server setups where API requests funnel through central servers, Workers can process crucial operations directly at edge nodes. This paradigm enhances the performance of APIs by reducing latency and offloading computational tasks from central servers.

Consider an example where a Worker functions as a preprocessing unit for API queries:

```
addEventListener('fetch', event => {
  event.respondWith(handleRequest(event.request))
})

async function handleRequest(request) {
  const { pathname, searchParams } = new URL(request.url)

  // Manipulate query params before proceeding
  searchParams.append('apikey', 'YOUR_API_KEY')

  const modifiedUrl = '${pathname}?${searchParams.toString()}'

  // Forward modified request to the origin server
  const response = await fetch(modifiedUrl, request)
  return response
}
```

In this Worker script, API requests directed through the edge node have their query parameters adjusted to append an API key before engaging the origin server. This can centralize authentication processes or key-based access control mechanisms close to the client-side, minimizing delay and preserving server load.

- **Content Personalization and Localization**

Cloudflare Workers allow for dynamic content delivery that tailors web page responses based on user specifics. Personalizing user experiences enhances engagement by presenting content that reflects individual user preferences, geographic location, or device characteristics.

Here is an example demonstrating how Workers can customize content based on user location:

```
addEventListener('fetch', event => {
```

```
    event.respondWith(handleRequest(event.request))
})

async function handleRequest(request) {
  const country = request.cf.country || 'US'

  const contentResponses = {
    US: 'Welcome to our US site!',
    FR: 'Bienvenue sur notre site français!',
    default: 'Welcome to our global site!'
  }

  const message = contentResponses[country] || contentResponses.default

  return new Response(message, {
    headers: { 'content-type': 'text/plain' }
  })
}
```

By accessing Cloudflare's 'cf.country' parameter, this Worker script adjusts its response to user requests based on country code, showcasing dynamic content updates to cater uniquely to each region's audience.

- **Performance Optimization and Asset Handling**

Workers can also enhance web performance by managing assets such as scripts and stylesheets. By optimizing these assets at the edge, users experience reduced loading times, benefitting from minified resources and the elimination of redundant data transfer.

Consider the following Worker script, responsible for serving minified CSS resources:

```
addEventListener('fetch', event => {
  const url = new URL(event.request.url)

  if (url.pathname.endsWith('.css')) {
    event.respondWith(minifyCss(event.request))
  } else {
    event.respondWith(fetch(event.request))
  }
})

async function minifyCss(request) {
  const response = await fetch(request)
  const cssText = await response.text()

  // Basic inline minification
  const minifiedCss = cssText.replace(/\s+/g, ' ').replace(/;\s/g, ';')

  return new Response(minifiedCss, {
    headers: { 'content-type': 'text/css' }
```

```
  })
}
```

Using this tactic, CSS files are minified in-flight as they pass through the Worker, reducing size before reaching client browsers. By automating this process at the edge, application aesthetics and performance benefited without compromising maintainability.

- **Security and Access Controls**

Beyond enhancing performance and personalization, Workers stand as a critical part of implementing security measures. They provide an initial line of defense by managing authentication, applying rate limits, and filtering malicious requests before they hit centralized servers.

Here's a strategy showcasing how to create a simple IP rate-limiting mechanism:

```
addEventListener('fetch', event => {
  event.respondWith(rateLimitedRequest(event.request))
})

async function rateLimitedRequest(request) {
  const clientIp = request.headers.get('CF-Connecting-IP')
  const url = new URL(request.url)

  const cacheKey = 'rate-limit-${clientIp}-${url.pathname}'
  const cache = caches.default

  const requestCountResponse = await cache.match(cacheKey)
  let requestCount = parseInt(await requestCountResponse?.text()) || 0

  if (requestCount > 100) {
    return new Response('Too Many Requests', { status: 429 })
  }

  // Increment counter
  event.waitUntil(cache.put(cacheKey, new Response((requestCount + 1).toString())))

  // Serve request
  const response = await fetch(request)
  return response
}
```

This solution uses Cloudflare's cache API for transient data storage, limiting the number of requests an IP address can make under set path conditions. Techniques like these inhibit abusive behaviors, ensuring system stability amidst varying traffic conditions.

201

- ## Serverless Cron Jobs and On-Demand Processing

In addition to real-time processing, Workers can power scheduled tasks, functioning as serverless cron jobs with Cloudflare's service integrations. Common applications include cleanup scripts, data synchronization, or report generation.

Here's a conceptual worker creating on-demand data aggregation:

```
addEventListener('scheduled', event => {
  event.waitUntil(handleScheduledTask(event))
})

async function handleScheduledTask(event) {
  const aggregatedData = await fetchAggregateData()

  await pushAggregatedData(aggregatedData)
}

async function fetchAggregateData() {
  const dataSources = [
    'https://example.com/api/data1',
    'https://example.com/api/data2',
  ]

  const results = await Promise.all(dataSources.map(url => fetch(url).then(res => res.
      json())))
  return results.reduce((total, current) => ({ ...total, ...current }), {})
}

async function pushAggregatedData(data) {
  const storageUrl = 'https://example.com/api/store'
  await fetch(storageUrl, {
    method: 'POST',
    headers: { 'Content-Type': 'application/json' },
    body: JSON.stringify(data)
  })
}
```

This Worker script defines a scheduled task to fetch and synchronize data from several APIs, aggregating and relaying it to a defined storage endpoint. By offloading scheduled computations to the edge, cloud resources remain untaxed until required for aggregated insights.

- ## E-commerce and Transactional Processing

In e-commerce applications, Workers can swiftly handle aspects of transactions, such as discount code validation, inventory updates, and personalized deal generation.

Below is a Worker script exemplifying real-time discount validation:

```
addEventListener('fetch', event => {
  event.respondWith(validateDiscount(event.request))
})

async function validateDiscount(request) {
  const discountCode = new URL(request.url).searchParams.get('code')

  if (!discountCode) {
    return new Response('Missing discount code.', {status: 400})
  }

  const validCodes = ['SAVE10', 'WELCOME20']
  const isValid = validCodes.includes(discountCode.toUpperCase())

  const message = isValid ? 'Code applied' : 'Invalid code'
  const status = isValid ? 200 : 403

  return new Response(message, {status})
}
```

The script verifies discount code legitimacy against pre-defined options, engaging clients directly at the edge. Speed and reliability are enhanced as transactions are not bottlenecked by central server checks.

These use cases exemplify Cloudflare Workers' profound utility in modern network and application designs. Maximizing edge computing advantages, workers underpin processes spanning domains from performance optimization to transactional integrity. This enhances responsiveness, overall intelligibility, and adaptability, leading to transformative user experiences alongside sustainable operational models.

Exploratory innovations grounded in these edge capabilities help position organizations at the forefront of technology advancement, addressing digital evolution dynamics proactively. Further sections will resolve potential constraints, identifying optimal resolution pathways in these fast-paced development environments.

7.7 Debugging and Testing Workers

Ensuring the reliability and performance of Cloudflare Workers is vital to robust edge deployment. Debugging and testing, however, can pose unique challenges akin to those encountered in other asynchronous and serverless environments. This section provides meticulous insights into debugging strategies, testing methodologies, and best practices to identify and rectify issues while optimizing performance. Through comprehensive examples and methodical analysis, developers can enhance their workflow in developing, testing, and maintaining Cloudflare Workers.

Understanding the Debugging Environment

Debugging Cloudflare Workers involves navigating an asynchronous, event-driven environment hosted across distributed nodes. Unlike traditional server debugging, there's no central server log or direct terminal. Instead, Workers are executed inside sandboxed V8 runtimes with limitations on logging and error inspection, necessitating innovative approaches for fault isolation and tracing.

Log-based Debugging

Logging remains a primary means of monitoring Workers' behavior during execution. Incorporating console statements provides real-time insights into data processing, decision branches, and error states. However, console output from Workers is captured via Cloudflare's logs, accessible through Wrangler CLI or the Cloudflare dashboard.

Here's an example illustrating how to use logging effectively:

```
addEventListener('fetch', event => {
  event.respondWith(logRequestDetails(event.request))
})

async function logRequestDetails(request) {
  console.log('Request URL: ${request.url}')
  console.log('Request Method: ${request.method}')

  try {
    const response = await fetch(request)
    return response
  } catch (error) {
    console.error('Fetch Error: ', error)
    return new Response('Internal Server Error', { status: 500 })
  }
}
```

The above example logs essential information such as request URLs and methods, while also capturing any errors during fetch operations. This provides a basic framework for testing hypotheses about script behavior and performance.

Using Wrangler tail

Wrangler tail is a Wrangler CLI command designed for direct log access, enabling developers to stream Worker logs in real-time. To initiate tail, use:

```
wrangler tail
```

This naturally integrates into the local development process to diagnose issues promptly without the overhead of repeated deployment cycles.

Error Boundary Strategies

Implementing error boundaries captures unexpected behaviors, easing the troubleshooting process. Wrapping Worker logic in try-catch blocks offers controlled handling for both anticipated and unforeseen errors.

```
addEventListener('fetch', event => {
  event.respondWith(handleFetchEvent(event).catch(handleError))
})

async function handleFetchEvent(event) {
  const response = await fetch(event.request)

  if (!response.ok) {
    throw new Error('Fetch failed with status: ${response.status}')
  }

  return response
}

function handleError(error) {
  console.error('Error caught: ', error)
  return new Response('An error occurred. Please try again later.', { status: 502 })
}
```

Using a clean failover pathway such as displaying a friendly fallback message can protect service integrity during periods of intermittent errors or latency.

Testing Strategies and Methodology

Testing Workers individually requires handling both their unique execution characteristics and the consistency of outcomes across unpredictable network environments. Here, we examine strategies to test worker logic effectively:

Local Testing and Wrangler dev

Wrangler dev facilitates local execution of Workers, simulating production-like environments on developer machines. By providing a proxied interface for debugging locally, developers can interact with Workers as though in production, accessing logs, errors, and console output.

Start the local testing server using:

```
wrangler dev
```

This command enables interactive testing, including editing and refreshing scripts live to diagnose and resolve issues.

Unit Testing with Mocks

For granular logic testing, integrating unit tests that utilize mocking libraries to simulate fetch requests and global variables is critical. Libraries such as Mocha and Sinon provide an ideal framework to create controlled environments.

Consider a unit test skeleton utilizing mocks:

```
const sinon = require('sinon')
const { handleFetchEvent } = require('./worker')

describe('Cloudflare Worker Test Suite', () => {
  let fetchStub;

  beforeEach(() => {
    fetchStub = sinon.stub(global, 'fetch')
  })

  afterEach(() => {
    fetchStub.restore()
  })

  it('should fetch resource successfully', async () => {
    fetchStub.resolves(new Response('OK', { status: 200 }))

    const event = { request: new Request('https://api.example.com/data') }
    const response = await handleFetchEvent(event)

    sinon.assert.calledOnce(fetchStub)
    expect(response.status).to.equal(200)
  })

  it('should return error message on failure', async () => {
    fetchStub.rejects(new Error('Network error'))

    const event = { request: new Request('https://api.example.com/data') }
    const response = await handleFetchEvent(event).catch(err => err)

    sinon.assert.calledOnce(fetchStub)
```

```
    expect(response).to.equal('An error occurred. Please try again later.')
  })
})
```

This example demonstrates crafting unit tests with Mocha and Sinon to mock fetch requests, validating expected outcomes from diverse code paths while isolating external variables.

Integration Testing with Live Environments

Using staging environments for integration testing authenticates interaction among components (e.g., Workers, KV storage, CDN, third-party APIs). Here, full-fledged testing of API calls, data manipulation, and integration logic validate cumulative behavior through system-wide tests.

Developers can execute integration suites using tools such as Cypress, which automates end-to-end browser interactions to verify real-world operation.

```
describe('API End-to-End Test', () => {
  it('successfully loads the API endpoint', () => {
    cy.visit('https://staging.example.com/api')
    cy.request('GET', '/data')
      .should((response) => {
        expect(response.status).to.eq(200)
        expect(response.body).to.have.property('key')
      })
  })
})
```

Such practices afford full stack level assurance that a system behaves as expected within real conditions, mitigating the risk of production issues.

Performance and Load Testing

Performance testing evaluates script efficiency, particularly under scaled conditions. Services like Artillery and benchmarking tools help simulate high-load scenarios and reveal potential bottlenecks.

Example Usage of Artillery for Load Testing:

```
config:
  target: 'https://example.com/worker-endpoint'
  phases:
    - duration: 300
      arrivalRate: 10
scenarios:
```

207

```
- flow:
  - get:
      url: '/test-load'
```

The configuration sets up a 5-minute duration test, gradually increasing the request rate to simulate real-world load, consequently identifying latency excursions and resilience concerns.

Best Practices for Debugging and Testing

- Structured Logs: Implement structured JSON logging to simplify log search and filter operations within Cloudflare's logging services.

- Version Control and CI/CD: Utilize branch-driven CI/CD processes to automate testing on each code revision, maintaining consistent quality checks.

- Iterative Development: Merge iterative improvements and lean checkpoints where feasible, combining logs, tests, and metrics into a seamless feedback loop.

This comprehensive overview of debugging and testing Workers ensures that applications remain reliable, performant, and scalable. By embodying architectures grounded in best practices, developers can safely innovate at the edge, managing both uncertainty and opportunity within distributed systems environments. Subsequent discussions will further address cost management and optimization strategies to complement technical employment efforts.

7.8 Billing and Cost Considerations

The financial implications of deploying Cloudflare Workers significantly influence how organizations adopt and scale serverless functions at the edge. With Cloudflare's flexible billing structures, applications can scale efficiently, yet caution is advised to ensure that cost models align with deployment strategies. This section provides an in-depth explanation of Cloudflare Workers' billing mechanisms, identifies potential cost drivers, and offers optimization strategies to maintain fiscal oversight while maximizing computational capacity.

- **Understanding Cloudflare Workers Billing Model**

At its core, Cloudflare Workers operates under a consumption-based pricing model, differing significantly from traditional server hosting costs. This approach aligns expenses closely with concurrent usage, charging based on quantified request counts, compute time, and KV data operations.

- **Key Components of Worker Pricing**

1. Request Count: Charges are derived from the number of Workers invocations. Each incoming HTTP request that triggers a Worker script constitutes a billable request.

2. Duration: Workers billing also considers the compute time per request, with measurements typically rounded up to the nearest millisecond. The inherent efficiency of Workers often represents a significantly lower execution time compared to server-hosted counterparts.

3. Additional Features and Limits: Specific Worker features such as Durable Objects or KV storage possess distinct cost structures, separated from standard request handling fees. These costs are determined by read/write operations and data stored across Cloudflare's distributed network.

Here's an example breakdown of a hypothetical monthly Workers' bill for a mid-sized application:

Charges	Unit Count	Rate	Cost
Worker requests	5,000,000	$0.15 per million	$0.75
Duration (ms)	200 million	$0.30 per million	$60.00
KV operations	500,000 reads	$0.05 per million	$0.025
	200,000 writes	$0.50 per million	$0.10
Durable Objects	1,000,000 ops	$0.15 per million	$0.15
Total Monthly Cost	-	-	**$61.025**

- **Free Tier and Additional Services**

Cloudflare Workers offer a free tier with operational limits suitable for low-traffic applications or proof-of-concept projects. The free tier allows 100,000 requests per day before charging begins, empowering small teams to explore foundational serverless deployments without upfront cost commitments.

• Cost Drivers and Optimization Strategies

In the pursuit of cost efficiency and optimal resource utilization, understanding the main drivers of expenses is crucial. Identifying specific actions to offset or lower these costs can directly impact overall budget expenses.

• Key Cost Drivers

1. Request Frequency and Compute Intensity: High-request frequency or compute-heavy operations, such as complex algorithmic calculations or extensive data processing tasks, require more execution time, thus increasing costs.

2. Storage and KV Reads/Writes: Persistent storage usage and frequent read/write operations across Workers KV contribute to increasing prediction costs as data requirements grow beyond prime thresholds.

3. Extra Features: Advanced features like Durable Objects might introduce unpredicted variable costs, depending on usage trends and scaling scenarios.

• Techniques for Cost Optimization

1. Resource Throttling and Rate Limiting: Implement rate limiting within Workers to control the number of requests processed and prevent overuse. This can distribute compute loads, offering better financial outcomes and reducing peak incidents.

```
addEventListener('fetch', event => {
  event.respondWith(rateLimitCheck(event.request))
})

async function rateLimitCheck(request) {
  const url = new URL(request.url)
  const ip = request.headers.get('CF-Connecting-IP')
```

```
// Assume cache and rate limit logic integrated
const cacheKey = '${url.hostname}-${ip}'
const rateExceeds = await rateLimit.cacheGet(cacheKey) > 1000

if (rateExceeds) {
  return new Response('Too Many Requests', { status: 429 })
}

// Continue processing requests
return await fetch(request)
}
```

This example depicts limiting requests by IP, curbing spikes that potentially elevate costs without compromising user access effectively.

2. Efficient Data Transfer: Minimize direct KV or Durable Object operations to necessary data points. Use local Worker transformations over fetching computations to limit KV interactions.

3. Concurrency Management: Optimize parallel processing within acceptable parameters to maintain concurrency without exceeding predefined resource quotas, addressing billing implications of excessive CPU time and memory usage.

4. Task Segmentation and Caching: Decompose complex tasks into modular Worker scripts and leverage caching, both to improve response times and reduce redundant computation.

5. Network Strategy and Routing: Diligent use of Cloudflare's routing capabilities can optimize geographic data flows, ensuring content is served from the most cost-effective regions out of available edge nodes, using latency-based considerations.

- **Benchmarking and Monitoring Tools**

Prudent tracking and analytics tools can help monitor, anticipate, and optimize resource allocation. Comprehensive insights support data-driven decision-making, hinting at adjustments necessary for deployment harmony and cost stability.

- **Logging and Metrics**

Augment Workers with performance logging and metrics collection tools to measure execution patterns and predict cost-related anomalies:

```
addEventListener('fetch', event => {
  const startTime = Date.now()
  event.respondWith(logPerformanceMetrics(event.request, startTime))
})

async function logPerformanceMetrics(request, startTime) {
  // Mocking service measure
  const result = await fetch(request).then(res => res.text())
  const duration = Date.now() - startTime

  console.log('Request URL: ${request.url}, Duration: ${duration}ms')

  return new Response(result, {
    headers: { 'content-type': 'text/plain' }
  })
}
```

- **Employ Continuous Profiling**

Leverage tools that provide profiling capabilities across worker executions, displaying per-operation insights and high-level overview metrics. These enable the identification of hotspots for performance improvements conducive to cost-saving measures.

- **Utilize Cloudflare's Graphana Integration**

Thoughtful integration of Cloudflare Workers' metrics into continuous monitoring platforms like Grafana aids in real-time visualization of expenditures and trends, offering predictive analytics capacity for upcoming demands.

- **Collaborative Budget Planning**

Incorporate cross-departmental input to align development, operations, and financial expectations. Approaching budget discussions collaboratively with anticipated workload reports ensures stakeholders understand costs' origin and impact.

- **Strategic Expansion and Future Considerations**

Align current cost management principles with long-term scalability goals. With Cloudflare Workers evolving consistently alongside modern application needs, it's vital to anticipate future features and billing alterations within forward-looking infrastructure planning.

- **Flexibility in Scaling**

Consider burstable use cases and alternative edge computing strategies to adhere to changing traffic dynamics without overcommitting to specific resources beyond current requirements.

- **Exploring Complementary Cloudflare Products**

Cloudflare's extensive ecosystem includes additional security, analytics, and optimization products that can pair with Workers to enhance economy-of-scale effects, leading to further financial efficiencies.

- **Embrace Innovation and Continuous Evaluation**

Regularly revisit architectural designs and billing practices as part of an ongoing process. Adapting methodologies can safeguard from unseen financial risks while revamping to employ new features that Cloudflare adds to their suite.

Ultimately, through rigorous understanding and proactive management of pricing dynamics, it is possible to economically deploy Cloudflare Workers at scale while maintaining fiscal responsibility. Extending cloud expenditure strategies with precision-based optimizations ensures control over costs while preserving rapid, responsive service delivery capabilities. As industries increasingly adopt these edge technologies, development teams must appraise budgetary impacts proactively, matching the agility afforded by serverless computing with sound financial prudence.

214

Chapter 8

Monitoring and Analyzing Traffic with Cloudflare

This chapter details the methods and tools provided by Cloudflare for monitoring and analyzing web traffic to bolster security and performance management. It covers the utilization of the Cloudflare Analytics Dashboard, highlighting real-time and historical traffic data insights. The chapter demonstrates how to identify traffic anomalies, customize reports, and integrate Cloudflare data with third-party analytics solutions. By mastering these techniques, users can enhance their ability to manage and optimize web traffic effectively, ensuring a reliable and efficient online presence.

8.1   Importance of Traffic Monitoring

Web traffic monitoring is an essential activity in the domain of cyber-security and network management. Effectively monitoring web traffic

215

enables network administrators and stakeholders to understand the flow of data across networks, identify potential security threats, and optimize performance. This section explores the multifaceted importance of traffic monitoring, considering various perspectives such as security, performance, and user behavior insights.

Traffic monitoring is paramount for maintaining the integrity and security of a network. With the ever-increasing volume of cyberattacks that organizations face, monitoring web traffic helps detect anomalies that could signify malicious activities. Suspicious patterns, such as a sudden spike in traffic, can be indicative of Distributed Denial-of-Service (DDoS) attacks, while unusual access requests might signify data breach attempts. By implementing continuous monitoring, organizations can quickly identify and mitigate these threats.

The following Python code demonstrates a basic approach to log and analyze network traffic statistics:

```
import socket

def log_packet(packet):
    with open('traffic.log', 'a') as log_file:
        log_file.write(f'{packet}\n')

def monitor_traffic(interface):
    sock = socket.socket(socket.AF_INET, socket.SOCK_RAW, socket.
        IPPROTO_TCP)
    sock.bind((interface, 0))

    while True:
        packet, addr = sock.recvfrom(65565)
        log_packet(packet)

monitor_traffic('eth0')
```

Using the code above, network operators can create a log file that records each packet received on a specific network interface. Analyzing the "traffic.log" file can help identify patterns associated with potential security issues.

Another essential aspect of traffic monitoring is performance optimization. By analyzing traffic patterns, organizations can determine peak usage times, understand load distributions, and make informed decisions about load balancing and resource allocation. Monitoring tools can capture data such as response times, throughput, and latency, allowing network administrators to pinpoint bottlenecks or performance

216

inefficiencies.

Consider the following code which simulates a basic performance analysis tool that records response times:

```python
import requests
import time

def analyze_response_time(url, num_requests=10):
    times = []
    for _ in range(num_requests):
        start_time = time.time()
        response = requests.get(url)
        end_time = time.time()

        if response.status_code == 200:
            times.append(end_time - start_time)

    average_response_time = sum(times) / len(times)
    return average_response_time

url = 'https://example.com'
average_time = analyze_response_time(url)
print(f'Average response time for {url} is {average_time} seconds')
```

Running this tool against a web service can yield insights into latency issues, helping systems administrators make adjustments on the server side to improve user experiences.

In addition to security and performance, monitoring traffic can offer significant insights into user behavior. Data regarding how users interact with a website, including time spent on pages, navigation paths, and interaction rates, can be collated and analyzed to understand user preferences and behaviors. By leveraging this data, organizations can enhance website design and content to better meet the needs and expectations of their audience, ultimately increasing engagement and conversion rates.

Web analytics tools, such as those provided by Cloudflare, offer extensive reporting capabilities that enable analysis of visitor behavior with metrics such as:

Metric	Description
Page Views	Number of times a page is viewed
Bounce Rate	Percentage of single-page sessions
Session Duration	Average time users spend on the site

By tracking these metrics, organizations can deduce which content is most engaging, which pages lead to user exit, and how overall navigation can be improved.

217

Critical to the process of traffic monitoring is the ability to distinguish between different types of traffic. This includes separating legitimate user traffic from potential attacks or crawler bots. Various techniques, such as IP filtering and user-agent validation, are employed in refining traffic analysis. This refinement ensures that data insights are not skewed by non-human interaction, which could otherwise lead to inaccurate conclusions about user behavior and system performance.

Traffic monitoring involves real-time analysis as well as post-event examination. Real-time monitoring allows for immediate response to adverse conditions such as DDoS attacks or server failures, while historical analysis aids in understanding long-term trends and patterns. For this purpose, a combination of inline and out-of-band monitoring is often used. Tools such as intrusion detection/prevention systems capture real-time data, whereas systems like Security Information and Event Management (SIEM) platforms provide post-event analysis.

```
from scapy.all import *

def packet_callback(packet):
    if packet.haslayer(TCP) and packet.getlayer(TCP).dport == 80:
        print(f"HTTP Request: {packet.summary()}")

sniff(iface="any", filter="tcp", prn=packet_callback, store=0)
```

This Python script utilizes the Scapy library to sniff HTTP traffic and prints a summary of each packet. Adaptations of such tools can be extended for both live monitoring and the collection of data for subsequent analysis.

The regulatory environment also highlights the necessity of traffic monitoring. Compliance with standards like General Data Protection Regulation (GDPR) and the Health Insurance Portability and Accountability Act (HIPAA) requires organizations to maintain proactive monitoring practices to ensure data integrity and security. Compliance with these regulations entails monitoring to prevent data breaches and unauthorized access, as well as maintaining logs for audit trails.

Cost efficiency is another pertinent reason for traffic monitoring. The ability to predict and allocate resources where they are needed can significantly reduce operational costs. Moreover, by identifying and blocking malicious traffic or non-essential access, organizations can save bandwidth and reduce the load on infrastructure, enhancing efficiency and potentially reducing costs related to cloud services or network bandwidth usage.

Little inspection mechanisms such as Deep Packet Inspection (DPI) are often employed to provide detailed traffic analysis, including payload examination and protocol validation. DPI can help in identifying malicious packets or unauthorized data transfers, reinforcing network security posture. The employment of such techniques is however balanced with privacy concerns and the potential impacts on network latency.

Traffic monitoring therefore is a proactive approach that both protects and optimizes. It is a cornerstone of modern internet infrastructure, contributing to the control and stabilization of network operations, ensuring compliance with international standards, optimizing resource allocation, and providing insights that steer strategic business operations. Monitoring provides visibility into complex network infrastructures where traditional oversight may fail, enabling organizations to act defensively and efficiently in the digital landscape.

8.2 Cloudflare Analytics Dashboard

The Cloudflare Analytics Dashboard is an essential tool for website administrators and network managers, providing a comprehensive overview of web traffic and security metrics. By offering real-time data visualization and historical insights, the dashboard empowers users to make informed decisions to enhance security, performance, and user experience. This section delves into the functionalities of the Cloudflare Analytics Dashboard, exploring the types of data available and how they can be leveraged to optimize web operations.

At the core of the Cloudflare Analytics Dashboard is its ability to present a detailed summary of traffic statistics. This includes metrics such as the total number of requests, bandwidth usage, and unique visitors. These metrics are displayed in interactive graphs and charts that allow users to analyze data over various time periods, ranging from the last 24 hours to the previous year. Understanding the flow and magnitude of requests can help identify trends in user activity and content demand.

The dashboard also provides insights into the geographical distribution of traffic. This feature displays a world map illustrating where requests originate, enabling administrators to identify key markets and tailor infrastructure to optimize performance in those regions. By analyzing geographical data, organizations can prioritize server deployments or Content Delivery Network (CDN) strategies to meet user demand efficiently.

Security insights form a critical component of the Cloudflare Analytics Dashboard. These insights cover data on security events, such as blocked threats, which include DDoS attacks, Firewall rule matches, and Bot Defense events. By visualizing this data, administrators can assess the efficacy of security configurations and adjust their rulesets to improve threat mitigation. The following Python snippet demonstrates how one might simulate logging security events for analysis:

```python
import random
import time

security_events = ['DDoS Attack Blocked', 'Suspicious IP Blocked', 'SQL Injection
    Attempt Detected']

def log_security_event():
    event = random.choice(security_events)
    timestamp = time.strftime("%Y-%m-%d %H:%M:%S", time.gmtime())
    with open('security_events.log', 'a') as log_file:
        log_file.write(f'{timestamp} - {event}\n')

for _ in range(10):
    log_security_event()
    time.sleep(1)
```

The "security_events.log" file generates a simulated log of security incidents, illustrating the types of events typically monitored within the Cloudflare Dashboard.

Performance metrics offered by the Cloudflare Analytics Dashboard include average request response time, cache hit rates, and origin and edge server latencies. These metrics allow administrators to evaluate content delivery efficiency and identify potential bottlenecks. Cache performance metrics, for instance, display the percentage of requests that were served from Cloudflare's cache rather than being fetched from the origin server. A high cache hit rate indicates efficient content delivery, contributing to faster load times for users.

As depicted in Figure 8.1, tracking changes in cache hit rates can provide insights into traffic and content delivery efficacy over the course

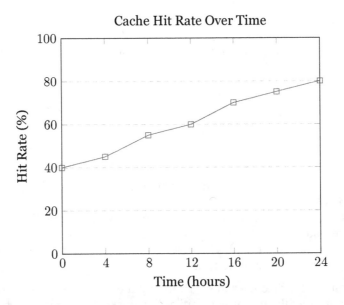

Figure 8.1: Visual representation of Cache Hit Rate across a 24-hour period.

of a day.

Another feature of the Analytics Dashboard is its advanced report generation capability. Users can create customized reports by selecting specific metrics and applying filters or segments. These reports can be tailored to focus on traffic patterns during marketing campaigns or seasonal peaks, providing critical data to enhance strategic planning.

The API functionality of Cloudflare allows users to automate data extraction and integrate dashboard data into third-party applications for deeper analysis or presentation. For example, a Python script can be crafted to perform automated data retrieval using the Cloudflare API, enabling dynamic data integration into data visualization platforms like Tableau:

```
import requests

api_token = 'your_api_token'
headers = {
    'Authorization': f'Bearer {api_token}',
```

```
    'Content-Type': 'application/json',
}

url = 'https://api.cloudflare.com/client/v4/zones/your_zone_id/analytics/dashboard'

response = requests.get(url, headers=headers)
data = response.json()

with open('cloudflare_data.json', 'w') as f:
    f.write(response.text)
```

This script contacts the Cloudflare API, retrieves data, and stores it in a "cloudflare_data.json" file for further analysis or visualization.

The dashboard's ability to handle both real-time and historical data enables a holistic view of web performance and security. Real-time analytics allow for immediate identification of traffic anomalies or performance issues, ensuring rapid incident response. Historical data analysis, on the other hand, aids in detecting long-term trends and assessing the impact of past interventions.

Operational efficiencies are further enhanced through the Cloudflare Analytics Dashboard by its intuitive alerting systems and proactive performance tuning suggestions. For example, automatic alerts can be set up to notify administrators about thresholds for request rates, error rates, or security events, prompting swift action to maintain service availability and integrity.

Considering scalability, Cloudflare's analytics infrastructure is robust, making it capable of handling vast datasets without degrading performance. This aspect is especially crucial for businesses experiencing rapid growth or high traffic levels, ensuring that they continue to receive actionable insights without latency.

Cloudflare Analytics Dashboard is a tool not only significant for its ability to provide in-depth traffic and security insights but also due to its contribution to enhancing user experience by offering various performance improvement techniques. The dashboard's user-friendly interface, rich data presentation capabilities, and extensive integration options make it an integral aspect of modern web administration strategies. Through comprehensive analysis and informed decision-making facilitated by Cloudflare Analytics, organizations are better equipped to optimize their online operations and secure their digital assets efficiently.

8.3 Real-Time and Historical Traffic Analysis

The ability to conduct both real-time and historical traffic analysis is crucial for maintaining an effective, secure, and efficient online presence. This section examines the methodologies and tools available for analyzing web traffic through Cloudflare, emphasizing the importance of both immediate, actionable insights and longer-term data trends. By leveraging these analyses, organizations can optimize web performance, enhance user experience, and bolster security defenses.

Real-time traffic analysis focuses on the immediate observation and interpretation of data as it flows through the network. This kind of analysis allows for the prompt detection of irregularities or threats such as DDoS attacks, sudden surges in traffic due to viral content, or even technical malfunctions on the server side. Techniques such as packet sniffing and logging are pivotal for acquiring real-time data. Tools like Cloudflare's threat intelligence system are integral in this context, as they facilitate rapid responses to security incidents.

Real-time monitoring can be conducted using various tools and scripting methods. The following Python code snippet demonstrates how to capture and analyze network packets in real time using the Scapy library:

```python
from scapy.all import sniff

def process_packet(packet):
    print(f'Packet: {packet.summary()}')
    if packet.haslayer('IP'):
        ip_src = packet['IP'].src
        ip_dst = packet['IP'].dst
        print(f'Source IP: {ip_src}, Destination IP: {ip_dst}')

sniff(filter="ip", prn=process_packet)
```

This script utilizes packet sniffing to display each packet along with its source and destination IP addresses, providing elemental building blocks for developing more complex real-time analysis systems.

Moreover, real-time analytics dashboards, such as those offered by Cloudflare, provide visualization tools that aggregate data into intuitive, dynamic panels. These dashboards are essential for easily moni-

223

toring key metrics such as request rates and error rates, giving network administrators the ability to track and interpret data with minimal delay.

Besides immediate threats, real-time analysis also aids in managing traffic flow. Automated rules can be set up to throttle traffic, redirect users, or cache content dynamically based on present conditions. Cloudflare's Page Rules and Traffic Control features offer such automation, minimizing downtime and maximizing resource utilization.

Contrastively, historical traffic analysis involves the examination of data collected over time, allowing organizations to identify patterns, evaluate the effectiveness of past interventions, and plan for future demands. This form of analysis is invaluable for long-term strategic planning, providing insights into user behavior, peak traffic periods, and recurring security threats.

Historical data analysis requires robust data storage and processing capabilities to handle large datasets. Cloudflare supports this through a comprehensive logging service that captures detailed request data. This data can be exported to third-party storage solutions like Google Cloud Storage or Amazon S3 for further analysis.

Consider the following example, which uses Python's pandas library to analyze historical traffic data exported from Cloudflare:

```
import pandas as pd

# Load historical traffic data from a CSV file
data = pd.read_csv('cloudflare_traffic_data.csv')

# Convert timestamps to datetime objects
data['timestamp'] = pd.to_datetime(data['timestamp'])

# Set the timestamp column as the index
data.set_index('timestamp', inplace=True)

# Calculate daily traffic statistics
daily_stats = data.resample('D').agg({
    'requests': 'sum',
    'unique_visitors': 'mean',
    'bandwidth': 'sum'
})

print(daily_stats)
```

This code snippet reads a CSV file containing exported traffic data, processes it to provide daily summaries, and displays key metrics, such as the total requests and bandwidth usage over time.

One of the most critical components of historical analysis is trend identification. Recognizing trends can highlight growth opportunities and
predict future resource requirements. For example, observing an up-
ward trend in mobile access can prompt a reallocation of development
budget towards mobile interface improvements.

Additionally, historical data can be instrumental in refining security
posture. By reviewing logs of past security incidents, organizations can
identify recurring vulnerabilities or attack vectors and take proactive
steps to mitigate these issues.

Predictive analytics, a subset of historical traffic analysis, uses historical data to make predictions about future events. Machine learning
algorithms can analyze past data to forecast traffic spikes, detect potential security threats before they occur, or anticipate system overloads.
This enables proactive management strategies that improve reliability
and user satisfaction.

Combining real-time and historical analysis provides a comprehensive
view of network conditions. While real-time analysis addresses immediate needs and threats, historical analysis informs long-term strategies and resource planning. Together, they create a robust framework
that supports efficient decision-making across multiple operational
facets.

To further illustrate the integration of real-time and historical data,
consider the following Python script employing machine learning for
traffic prediction. This example uses a simple linear regression approach:

```
from sklearn.linear_model import LinearRegression
import numpy as np

# Example historical data
historical_data = np.array([[1, 100], [2, 150], [3, 200], [4, 250]])

# Separate features and labels
X = historical_data[:, 0].reshape(-1, 1) # Time units, e.g., days
y = historical_data[:, 1] # Number of requests

# Train the linear regression model
model = LinearRegression().fit(X, y)

# Predict future traffic
future_time = np.array([[5]])
```

```
predicted_traffic = model.predict(future_time)
print(f'Predicted traffic for day 5: {predicted_traffic[0]}')
```

Here, a linear regression model predicts traffic levels based on simple historical data. While simplistic, this represents the fundamental process behind more sophisticated machine learning applications used in traffic analysis.

The adoption and implementation of real-time and historical traffic analysis require meticulous planning and execution. Organizations should ensure that their analysis tools are properly configured and integrated with existing infrastructure. Investment in skilled personnel and advanced technologies, such as AI-driven analytics, significantly enhances the capacity to extract actionable insights from traffic data.

The union of real-time and historical traffic analysis through platforms like Cloudflare provides indispensable capabilities for managing network operations, optimizing performance, and strengthening defenses against threats. By systematically applying these analytical techniques, organizations can achieve heightened situational awareness, allowing them to anticipate and adapt to both immediate and evolving challenges in the digital landscape.

8.4   Identifying and Responding to Traffic Anomalies

Effectively identifying and responding to traffic anomalies is a critical aspect of maintaining robust cybersecurity and optimal network performance. Traffic anomalies can encompass a wide spectrum of unexpected or unusual events, including sudden surges in traffic, signs of potential attacks, or deviations from typical user behavior. This section explores the techniques and approaches for detecting these anomalies using Cloudflare, and the strategic responses necessary to mitigate risks and improve site reliability.

Traffic anomalies are often early indicators of security threats such as Distributed Denial-of-Service (DDoS) attacks, unauthorized access attempts, or malware spread. Identifying these patterns promptly allows organizations to execute defensive strategies that protect data integrity and maintain service availability. This begins with the implementation of monitoring solutions capable of distinguishing normal traffic from potential malicious activities.

The foundation of anomaly detection lies in understanding what constitutes normal operation for any given system. Statistical models and machine learning algorithms can establish baselines based on historical data. Anomalies are detected when current activity deviates significantly from these baselines.

Cloudflare provides advanced security features like the Web Application Firewall (WAF) that automatically detects and responds to abnormal traffic patterns. For instance, it can block or challenge requests that deviate from established rules. Additionally, Cloudflare's Bot Management identifies good versus bad bots, mitigating the risk of bot-driven attacks like credential stuffing or scraping.

To demonstrate a simplified approach to anomaly detection, consider the following Python program that uses statistical thresholds:

```python
import numpy as np

# Sample traffic data: number of requests per interval
traffic_data = [100, 102, 98, 105, 110, 115, 150, 300, 102, 108, 110]

# Calculate mean and standard deviation
mean_traffic = np.mean(traffic_data)
std_dev = np.std(traffic_data)

# Define anomaly threshold as mean + 2*std_dev
threshold = mean_traffic + 2 * std_dev

# Identify anomalies
anomalies = [x for x in traffic_data if x > threshold]
print(f'Traffic anomalies: {anomalies}')
```

This code calculates the mean and standard deviation of a sample dataset, identifying anomalies as values exceeding the defined threshold. While simplistic, it offers an intuitive approach to understanding how statistical anomalies are detected.

Responses to traffic anomalies depend on the nature and severity of the detected issue. In scenarios suggestive of a DDoS attack, rate limiting and IP filtering are effective countermeasures. Cloudflare's Rate Limiting rules can limit access from high-frequency IP addresses or client types, thus minimizing the impact of automated attacks without disrupting legitimate user access.

227

Cloudflare also boasts enhanced DDoS protection, leveraging automatic mitigation efforts powered by its global network. This includes identifying flood attacks through pattern recognition and implementing traffic diversion strategies that absorb or mitigate attack impacts in real-time.

Another critical realm of response involves adjusting WAF policies to block suspicious request patterns. Refining WAF rules involves analyzing attack signatures and adjusting filters to block potentially harmful traffic. This can include blocking requests originating from untrusted locations or containing malicious payloads.

To better apprehend malicious payload indicators, the following Python code snippet illustrates simple payload analysis in HTTP requests. This tool can be used to detect SQL injection attempts by inspecting payloads for common attack patterns:

```
def is_sql_injection(payload):
    # Simplistic pattern matching for SQL injection
    patterns = ["'", "--", ";", "/*", "*/", " OR ", " AND "]
    return any(pattern in payload for pattern in patterns)

http_requests = [
    "SELECT * FROM users WHERE username = 'admin'",
    "http://example.com/page.php?id=1 OR 1=1",
    "http://example.com/page.php?id=5",
    "Union SELECT * FROM passwords"
]

for request in http_requests:
    if is_sql_injection(request):
        print(f'SQL Injection detected: {request}')
```

Detection of SQL injection attacks, as shown in the example, highlights the importance of analyzing request payloads to identify and respond to anomalies.

User behavior analytics is another dimension of anomaly detection. Significant deviations from normal user behavior, such as unusual login times or unexpected geographical access points, can signal credential theft or compromised accounts. Cloudflare provides tools to observe these behavioral metrics and implement risk-based authentication or enhanced scrutiny of flagged accounts.

By performing behavioral analysis, organizations can identify patterns that suggest compromise or policy violations. Machine learning models enhance this detection by evaluating complex behavioral datasets

228

and producing actionable intelligence.

In terms of proactive anomaly management, a comprehensive incident response plan is mandatory. This includes crafting a set of playbooks that detail actions to be taken for various anomaly scenarios, such as contact protocols, notification requirements, and recovery procedures. Regular testing and updating of these playbooks ensure readiness for emerging threats.

Moreover, a secure communication channel is vital during anomaly response to ensure the integrity and confidentiality of crisis management discussions. Secure channels prevent adversaries from intercepting or manipulating communication efforts during critical response operations.

Lastly, periodic review and adaptation of detection mechanisms and response strategies reflect the constantly evolving threat landscape. Organizations should maintain threat intelligence systems that update security configurations based on known risk trends, enabling faster recognition of new attack patterns.

Identifying and responding to traffic anomalies involves a multi-stage approach including effective detection mechanisms, rapid and strategic responses, and a thorough understanding of normal traffic patterns. Cloudflare equips organizations with resilient tools and capabilities to manage these processes efficiently, ensuring a secure and performant network environment. By integrating technology-driven solutions with strategic planning, organizations enhance their protection against anomalies that threaten operational integrity and security.

8.5 Customizing Traffic Reports

Customizing traffic reports is a critical task for network administrators and analysts who need to extract specific insights from web traffic data. Tailoring reports to focus on particular metrics, timeframes, or segments allows organizations to gain a precise understanding of their web performance and security posture. This section explores the methodologies enabled by Cloudflare's reporting tools to create customized traffic reports and the implications such customization has for strategic decision-making and operational optimization.

The cornerstone of customized traffic reporting lies in defining the purpose of the report. Reports can serve various objectives, such as performance optimization, security assessment, user behavior analysis, or compliance verification. Once the goal is clear, the next step involves determining which metrics or data points will convey relevant insights. Commonly monitored metrics include request count, bandwidth usage, latency, cache performance, and security threats.

Cloudflare's Analytics API is a robust tool that allows users to programmatically generate reports customized to their specific needs. By leveraging this API, organizations can create scripts that automate the retrieval and analysis of data. This capability is vital for enterprises requiring frequent and consistent reporting.

Here is an example of a Python script using the Cloudflare API to create a tailored report on request count and bandwidth usage for the past week:

```python
import requests
import datetime

# Configuration
api_endpoint = 'https://api.cloudflare.com/client/v4/zones/{zone_id}/analytics'
api_key = 'your_api_key'
zone_id = 'your_zone_id'

# Set headers for API request
headers = {
    'Authorization': f'Bearer {api_key}',
    'Content-Type': 'application/json',
}

# Define the timeframe for the past week
end_date = datetime.datetime.now()
start_date = end_date - datetime.timedelta(days=7)

# Make the request
params = {
    'since': start_date.strftime('%Y-%m-%dT%H:%M:%SZ'),
    'until': end_date.strftime('%Y-%m-%dT%H:%M:%SZ'),
    'metrics': 'requests,bandwidth',
}

response = requests.get(api_endpoint.format(zone_id=zone_id), headers=headers,
        params=params)
data = response.json()

# Print report
print(f"Traffic Report for {zone_id}")
for result in data['result']:
    print(f"Date: {result['date']}, Requests: {result['requests']}, Bandwidth: {result['
        bandwidth'] / (1024**2):.2f} MB")
```

The script above retrieves the request count and bandwidth data for a specified Cloudflare zone, offering a foundational approach for creating more complex reports.

Customizing timeframes is another valuable aspect of report creation. While some stakeholders might be interested in daily reports to spot trends more quickly, others may need monthly summaries to assess long-term changes. The flexibility of Cloudflare's tools allows for easy adjustments to reporting periods, providing relevant data aligned with organizational needs.

In addition to timeframes, filtering options enable the exclusion or inclusion of certain types of traffic. For example, removing bot traffic from analytics can offer a clearer picture of genuine user engagement, while geographic filters help assess performance or adoption in specific regions.

Integration with Business Intelligence (BI) tools enhances the visualization and interpretation of customized reports. By exporting Cloudflare analytics data to platforms like Tableau or Power BI, organizations can create dynamic dashboards that provide richer insights. Advanced visualization aids in detecting patterns or correlations that may not be immediately apparent in raw data outputs.

Moreover, segmented reports focusing on particular traffic streams, such as mobile users, specific geographic locations, or traffic referred from particular marketing campaigns, reveal targeted insights. These segments help in understanding how different parts of an audience interact with the site and provide data for allocation of resources or ad spend.

Advanced scripts can deploy machine learning models to automatically process and enhance report datasets. For instance, predicting user churn based on traffic patterns involves complex data transformation and analysis, which can be effectively managed through automation pipelines. Here is an example illustrating the classification of user behavior patterns within custom traffic reports:

```
from sklearn.cluster import KMeans
import numpy as np

# Sample dataset: features are [average session duration, page views per session]
user_data = np.array([
    [5.5, 4], [7.8, 2], [10.1, 9], [3.5, 10], [12.2, 8],
```

```
   [11.5, 5], [9.2, 7], [3.0, 4], [4.8, 6], [6.9, 3]
])

# K-Means clustering to classify patterns
kmeans = KMeans(n_clusters=3, random_state=0).fit(user_data)
print(f"Cluster labels: {kmeans.labels_}")

# Display centers of clusters
print(f"Cluster centers: {kmeans.cluster_centers_}")
```

The KMeans clustering algorithm categorizes sessions into distinct groups based on interaction features, such as session duration and page views, providing insights into potential user segments.

Another vital element of customized reports is compliance with legal or organizational requirements. Tailoring reports for governance requires activation of specific features in Cloudflare, such as enhanced logging, encryption, or adherence to compliance frameworks like GDPR. This ensures that data handling processes meet stringent security and privacy standards.

The final presentation of custom traffic reports requires consistent formatting and clear visual representation to communicate findings effectively. Well-crafted reports combine quantitative data with qualitative narratives that contextualize the figures and suggest actionable insights.

In addressing the ever-growing complexity of web traffic management, it is crucial that reports evolve in parallel with new analytical tools and data processing techniques. As Cloudflare continues to develop enhanced capabilities for traffic monitoring and analytics, continued education and adaptation of reporting methodologies ensure that organizations maintain competitive advantage through insightful data analysis.

Tailoring traffic reports is not merely about data extraction; it is an ongoing process of interpretation and adaptation to ever-changing web landscapes. By mastering the ability to create and utilize customized reports, organizations gain unparalleled visibility into their operations, enabling smarter, data-driven decisions that foster growth and resilience in digital environments.

8.6 Integrating Cloudflare Data with Third-Party Tools

Integrating Cloudflare data with third-party tools enhances the capabilities of network administrators and data analysts by allowing them to leverage insights beyond the Cloudflare platform. This integration facilitates comprehensive data analysis, improved visualization, and advanced alerting and reporting functionalities. By connecting Cloudflare data with external analytics platforms, organizations can significantly augment their ability to monitor, analyze, and optimize web traffic and security measures.

One primary reason for integrating Cloudflare data with other tools is to enable centralized data management and improve data accessibility. Analytics platforms, such as Google Analytics, Azure Data Studio, and Tableau, provide advanced capabilities for data aggregation and visualization, thus enriching the breadth and depth of insights derived from Cloudflare data.

The use of Cloudflare's robust API facilitates seamless integration with these platforms. By utilizing the API, data can be retrieved programmatically and transformed to fit the target platform's structure. Integrations often involve the extraction of metrics like request count, bandwidth usage, and security event logs, followed by their deployment into custom dashboards or detailed reports.

The following is an example Python script showcasing how to retrieve Cloudflare data and prepare it for ingestion into a third-party analytics platform:

```
import requests
import json

# Cloudflare API credentials
api_token = 'your_api_token'
zone_id = 'your_zone_id'
api_url = f'https://api.cloudflare.com/client/v4/zones/{zone_id}/analytics/dashboard'

# Headers for the API request
headers = {
    'Authorization': f'Bearer {api_token}',
    'Content-Type': 'application/json',
}
```

233

```
# Make a request to Cloudflare API to fetch analytics data
response = requests.get(api_url, headers=headers)
data = response.json()

# Convert data to a format for a third-party tool, e.g., JSON
formatted_data = json.dumps(data, indent=4)

# Save to a file or send to a third-party system
with open('cloudflare_data.json', 'w') as file:
    file.write(formatted_data)
```

This script retrieves response data from the Cloudflare API, formats it in JSON, and saves it locally, establishing an essential step for further integration with any data handling system.

Integration with visualization platforms like Tableau leverages their sophisticated charting tools to build dynamic dashboards that provide real-time insights. Users can employ drag-and-drop interfaces to filter and dissect metrics, generating actionable business intelligence that supports decision-making processes.

Another compelling integration scenario is with monitoring and alerting systems such as Splunk or Nagios. By connecting Cloudflare data to these platforms, organizations can automate the surveillance of network activities and establish real-time notifications for critical security events or performance thresholds. For instance, Splunk can ingest Cloudflare logs, producing indices that allow rapid query and alert configurations when anomalies are detected.

In accommodating demand for machine learning applications, Cloudflare data can also be fed into platforms such as AWS SageMaker or Microsoft Azure's Machine Learning Studio. This potentiality enables advanced analyses like predictive modeling, anomaly detection, and customer segmentation. Here's an illustrative example of using Python's Pandas library to preprocess Cloudflare data for ML applications:

```
import pandas as pd

# Load Cloudflare data into a DataFrame
data = pd.read_json('cloudflare_data.json')

# Data preprocessing example: simplify columns for ML analysis
data['date'] = pd.to_datetime(data['time_series'].apply(lambda x: x['since']))
data['requests'] = data['totals'].apply(lambda x: x['requests']['all'])
data['threats'] = data['totals'].apply(lambda x: x['threats']['all'])

# Simplified DataFrame for Machine Learning
ml_ready_data = data[['date', 'requests', 'threats']]
```

```
print(ml_ready_data.head())
```

In this script, the Cloudflare data is processed to refine it into a machine learning-ready format. Data frames like these serve as base datasets to train models on historical trends or classify patterns.

In addition to analytics and alerting, integrating Cloudflare data supports improved automation in network management workflows. By enabling cross-platform data exchanges, repetitive administrative tasks can be streamlined, reducing manual intervention and enhancing operational efficiency. Automation platforms like Zapier or Apache NiFi facilitate creating workflows that trigger actions based on Cloudflare data interactions.

Data security and compliance considerations also play a vital role in integration strategies. As the transfer of data between Cloudflare and third-party tools occurs, ensuring encryption and security protocols are in place is necessary. Cloudflare offers its IPsec VPN tunneling methods and access policies to restrain data exposure during such integrations.

Integrating Cloudflare data often requires customized pipelines that transform and enrich data to satisfy specific business requirements. Such pipelines, built using ETL (Extract, Transform, Load) tools like Apache Airflow, empower organizations to continuously adapt to evolving analytical demands without macro interruptions.

Integrating Cloudflare data with third-party systems unlocks powerful cross-functional insights that enhance scalability, security, and sustainability of web solutions. Careful planning and execution ensure integrations align with organizational goals, ultimately driving innovation and delivering superior user experiences. Through these integrated environments, businesses harness the full potential of Cloudflare's data capabilities, forming an integral part of their data-driven strategies in today's digital landscape.

8.7 Best Practices for Traffic Management

Effective traffic management is a cornerstone of any successful web operation, influencing both security and performance outcomes. The strategic routing, monitoring, and control of web traffic can dramatically enhance user experience while safeguarding infrastructure from potential threats. This section delves into the best practices for traffic management through Cloudflare, offering detailed insights into optimizing routing, ensuring scalability, and employing security measures to maintain robust network operations.

One of the primary considerations in traffic management is load balancing, which involves distributing incoming network traffic across multiple servers to ensure no single server is overwhelmed. Cloudflare offers a robust load balancing feature that can accommodate non-invasive, seamless traffic distribution based on pre-defined rules. By implementing load balancing, organizations can maintain high availability and reliability, especially during traffic surges.

A typical load balancing setup involves configuring health checks to monitor server performance continuously. This ensures traffic is rerouted in the event of server failure or degradation:

```python
import requests

def health_check(server):
    try:
        response = requests.get(f'http://{server}/health')
        if response.status_code == 200:
            return True
        else:
            return False
    except requests.ConnectionError:
        return False

servers = ['server1.example.com', 'server2.example.com', 'server3.example.com']
healthy_servers = [server for server in servers if health_check(server)]

print(f'Healthy servers: {healthy_servers}')
```

This script handles health checks for a list of servers, determining which are responsive and healthy, and thus eligible to receive traffic.

Another crucial practice involves setting up appropriate DNS configu-

236

rations, particularly using Cloudflare's managed DNS service. Proper DNS setup enhances resolution speed and supports failover capabilities, ensuring that traffic is directed towards the optimal endpoint. Implementations of DNS Layer 3 Anycast routing improve performance by dynamically routing users to the closest available server, reducing latency.

Traffic prioritization is another vital aspect of effective management. By using Quality of Service (QoS) rules, administrators can allocate bandwidth to critical applications or users, preventing less essential traffic from consuming excessive resources. Through Cloudflare's intuitive interfaces, these rules can be applied easily, offering dynamic control over how traffic is processed.

Caching strategies also play a vital role in managing traffic efficiently. Effective caching reduces server demand and speeds up content delivery by serving requests from the intermediary cache rather than the origin server. Cloudflare's CDN capabilities offer robust caching options, including static content caching and custom cache keys to optimize cache use.

Security-centric traffic management strategies include DDoS protection and firewall configurations. Given the rise of sophisticated cyber threats, deploying a strong Web Application Firewall (WAF) that identifies and blocks malicious traffic helps protect user data and maintain service availability. Carefully crafted firewall rules ensure that only legitimate traffic reaches critical infrastructure:

```
# Example: Setting up Cloudflare firewall rules using the command line
gcloud compute firewall-rules create allow-ssh \
    --allow tcp:22 \
    --network your-network-name \
    --source-ranges 198.51.100.0/24 \
    --description "Allow SSH traffic from trusted IPs"

gcloud compute firewall-rules create deny-invalid-traffic \
    --action DENY \
    --rules tcp,udp,icmp:all \
    --destination-ranges 0.0.0.0/0 \
    --priority 1000 \
    --description "Deny all invalid traffic"
```

This shell command creates a firewall rule to allow SSH access from a trusted IP range while denying all other traffic, exemplifying a fundamental security configuration.

Adapting for scalability is an intrinsic part of traffic management. Organizations should anticipate traffic growth and scale infrastructure accordingly, leveraging Cloudflare's flexible and automated scaling solutions to adapt to demand without manual intervention. Auto-scaling strategies minimize latency increases during demand peaks and maintain consistent performance levels.

Communication through strategically implemented alerts and monitoring systems helps administrators respond swiftly to traffic anomalies or performance dips. Cloudflare's integration with platforms like PagerDuty can automate alerting as part of an Incident Response strategy, ensuring problems are resolved quickly before they escalate.

Considering geographical distribution when routing traffic can also have significant performance benefits. As Cloudflare's global network consists of multiple data centers spanning different geolocations, setting up geo-redundancy and directing users to the nearest data center mitigates latency, elevating user experience globally.

Finally, adopting an integrative orchestration approach aligns traffic management practices with broader organizational objectives. Implementing orchestration tools, like Kubernetes for containerized applications, provides standardized management protocols that automatically ensure balanced traffic distribution according to system metrics.

Effective traffic management with Cloudflare results in improved performance, reliable security, and scalable web operations. Applying these best practices ensures that networks support business continuity, delivering seamless user experiences and upholding the integrity of online entities. By balancing technological innovations with strategic planning, organizations can excel in handling diverse and dynamic web traffic scenarios.

Chapter 9

Integrating Cloudflare with Web Applications

This chapter addresses the processes involved in seamlessly integrating Cloudflare's services with web applications to enhance security, performance, and scalability. It outlines the steps for configuring DNS settings, implementing SSL/TLS for encrypted connections, and utilizing Cloudflare's API for automation. The chapter also discusses optimization techniques using Cloudflare features and provides strategies for addressing integration challenges. By leveraging these integration strategies, developers can maximize the operational efficiency and resilience of their web applications.

9.1 Preparing Your Application for Cloudflare Integration

Preparing your application for integration with Cloudflare demands a strategic approach that encompasses a thorough evaluation of your current infrastructure, understanding the specific requirements of your application, and establishing a robust integration plan. Cloudflare acts as a powerful conduit through which your application's performance, security, and scalability can be significantly enhanced. As such, this preparation phase is critical for ensuring that the transition to Cloudflare's services is both seamless and effective.

Initially, it is essential to conduct an exhaustive assessment of your existing web application architecture. This involves understanding the present deployment environment, the underlying web server configurations, and the network characteristics that will interact with Cloudflare's network. Begin by cataloging all web service endpoints, identifying resource consumption patterns, traffic distribution, and security policies already in place. Such an audit helps in recognizing which aspects of the application could benefit most from Cloudflare's features, such as caching and security enhancements.

Moreover, comprehend the degree of dependency between various components of your application. Integration with Cloudflare may alter the request and response flow, thus affecting interconnected components if not appropriately managed. Scrutinize how these components communicate within your network stack and document any intrinsic assumptions your application makes regarding direct client-server interaction. Given that Cloudflare operates as a reverse proxy, this understanding will mitigate potential disruptions during transition.

It is beneficial to involve Cloudflare-compatible tools for testing and evaluation purposes. Use network diagnostic utilities to analyze how requests are processed and how network latency affects user experience. You might utilize tools such as traceroute or ping to map the route taken by packets between client and server under current configurations.

```
traceroute example.com
ping example.com
```

The output helps identify existing network bottlenecks, which Cloudflare's global distributed network could alleviate through efficient traffic routing.

A key step is configuring development and staging environments to mirror the planned production setup involving Cloudflare. This includes replicating DNS configurations and SSL requirements where possible. This pre-deployment strategy aids in identifying potential inconsistencies early in the process and provides a controlled environment to test Cloudflare's features before full-scale deployment.

Emphasizing security, developers should review current data protection and encryption mechanisms. Cloudflare provides several layers of security enhancements, including DDoS protection and Web Application Firewall (WAF) services. Identify any gaps where your application might be vulnerable to outside threats and how Cloudflare's features could fortify these areas. Revise security policies as needed to accommodate new features and ensure compliance with organizational legal and security guidelines.

In this preparatory phase, decision makers must also consider data privacy policies and regulatory compliance requirements such as GDPR or HIPAA, particularly when leveraging Cloudflare's data services. Cloudflare's network often routes traffic through multiple jurisdictions, causing potential conflicts with regional data protection laws if not adequately managed.

Furthermore, explore the potential impact of Cloudflare's caching features on dynamic content delivery. Cloudflare's content delivery mechanism offers significant performance improvements but may necessitate changes in cache-control headers to prevent unintended caching of dynamic content. Understand how to configure cache rules and employ fine-grained cache control to meet your application's needs.

Assess existing application logging and monitoring frameworks; integrating Cloudflare might necessitate changes to log collection methods, especially when Cloudflare directly handles incoming traffic redirects. Alter your monitoring scripts and alerts to ensure they accommodate the additional layer introduced by Cloudflare.

Prepare detailed plans for DNS changes, as these are integral to Cloudflare integration. Cloudflare provides a DNS service that becomes the primary interface managing internet traffic of your application. Document existing DNS records and configurations, using tools like dig to retrieve DNS information systematically.

```
dig example.com +short
dig example.com ANY
```

Effective preparation also involves deeper analysis of performance expectations and SLAs defined internally or with clients. Properly quantify baseline performance metrics to measure improvements post-Cloudflare integration accurately. These include response times, throughput levels, and resource utilization patterns.

Communicating with stakeholders, including technical, customer service and management teams, is paramount during this phase. Facilitate understanding of both the technical integration details and the improvements expected in terms of user experience and operational benefits. Workshops or documentation reinforce knowledge transfer within the organization and assure stakeholders that risks are accounted for and performance objectives align with broader business goals.

This in-depth preparation, involving cross-functional examination and robust planning, will lay a strong foundation for subsequent configuration processes, ensuring that your application harnesses the full capacity of what Cloudflare offers. Through meticulous assessment and planning, the transition to using Cloudflare becomes an opportunity to enhance every facet of your application's infrastructure.

9.2 DNS Configuration for Application Integration

Configuring DNS (Domain Name System) settings is a pivotal step in integrating your application with Cloudflare. This process ensures that traffic destined for your application is routed through Cloudflare's network, enabling you to leverage its various features for enhanced performance and security. Proper DNS configuration aligns the user-facing domain with Cloudflare's reverse proxy, making it essential to execute these adjustments with precision and care.

Initially, familiarize yourself with your existing DNS provider's settings and understand the roles of various DNS records. DNS records are critical for directing traffic, providing key information about your domain's structure and pointing clients to the correct resources. Key DNS record types include A records, CNAME records, MX records, and TXT records. Each type serves distinct purposes, from associating domain names with IP addresses to specifying mail servers and verifying domain ownership.

242

In preparation for DNS configuration, create a comprehensive inventory of current DNS records. This involves noting down existing A and CNAME records, ensuring you comprehend how they direct traffic under current conditions. The dig command can be instrumental for retrieving and cataloging this information.

```
dig example.com A +short
dig example.com CNAME +short
dig example.com MX +short
```

Once you have documented the existing DNS setup, initiate the integration process by adopting Cloudflare's nameservers. Cloudflare acts as an authoritative DNS provider, meaning you will need to replace your current provider's nameservers with those provided by Cloudflare. This change will direct all DNS queries for your domain to Cloudflare.

Log in to your domain registrar's portal and locate the DNS settings or name server management section. Replace the existing nameserver entries with Cloudflare's nameservers, which are specified within your Cloudflare account dashboard upon domain addition. This alteration typically takes about 24-48 hours to propagate across the internet.

With Cloudflare functioning as your DNS provider, migrate the DNS records you documented earlier into Cloudflare's platform. Their streamlined interface facilitates the manual addition, deletion, and management of DNS records.

```
<div class="dns-add-record">
    <h3>Add DNS Record</h3>
    <!-- Record Type Selection -->
    <select id="record-type">
        <option value="A">A</option>
        <option value="CNAME">CNAME</option>
        <option value="MX">MX</option>
        <!-- More records as necessary -->
    </select>
    <!-- Value Entry -->
    <input type="text" id="record-value" placeholder="Enter value here">
</div>
```

The transition to Cloudflare's DNS platform introduces potential configuration changes due to their expansive feature set. Cloudflare's network uses a combination of Anonymizer, Load Balancer, and Rate Limiting features, which determine DNS resolution and service functionality.

Activate Cloudflare's Proxy Status (indicated by an orange cloud icon) on records that you wish to route through Cloudflare's layer. This ensures that traffic is passed through Cloudflare servers, which has implications for caching, security, and content delivery performance. Conversely, disable the Proxy Status (indicated by a gray cloud icon) for records that should bypass Cloudflare, such as internal APIs or services incompatible with proxying.

Be mindful of the TTL (Time to Live) configurations during this setup phase. TTL values determine the duration DNS records are cached before fresh resolution occurs. Adjust TTL settings with consideration to how frequently records change within your infrastructure to optimize DNS propagation without introducing unnecessary delays.

To enhance security, implement DNSSEC (DNS Security Extensions) via Cloudflare. DNSSEC adds a layer of verification between your DNS records and resolvers, preventing certain types of attacks such as cache poisoning. Activate DNSSEC within Cloudflare and provide the generated DS (Delegation Signer) record to your registrar to ensure thorough security for your DNS authentication chain.

Understanding and configuring aliases with CNAME records involves special considerations under Cloudflare's architecture. Certain validations, SSL certificate resolutions, and redirects are inherently managed by Cloudflare's intelligent network handling CNAME flattening. This process allows root domains to leverage CNAME features without typical restrictions posed by standard DNS setups.

Consider scenarios where Cloudflare's Layer 3 and 4 DDoS protection might impact record accessibility. Adjust configurations to account for the robust defenses that Cloudflare provides, particularly if your application is prone to volumetric attacks targeting specific endpoints. Incorporate fallback or redundancy measures in your DNS records, mitigating the impact of any unexpected disruptions.

Regularly validate all DNS configurations post-integration. Utilize verification methods such as checking DNS propagation status through online DNS checker tools to confirm successful integration and proper record resolution.

```
Domain: example.com
  Type: A
  Value: Node location
```

```
TTL: Auto
Status: Proxy enabled (orange cloud)
DNSSEC: Active
```

Effective DNS management is integral not only for traffic routing but also for optimizing availability and performance across Cloudflare's CDN and other feature sets. Reassess DNS configurations periodically, especially when introducing new services or altering existing ones within your application, to maintain a smooth and secure network topology.

This thorough DNS configuration process aligns your application traffic with Cloudflare's network, unleashing the potential for a secure, performant, and reliable broadcasting of your application across global networks. The meticulous consideration of DNS settings is foundational to ensuring robust and resilient integration outcomes with Cloudflare's extensive capabilities.

9.3 Setting Up SSL/TLS for Secure Connections

Establishing secure connections between web applications and their users is a critical component of modern web infrastructure. Configuring SSL/TLS (Secure Sockets Layer/Transport Layer Security) with Cloudflare ensures encrypted communications, providing both confidentiality and integrity for data in transit. SSL/TLS protects against various attacks, enhancing the trust users place in interacting with your application.

The initial step in configuring SSL/TLS involves understanding the current security landscape of your application, identifying the existing SSL/TLS certificates in use, and determining compatibility with Cloudflare's certificates and security policies. Begin by auditing current certificate details, including the issuer, expiration dates, and cryptographic strength.

To inspect certificates, use utilities such as openssl to verify certificate chains and validation periods, ensuring there are no imminent expiration concerns.

```
openssl s_client -connect example.com:443 -showcerts
```

Upon initiating the Cloudflare SSL/TLS setup, decide which mode of SSL/TLS operation best aligns with your application's security needs. Cloudflare offers several SSL/TLS encryption modes: Off, Flexible, Full, and Full (Strict). Each provides varying degrees of encryption assurance, ultimately guiding how data is encrypted from the client browser to the server.

- Off: Disables SSL/TLS, allowing connections in the plaintext HTTP protocol. Use this solely for applications where encryption isn't feasible.

- Flexible: Encrypts traffic between the browser and Cloudflare. This mode requires no SSL certificate at the origin but is suboptimal for full encryption as it doesn't secure the connection end-to-end.

- Full: Provides encryption from the browser to Cloudflare and Cloudflare to the server. This mode needs a valid SSL certificate at the origin, though self-signed certificates are sufficient.

- Full (Strict): Similar to Full, but requires valid CA-signed certificates at the origin, offering the highest security assuredness through SSL/TLS.

After selecting the appropriate SSL/TLS mode, configure certificate management within Cloudflare. This involves generating or uploading certificates, utilizing their universal SSL certificates or opting for advanced configurations with dedicated or custom certificates.

Generate SSL certificates using Cloudflare's user-friendly interface, or manage them via the API for bulk or automated deployments. Access the SSL/TLS settings in the Cloudflare dashboard under the "SSL/TLS" section to manage these credentials.

To issue a certificate, execute the Certificate Signing Request (CSR) generation and submission process. This includes defining certificate specifics, choosing completed CA, and designating Subject Alternative Names (SANs) crucial for multi-domain or subdomain applications.

246

```
openssl req -new -newkey rsa:2048 -nodes -keyout example.key -out example.csr
```

Following certificate acquisition, navigate Cloudflare's platform to either deploy new SSL certificates or confirm automatic provisioning of Universal SSL. This method offers immediate steps toward encrypting visits to your site via HTTPS.

For custom or enterprise-grade SSL needs, Cloudflare provides mechanisms to upload pre-existing certificates for individualized management. This route supports organizations with specific compliance guidelines or client trust mandates that dictate particular certificate vendor use.

Implement SSL settings such as Minimum TLS Version to align with best-practice standards and modern security directives. Decide on TLS 1.2 or higher for compliance and to enhance security against vulnerabilities in earlier protocol versions. Adjusting these settings is typically performed in the Cloudflare dashboard or via their API.

Cloudflare's SSL/TLS features extend to support advanced functions like HTTP/2 and the newer HTTP/3 protocols. These technologies augment web resource efficiency through multiplexing and decreased connection latency. They help improve load times and interactive experiences, all while under tighter security of encrypted communication channels.

Incorporate automated redirect rules to enforce HTTPS, guaranteeing safety by shifting user requests transparently from potentially insecure HTTP to HTTPS. This can be achieved by establishing page rules within the Cloudflare settings dashboard.

Engage with content security best practices, adopting HTTP Strict Transport Security (HSTS). Enabling HSTS ensures that browsers only connect over HTTPS for specified periods, defending against downgrade attacks and cookie hijacking. Set this up within Cloudflare's dashboard under the 'Edge Certificates' section, specifying max-age and other directives.

Maintenance of certificate validity and endpoint security forms another segment of securing SSL/TLS. Monitor and automate certificate renewals to avoid connections dropping due to unverified credentials. Consider agile DevOps practices, leveraging Cloudflare's APIs to script renewal processes as part of continuous deployment pipelines.

Periodically, execute in-depth tests using third-party tools like Qualys SSL Labs to assess SSL/TLS implementation thoroughness, including protocol support, key exchange strength, and cipher suite appropriateness.

Furthermore, delve deeper into configuring Origin CA certificates issued by Cloudflare, which serve as an intermediary in securing traffic from Cloudflare to your origin server in scenarios demanding stringent end-to-end encryption but where CA-signed certificates are impractical or costly.

```python
import requests

def get_ssl_status(zone_id, api_token):
    url = f"https://api.cloudflare.com/client/v4/zones/{zone_id}/settings/ssl"
    headers = {
        "Content-Type": "application/json",
        "Authorization": f"Bearer {api_token}",
    }
    response = requests.get(url, headers=headers)

    if response.status_code == 200:
        return response.json()
    else:
        raise Exception("Failed to get SSL status")

ssl_info = get_ssl_status("your_zone_id", "your_api_token")
print(ssl_info)
```

The comprehensive setup and management of SSL/TLS ensure your application interactions with users remain confidential and authentic, enabling a secure baseline for all subsequent Cloudflare driven optimization and performance enhancements. Proper SSL/TLS configuration reflects a commitment to protecting user data, supporting increased application credibility and trustworthiness across the internet landscape.

9.4 Utilizing Cloudflare's API for Automation

Leveraging Cloudflare's API is an effective strategy for automating the management of web application infrastructure, encompassing a wide

248

range of functionalities such as DNS management, security settings, and content caching. The Cloudflare API is RESTful, providing a robust platform that enables developers to programmatically control configuration details that can enhance efficiency, minimize manual intervention, and streamline workflows across web services.

To begin utilizing Cloudflare's API, it is crucial to understand the structure and requirements of API requests. Each API request requires authentication, which is commonly achieved using either an API token or an API key associated with your Cloudflare account. This authentication ensures secure communication and operation adjustments only from authorized entities.

Cloudflare offers extensive API documentation that provides detailed endpoints and response patterns. A typical API request structure to Cloudflare's RESTful service includes the base URL (https://api.cloudflare.com/client/v4), followed by specific paths to access different resources, and utilizes standard HTTP methods such as GET, POST, PUT, and DELETE for operations.

Authentication Configuration: Securely configures API access tokens in your development environments. Use API tokens with the least privilege necessary for designated tasks, with scopes tailored to precisely the targeted resources and actions.

```
# Define a new API token with permissions
cf_api_token="your_api_token_here"
export CF_API_TOKEN=$cf_api_token
```

DNS Management Automation: One of the prominent features allows developers to dynamically manage DNS records, automate changes, and ensure record integrity without manual input. Applications requiring dynamic DNS updates for distributed systems or rapid IP address changes benefit significantly from API automation.

Example: Automating DNS record creation using Python requests library.

```
import requests
import json

def create_dns_record(zone_id, api_token, record_type, record_name,
        record_content):
    url = f"https://api.cloudflare.com/client/v4/zones/{zone_id}/dns_records"
    headers = {
        "Content-Type": "application/json",
```

```
    "Authorization": f"Bearer {api_token}",
}
data = {
    "type": record_type,
    "name": record_name,
    "content": record_content,
    "ttl": 120,
}
response = requests.post(url, headers=headers, data=json.dumps(data))
return response.json()

zone_id = "your_zone_id"
api_token = "your_api_token"
record_type = "A"
record_name = "subdomain.example.com"
record_content = "192.0.2.1"

response = create_dns_record(zone_id, api_token, record_type, record_name,
        record_content)
print(response)
```

Cache Management and Optimization: Cloudflare's caching rules can be automated through the API, providing dynamic cache purging and customized caching logic to match application-specific requirements. These capabilities are vital for resource-intensive web applications seeking to optimize latency and server load.

To invalidate or purge cache for updated content, you can call the respective API allowing immediate propagation of latest changes:

```
def purge_cache(zone_id, api_token):
    url = f"https://api.cloudflare.com/client/v4/zones/{zone_id}/purge_cache"
    headers = {
        "Content-Type": "application/json",
        "Authorization": f"Bearer {api_token}",
    }
    data = {"purge_everything": True}
    response = requests.post(url, headers=headers, data=json.dumps(data))
    return response.json()

purge_response = purge_cache(zone_id, api_token)
print(purge_response)
```

Security Endpoint Integration: APIs enable on-the-fly adjustments to security settings like firewall rules, DDoS protection configurations, and access control policies. For applications needing responsive security setups adaptable to detected threats, API utilization facilitates swift deployment of countermeasures.

Example: Automating the creation of a firewall rule to block specific IP ranges:

```
def create_firewall_rule(zone_id, api_token, ip_range):
    url = f"https://api.cloudflare.com/client/v4/zones/{zone_id}/firewall/rules"
    headers = {
        "Content-Type": "application/json",
        "Authorization": f"Bearer {api_token}",
    }
    data = [{
        "expression": f"(ip.src in {{ {ip_range} }})",
        "action": "block",
        "description": "Block IP range",
    }]
    response = requests.post(url, headers=headers, data=json.dumps(data))
    return response.json()

firewall_response = create_firewall_rule("your_zone_id", "your_api_token",
    "192.0.2.0/24")
print(firewall_response)
```

Analytics and Monitoring: Cloudflare's API facilitates programmatic access to a wealth of performance and security analytics. Automating analytics retrieval enables detailed monitoring across application platforms, providing insights into traffic patterns, threat landscapes, and subsequent data-driven decision-making processes.

Periodically executing requests for analytics data supports creating dashboards that convey the health of infrastructure components or to inform security teams in real-time.

Automation Integration Strategies: Employ the principle of least privilege in access control, segment API usage among teams based on responsibilities, and implement monitoring to audit API invocation patterns for compliance and security posture.

Further integrate Cloudflare's API into CI/CD pipelines, enhancing infrastructure automation by adjusting DNS records, security mechanisms, and caching policies automatically in response to application lifecycle events such as deployments or updates.

Code Reusability and Maintenance: Organize code into modular scripts, developed with reusability and adaptability in mind, equipping teams to extend automation scripts easily for future needs. Leverage shared libraries and configuration templates to standardize the automation tools used across development environments.

Cloudflare's API for automation serves as a gateway to a dynamically adjustable infrastructure, empowering development organizations to achieve high efficiency, bulletproof security postures, and elastic scalability. The API enhances the ability to orchestrate complex operations with precision, fostering an environment where strategic deployments intersect seamlessly with user demands and business objectives.

9.5 Optimizing Application Performance with Cloudflare Features

Cloudflare offers a broad suite of features tailored to optimizing the performance of web applications, leveraging its global content delivery network (CDN), specialized routing protocols, and advanced caching mechanisms. Effective use of these features is integral to reducing latency, enhancing load times, and ensuring a seamless user experience across diverse geographical regions.

The cornerstone of performance optimization with Cloudflare is its Content Delivery Network (CDN). By distributing content across geographically dispersed servers, Cloudflare minimizes the distance between users and the server, significantly reducing latency. Integrating your application with Cloudflare's CDN involves selecting assets to be distributed (such as images, videos, and large JavaScript files) and configuring cache and purge settings.

Cloudflare's CDN supports highly dynamic and static content caching, requiring precise cache-control header configuration to define how resources are stored and invalidated.

Example: Setting cache-control headers using server-side configurations.

For Apache:

```
<FilesMatch "\.(html|css|js|jpeg|png)$">
    Header set Cache-Control "max-age=2592000, public"
</FilesMatch>
```

For Nginx:

```
location ~* \.(html|css|js|jpeg|png)$ {
    expires 30d;
    add_header Cache-Control "public, max-age=2592000";
}
```

Setting these headers effectively delegates caching responsibility to the CDN, freeing up origin server resources.

Another prominent feature is Cloudflare's Argo Smart Routing, which intelligently routes traffic across the fastest and most reliable network paths. Argo dynamically optimizes routes with real-time latency and congestion information to lower server response times.

Argo benefits applications with substantial global traffic, enabling more precise and efficient routing decisions that reduce time-to-first-byte (TTFB), a critical metric in user experience analysis.

Cloudflare also offers Load Balancing to distribute traffic evenly across multiple server instances or geographical locations, contributing to improved uptime, fault tolerance, and reduced stress on any single server.

Configure dynamic load balancers via Cloudflare's dashboard or API, specifying traffic steering policies, health check parameters, and failover triggers. This prevents uneven loads and mitigates the risk from single point failures.

Example: Implementing a load balancer through Cloudflare's API.

```python
import requests
import json

def create_load_balancer(account_id, api_token):
    url = f"https://api.cloudflare.com/client/v4/accounts/{account_id}/
        load_balancers"
    headers = {
        "Content-Type": "application/json",
        "Authorization": f"Bearer {api_token}",
    }
    data = {
        "name": "example-load-balancer.com",
        "origins": [
            {
                "name": "Primary Server",
                "address": "192.0.2.1",
                "enabled": True,
                "weight": 1
            },
            {
                "name": "Secondary Server",
                "address": "192.0.2.2",
                "enabled": True,
                "weight": 1
            }
        ],
        "default_pools": ["pool-id-12345"],
        "check_regions": ["WNAM", "ENAM", "EU"],
        "fallback_pool": "pool-id-67890"
```

```
    }
    response = requests.post(url, headers=headers, data=json.dumps(data))
    return response.json()

load_balancer_response = create_load_balancer("your_account_id", "
    your_api_token")
print(load_balancer_response)
```

Image Optimization: Cloudflare's 'Polish' tool automatically compresses and optimizes images to speed up application rendering on clients. Employ options like lossless or lossy compression and the WebP format conversion to enhance image delivery efficiency.

HTTP/2 and HTTP/3 Protocol Support: Cloudflare supports modern web protocols, HTTP/2 and HTTP/3, offering performance improvements over HTTP/1.1 through multiplexing, header compression, and advanced stream prioritization. HTTP/3, with a foundation atop UDP, further reduces transport overheads and improves performance on unreliable networks.

Activating these features is a step toward reducing latency and optimizing bandwidth use for high-performance web applications.

Content Delivery Adjustments: Employ Cloudflare's Page Rules to tailor domain-specific performance settings. They enable granular execution of rules for caching, security, redirection, and performance. Customize settings to push maximum performance out of content delivery configurations according to underlying business logic or geolocation data.

Network Prioritization: For applications with critical service levels, explore 'Tiered Caching,' a Cloudflare offering that consolidates regional PoP traffic. This measure reduces origin bandwidth by maximizing cache hit ratios across Cloudflare's data center tiers.

Advanced Analytics: Detailed analytics and monitoring within Cloudflare's portals yield insights into traffic flows, cache usage, bandwidth consumption, and potential threats. These metrics support identifying bottlenecks, understanding user engagement patterns, and fine-tuning configurations for optimal performance.

Example: Extracting analytics data via Cloudflare's API for performance monitoring.

```
def fetch_analytics_data(zone_id, api_token):
```

```
url = f"https://api.cloudflare.com/client/v4/zones/{zone_id}/analytics"
headers = {
    "Content-Type": "application/json",
    "Authorization": f"Bearer {api_token}",
}
response = requests.get(url, headers=headers)
return response.json()

analytics_data = fetch_analytics_data("your_zone_id", "your_api_token")
print(analytics_data)
```

Service Worker Integration: For applications demanding personalized, low-latency user experiences, Cloudflare offers service workers to execute JavaScript logic within the Edge network. This fosters a serverless environment enabling logic execution close to users, streamlining real-time adaptations in content or service features without origin server interactions.

Code Scripting for Optimizations: JavaScript augmentation through Cloudflare Workers can reduce load times by transforming HTTP requests or intelligently separating critical resource requests, parsing adaptive delivery based on device profiles or network conditions.

These advanced features, when meticulously strategized and deployed, render Cloudflare an indispensable cog in high-performance web architecture. Tailored configuration and automation of these performance optimizations not only streamline operations but also render a significant competitive edge, opening avenues for innovation, scaling, and sustained service excellence.

9.6 Security Enhancements for Web Apps

Integrating robust security measures is paramount for safeguarding web applications against a wide spectrum of cyber threats. Cloudflare provides an integrative security framework to bolster web applications, significantly mitigating risks through its extensive range of security features. With threats continually evolving, Cloudflare's dynamic and adaptive security solutions are designed to shield web applications from modern threats such as DDoS attacks, malicious bots, and sophisticated web exploits.

A foundational security feature is Cloudflare's **Web Application Firewall (WAF)**, which acts as a barrier to filter and monitor HTTP traffic between web applications and the Internet. The WAF inspects incoming requests, allowing only those that meet specified rules, thereby blocking common attack patterns such as SQL injection, cross-site scripting (XSS), and cross-site request forgery (CSRF).

Cloudflare's WAF allows customization of rules to meet specific security needs. This is achieved by defining rule sets and applying them to traffic. Example: A custom WAF rule using JSON payloads to block potentially harmful requests.

```
{
  "description": "Block SQL injection attempts",
  "paused": false,
  "priority": 1,
  "action": "block",
  "filter": {
    "expression": "(http.request.uri.query contains 'SELECT' or http.request.uri.query
        contains 'INSERT')"
  }
}
```

Understanding how and when to implement tailored WAF rules is essential for both reactive and proactive security postures.

To resist **Distributed Denial of Service (DDoS) attacks**, Cloudflare offers multi-layered DDoS protection. This mechanism automatically detects and mitigates attack traffic, using over 30 Tbps of network capacity, without impacting legitimate traffic. The effectiveness lies in Cloudflare's expansive network that absorbs and dilutes malicious traffic.

Implement security settings to tailor DDoS mitigation strategies by specifying IP block settings, rate limiting, and challenge mechanisms. These features ensure that only intended traffic accesses the application.

Example implementation of a rate limiting rule employing Cloudflare's API:

```
import requests
import json

def create_rate_limit_rule(zone_id, api_token):
    url = f"https://api.cloudflare.com/client/v4/zones/{zone_id}/rate_limits"
    headers = {
        "Content-Type": "application/json",
```

```
        "Authorization": f"Bearer {api_token}",
    }
    data = {
        "match": {
            "request": {
                "methods": ["GET"],
                "schemes": ["HTTPS"],
                "url": "*example.com/*"
            }
        },
        "threshold": 1000,
        "period": 60,
        "action": {
            "timeout": 60,
            "response": {
                "content_type": "text/plain"
            }
        },
        "enabled": True,
        "description": "Limit requests to protect from DDoS"
    }
    response = requests.post(url, headers=headers, data=json.dumps(data))
    return response.json()

rate_limit_response = create_rate_limit_rule("your_zone_id", "your_api_token")
print(rate_limit_response)
```

Bot Management: Evil bots can scrape content, undertake credential stuffing attacks, or engage in carding activities, affecting application integrity and performance. Cloudflare Bot Management uses machine learning algorithms to identify, challenge, or allow web visitors based on their behavior, browser fingerprint, reputation, and infrastructure.

Configure bot fight mode to allow actionable insights into how bots interact with your application and minimize their negative impacts.

SSL/TLS Encryption: As previously discussed, SSL/TLS encrypts data in transit and is fundamental for ensuring data confidentiality and integrity. Employ the strongest SSL/TLS security practices by activating Always Use HTTPS, enabling TLS 1.3, and configuring HSTS with preloading, providing long-term assurance against downgrade and MITM attacks.

Security Analytics and Insights: Security insights and analytics provide comprehensive overviews of attacks and threats faced by your application. Such analytics guide informed enhancements to existing security measures.

257

Example of fetching firewall event logs through Cloudflare's API for enhanced security monitoring:

```
def fetch_firewall_events(zone_id, api_token):
    url = f"https://api.cloudflare.com/client/v4/zones/{zone_id}/firewall/events"
    headers = {
        "Content-Type": "application/json",
        "Authorization": f"Bearer {api_token}",
    }
    response = requests.get(url, headers=headers)
    return response.json()

firewall_events = fetch_firewall_events("your_zone_id", "your_api_token")
print(firewall_events)
```

Implement automation pipelines to dynamically adapt security postures, ensuring agility in threat response.

Access Control: Cloudflare's Access feature provides a zero-trust approach to security, ensuring that internal sites and applications are presented to authenticated users only. Use policies grounded on roles, IP addresses, or device posture to conditionally grant or deny access.

Integrate with identity providers (IdPs) to utilize Single Sign-On (SSO) and industry-standard authentication protocols like OAuth2, SAML 2.0, and OpenID Connect. Such hybrid access models incorporate identity management practice within a broader security fabric.

Threat Intelligence and Layered Security Solutions: Cloudflare offers Radar, a threat intelligence service, which aggregates data from the CDN to track and report on emerging threats.

By intelligently correlating data, Cloudflare's threat intelligence identifies potential vulnerabilities and initiates remedial actions. Integrating these insights into existing security frameworks fosters preemptive adjustments to security policies and infrastructure adaptations.

The efficacy of Cloudflare's security enhancements is realized through comprehensive deployment and configuration strategies, aligning technological advances with web application security needs. Balancing frontend performance gains with robust backend security cultivates a sustainable, secure environment fostering ecological growth and innovation.

258

9.7 Common Challenges and Solutions

Integrating a web application with Cloudflare introduces numerous benefits, including enhanced security, improved performance, and robust scalability. However, developers and operations teams may encounter a variety of challenges during the integration process. Understanding these challenges and exploring effective solutions is key to a smooth transition and continued optimization of Cloudflare's offerings. Addressing common obstacles upfront, such as DNS misconfigurations, SSL/TLS handshake failures, caching inconsistencies, and API rate limits, ensures that the integration enhances rather than disrupts application operations.

One prevalent challenge is DNS misconfiguration. Cloudflare's efficient DNS services act as the first point of contact for incoming traffic, critical for correctly routing requests. Misconfigurations can result in downtime, unreachable services, or even data breaches if subdomains remain unprotected. DNS management demands meticulous attention to detail, precise records inputting, and consistent monitoring.

- **Solution:** Regularly audit DNS records for accuracy using DNS tools. Tools like dig or nslookup help ensure DNS records are correctly configured. Additionally, Cloudflare's dashboard provides a streamlined interface for managing and updating records efficiently.

- **Example:** Checking DNS A records using dig.

```
dig example.com A
```

These commands can verify correct DNS resolution paths, ensuring that the intended IP addresses are returned.

Another frequent issue is managing SSL/TLS handshake failures. Secure connections fail when there are mismatched SSL/TLS configurations between the Cloudflare layer and the origin server. Such mismatches halt user access, displaying security errors.

- **Solution:** Verify consistency in SSL/TLS configuration, reviewing certificate paths, expiration dates, and complete certificate

259

chains. Ensure the correct mode is selected within Cloudflare's settings (e.g., Full or Full (Strict)), where SSL/TLS certificates at the origin must be valid and trusted by a CA.

- **Example:** Testing SSL connections using openssl.

```
openssl s_client -connect example.com:443 -showcerts
```

This command provides a full certificate chain, validating correctness and expiration status, facilitating smooth SSL handshakes.

Caching inconsistencies arise from conflicting cache-control headers or unplanned purges. These can lead to outdated content delivery or excessive origin requests, increasing latency.

- **Solution:** Implement explicit cache-control policies to ensure consistent content caching. Define caching levels and control header directives such as max-age and no-cache to achieve predictable cache behavior.

- **Example configurations for Apache and NGINX servers to manage caching policies:**

Apache configuration:

```
<FilesMatch "\.(jpg|jpeg|png|gif)$">
    Header set Cache-Control "max-age=2592000, public"
</FilesMatch>
```

NGINX configuration:

```
location ~* \.(jpg|jpeg|png|gif)$ {
    expires 30d;
    add_header Cache-Control "public, max-age=2592000";
}
```

These settings propagate consistent caching policies, optimizing resource delivery across all served content.

Developers often face API rate limits during integration efforts, where excessive requests to Cloudflare's API result in throttled responses, delaying automated workflow processes.

- **Solution:** Scale API usage effectively by spacing out requests, implementing exponential backoff strategies, and optimizing data retrieval methods.

- **Example of managing API request intervals using Python's** time **module:**

```
import requests, time

def safe_api_call(url, headers, attempts=5):
    for i in range(attempts):
        response = requests.get(url, headers=headers)
        if response.status_code == 429: # Too Many Requests
            time.sleep((2 ** i) * 0.1) # Exponential backoff
        else:
            return response
    return None

api_headers = {"Authorization": "Bearer your_api_token"}
response = safe_api_call("https://api.cloudflare.com/client/v4/zones", api_headers)
```

Implementing exponential backoff mitigates API rate limiting issues by regulating request flow.

Security misconfigurations can lead to vulnerable entry points for malicious actors. Overly permissive firewall rules, poorly configured SSL settings, and inadequate bot mitigation strategies place applications at risk.

- **Solution:** Regular security audits, using Cloudflare's security analytics and external pentesting services, can identify and rectify misconfigurations. Configure WAF rules to mitigate common vulnerabilities, and employ bot management mechanisms to limit non-human traffic.

- **Example of querying WAF configurations via Cloudflare's API:**

```
def get_waf_settings(zone_id, api_token):
    url = f"https://api.cloudflare.com/client/v4/zones/{zone_id}/firewall/waf/
        packages"
    headers = {
        "Content-Type": "application/json",
        "Authorization": f"Bearer {api_token}"
    }
    response = requests.get(url, headers=headers)
    return response.json()
```

```
waf_settings = get_waf_settings("your_zone_id", "your_api_token")
print(waf_settings)
```

The use of APIs to regularly retrieve and verify configurations ensures optimal security posture.

Developers may notice performance degradation problems if CDN configurations inadvertently bypass caching or fail to leverage Smart Routing features.

- **Solution:** Reevaluate page rules and routing policies to ensure optimal use of CDN features, potentially employing Argo Smart Routing to enhance traffic paths based on real-time data.

Check Cloudflare's analytics for average latency and cache hit rates to identify performance bottlenecks and adjust routing or caching strategies accordingly.

Client-side or UX issues may emerge post-migration if legacy dependencies clash with modern security protocols (e.g., deprecated browsers unable to handle HTTP/2 or TLS 1.3). Such discrepancies can alienate segments of users.

- **Solution:** Conduct thorough user testing across various devices and browsers, leveraging analytics to identify and address compatibility woes swiftly; ensure that fallbacks or alternative paths are available for unsupported client setups.

Finally, ensure continuous improvements by engaging Cloudflare's community forums and online resources to expedite solutions for emerging integration challenges. Community feedback and updates from Cloudflare can yield valuable insights into change management in adaptive web ecosystems.

Proactively addressing these common integration challenges transforms the Cloudflare integration endeavor from a potential source of disruption into a lever for agility and security, ultimately creating a resilient, secure, and high-performing application that scales effectively with user demands. Continuous learning and adaptation forge a seamless path for tackling inevitable challenges in an ever-evolving cyber landscape.

Chapter 10

Advanced Configuration and Troubleshooting in Cloudflare

This chapter delves into advanced configuration options and troubleshooting techniques within Cloudflare, empowering users to fine-tune settings for optimal performance and resiliency. It covers complex DNS management capabilities, custom rule creation, and network optimization strategies. The chapter provides guidance on enhancing security configurations, diagnosing connectivity issues, and resolving cache-related performance problems. Additionally, it emphasizes using Cloudflare's monitoring tools for effective problem-solving, enabling users to maintain a robust and efficient web infrastructure.

10.1   Advanced DNS Management

Advanced DNS management is vital for optimizing web performance and ensuring security in digital environments. Cloudflare, a prominent content delivery network and DNS management service, offers several sophisticated DNS features, including DNSSEC, CNAME flattening, and custom nameservers. This section explores these concepts in depth, detailing their implementation and impact on performance and security.

Cloudflare's DNS services offer both authoritative DNS management and foundational performance improvements. By maintaining a direct line between domain names and their corresponding IP addresses, Cloudflare ensures efficient and secure DNS resolution. Let's explore some of the advanced features that Cloudflare provides.

- **DNSSEC: Enhancing DNS Security**

  DNSSEC (Domain Name System Security Extensions) is a suite of extensions to DNS that provides to DNS clients (resolvers) origin authentication of DNS data, authenticated denial of existence, and data integrity. It is implemented as a chain of trust. DNSSEC adds cryptographic signatures to existing DNS records, allowing the client or a validating server to ensure that responses to a query come from an authoritative source and are not tampered with.

  To enable DNSSEC in Cloudflare for your domain, the following procedures are typically utilized. Each step is vital to a seamless integration and proper functioning of DNSSEC.

  ```
  # Enable DNSSEC via Cloudflare dashboard
  1. Log into your Cloudflare account.
  2. Select the appropriate domain.
  3. Navigate to the 'DNS' section on the Cloudflare dashboard.
  4. Click on 'DNSSEC' and then 'Enable DNSSEC'.
  ```

  Once DNSSEC is enabled, Cloudflare will provide a DS (Delegation Signer) record. This record must be added to your domain registrar's DNS settings to complete the DNSSEC configuration.

- **CNAME Flattening: Simplifying DNS CNAME Records**

CNAME flattening is a feature that allows root domains (e.g., example.com) to be mapped via CNAME records, which traditionally can only be assigned to subdomains. This is particularly useful when a CDN is involved, where a root domain needs to point directly to a CDN.

This technique can solve the difficulty surrounding the CNAME record restriction at the domain apex. Cloudflare's CNAME flattening restructures these DNS queries for optimal functionality, resulting in a flattened response that appears as an A or AAAA record.

```
# Enable CNAME Flattening through Cloudflare interface
1. Access your Cloudflare account and open the desired domain.
2. Go to the 'DNS' settings.
3. Find the CNAME record you need to flatten.
4. Enable CNAME Flattening through the settings provided for that specific
   record.
```

CNAME flattening optimizes DNS resolution by reducing lookup times, ensuring that even apex domains benefit from the same performance enhancements that CNAME records offer subdomains.

- **Custom Nameservers: Tailored DNS for Flexibility**

Creating custom nameservers is paramount for branding purposes and DNS stability. Cloudflare permits the configuration of personalized nameservers, enhancing the professional appearance of your domain's DNS configuration.

The process typically involves registering your nameservers with your domain registrar. Cloudflare's setup includes providing your domain with specific nameserver labels and IP addresses, which your registrar must recognize as authoritative.

```
# Steps to configure custom nameservers in Cloudflare:
1. Log in to your Cloudflare account.
2. Go to the 'DNS' settings of the desired domain.
3. Select 'Custom Nameservers'.
4. Follow the on-screen instructions to set up and register your custom
   nameservers with your domain registrar.
```

Custom nameservers allow for cohesive DNS branding by maintaining the domain's identity even through third-party DNS services. Such measures are crucial for enterprises requiring consistent representation across web infrastructure components.

- **TTL Management and DNS Load Balancing**

  Time To Live (TTL) is an attribute of DNS records that defines their validity period, thus dictating how long a resolver can cache the query before re-checking. Proper management of TTL values can vastly influence traffic and load on your servers.

  In environments managed via Cloudflare, TTL optimization is essential to balanced load distribution and improved service resilience. DNS load balancing dynamically distributes incoming traffic to various server resources efficiently.

```
# TTL configuration and load balancing via Cloudflare API
{
  "type": "A",
  "name": "example.com",
  "content": "192.0.2.1",
  "ttl": 120,
  "proxied": true
}

# Load balancing configuration
{
  "pool": {
    "name": "Primary Pool",
    "origin": [
      {"ipv4": "192.0.2.1"},
      {"ipv4": "192.0.2.2"}
    ]
  }
}
```

  Choosing optimal TTL settings balances the need for up-to-date DNS answers and the performance cost of frequent DNS lookups. Proper configuration leads to increased cache hits and decreased latency for user requests.

- **Ensuring DNS Redundancy and Reliability**

  Reliability within DNS infrastructure is vital to preventing disruptions or downtime. Cloudflare provides DNS redundancy practices that ensure your DNS setup has numerous resolvers actively functioning as backup.

  Redundancy in the DNS context typically involves deploying multiple DNS servers across different geo-locations. Cloudflare's global network is inherently beneficial, as it allows diverse geographical DNS querying, minimizing latency and maximizing availability.

```
# Setup for DNS redundancy with Cloudflare's geographic distribution
1. Enable Anycast routing for minimized latency and improved speed.
2. Utilize Cloudflare dashboard to configure backup DNS settings.
3. Routinely audit configurations for consistency with Cloudflare's best
   practices.
```

Such strategies guarantee continuity and accessibility even in cases of localized outages, enhancing the reliability of the domain's online presence.

- **Analyzing DNS Query Logs for Insights**

Analyzing DNS query logs contributes valuable insights into user behavior, potential security threats, and infrastructure efficiency. Cloudflare provides robust logging tools capturing various DNS-related metrics.

These logs can be analyzed to assess factors such as query frequency, common failing queries, and latency metrics. Understanding patterns within these logs aids organizations in decision-making regarding infrastructure adjustments and optimizations.

```python
# Example Python code to parse DNS logs for frequent queries
import json

def parse_dns_logs(file_path):
    with open(file_path, 'r') as file:
        logs = json.load(file)
        frequency_count = {}
        for log in logs:
            query = log['queryName']
            frequency_count[query] = frequency_count.get(query, 0) + 1
        return sorted(frequency_count.items(), key=lambda x: x[1], reverse=
            True)

dns_frequencies = parse_dns_logs('dns_log.json')
print(f"The most frequent DNS query is: {dns_frequencies[0][0]} with {
    dns_frequencies[0][1]} queries")
```

Analyzing query logs also pinpoints suspicious behavior potentially indicative of DDoS attacks or unauthorized accesses, facilitating prompt responses to cybersecurity issues.

Each facet of advanced DNS management in Cloudflare—from the deployment of DNSSEC to effectively handling custom nameservers and monitoring—works in concert to provide robust DNS capabilities. This integrated approach enhances both the resilience and security of domain management, ensuring that digital infrastructures perform optimally across varied scenarios.

10.2 Custom Page Rules and Transform Rules

Custom Page Rules and Transform Rules in Cloudflare offer significant control over a website's behavior, enabling fine-grained management of HTTP requests and responses to optimize performance and customize user interaction. This section examines the creation and implementation of these rules, focusing on their impact on URL behavior and site performance optimization.

Understanding Custom Page Rules

Page Rules in Cloudflare allow webmasters to tailor how content is served to users. By defining custom URL patterns, you can specify integral modifications to the caching policies, security settings, URL forwarding, and more.

Page Rules operate by evaluating the incoming HTTP requests and determining whether they match the conditions defined within the rule. If a match is found, the modifications specified in the rule are applied to that session. These rules provide capabilities such as enforcing secure connections, optimizing bandwidth usage, and refining caching strategies.

```
# Example: Creating a Page Rule to always use HTTPS
1. Log into your Cloudflare account.
2. Navigate to the desired domain and go to the 'Page Rules' tab.
3. Click 'Create Page Rule'.
4. Enter the URL pattern *example.com/*
5. Select the setting 'Always Use HTTPS'.
6. Save and Deploy rule.
```

This Page Rule ensures that all traffic to 'example.com' is securely encrypted, enhancing user data protection and aligning with search en-

268

gine optimization practices which favor secure sites.

Configuring Caching with Page Rules

Caching is a pivotal aspect of site performance, reducing server load and improving response times. Through Cloudflare's Page Rules, one can dictate how content is cached to balance freshness and load reduction.

Rules may specify cache levels, determine content-specific caching policies, or create exceptions for dynamic content:

```
# Configuring advanced caching with Page Rules
1. Create a Page Rule targeting static assets: *example.com/static/*
2. Set 'Cache Level' to 'Cache Everything'.
3. Define 'Browser Cache TTL' to 1 month.
4. Save and deploy the rule.
```

By caching static elements extensively, server requests are minimized, and pages load faster, creating a streamlined user experience.

Implementing Transform Rules for URL Management

Transform Rules reshape request and response attributes. These rules are crucial in adjusting URL paths, headers, and query strings before they reach your server or after they leave it. Transform Rules can be instrumental in incoming request sanitization, logging uniformity, and response modification.

Transform Rules support operations such as:

- Adding, removing, or rewriting HTTP headers

- URL rewriting for route handling

- Modifying cookies for privacy adjustments

```
# Transform Rule to append security headers
1. Log into Cloudflare and select the domain.
2. Navigate to 'Rules' and select 'Transform Rules'.
3. Create a new rule.
4. Define a condition for all requests.
5. Add a transformation: Insert HTTP Header 'X-XSS-Protection: 1; mode=block'.
6. Activate the rule.
```

Security enhancements via HTTP headers are critical in mitigating risks like XSS (Cross-Site Scripting), as exemplified by the added header above.

Detailed Use Case Scenarios of Page and Transform Rules

URL Forwarding and Redirection

URL forwarding is beneficial for forwarding traffic from obsolete or re-
named URLs, thus maintaining SEO value and user accessibility without disruption.

```
# Setting up a redirect from old site to new site
1. Define a Page Rule for *oldsite.com/*
2. Set 'Forwarding URL' with Status Code 301 (permanent redirect)
3. Target new URL: https://newsite.com/$1
4. Deploy the rule
```

A 301 redirection ensures link value is preserved when moving content
between domains, thereby safeguarding search rankings and visitor
navigation continuity.

Geo-Targeting Content Delivery

Cloudflare's edge network allows routing queries based on geolocation
to serve geographically relevant content—an advantageous strategy in
regions with diverse linguistic or cultural contexts.

```
# Implementing Geo-based content with Transform Rules
1. Create a Transform Rule targeting visitor's country
2. Example condition: 'cf-ipcountry' Header equals 'FR'
3. Transform operation: Rewrite URL path to /fr/*
4. Apply rule and observe geographical targeting in action.
```

Geo-targeted delivery enhances local relevance and engagement, improving conversion rates and user satisfaction.

Optimizing Performance through Targeted Rules

Targeted application of Page and Transform Rules can deliver substantial performance gains, especially for sites experiencing high traffic or
requiring precise delivery optimizations.

Through advanced caching rules, sites benefit from reduced server load
and increased response speed. Intellectual placement of Transform
Rules can sanitize user inputs, reduce payload size by altering headers,
and compress responses dynamically, creating fluid user experiences.

```
# Example: Dynamic compression with Transform Rules
1. Define a condition for mime type 'text/html'
2. Add header 'Content-Encoding: gzip'
3. Reduce response size and improve load time for textual content.
```

Dynamic content compression minimizes bandwidth usage, cost, and timespan necessary for full content delivery.

Automating Reactionary Behavior with Rules

Rules at Cloudflare can be automated, reacting to traffic patterns or DDoS activity automatically with the right conditions set, thus aiding reactive measures without manual intervention, crucial for maintaining service continuity during unexpected traffic surges.

```
# Automatically throttle traffic with Page Rules
1. Create a Cloudflare Worker detecting high-volume requests.
2. Activate associated Page Rule when thresholds exceed limits.
3. Example: Limit requests per IP to 100 per minute.
4. Automatically safeguard against overloading the server.
```

These automated proactive measures are instrumental in preserving website uptime and preventing server breaches.

Through comprehensive manipulation of Page Rules and Transform Rules, Cloudflare provides a robust toolset for the tailored management of website performance, user interaction, and resource security. By effectively configuring these elements, websites can significantly enhance their operational efficiency, user satisfaction, and adherence to policy-guided web standards. Utilizing these rules, administrators are empowered to fine-tune web infrastructure behavior responsively and efficiently, facilitating a balance between strategic resource use and leading-edge user experience enhancement.

10.3 Network Optimizations with Cloudflare

Network optimization aims to enhance the performance, reliability, and efficiency of data transmission across web-based infrastructures. Leveraging Cloudflare's advanced networking capabilities, including Argo Smart Routing, HTTP/2 Prioritization, and custom IP Firewall rules, can significantly improve network performance. This section provides a comprehensive examination of these features and offers strategies for implementing them to meet diverse organizational needs.

Argo Smart Routing: Intelligent Path Optimization

Argo Smart Routing automatically optimizes the path data takes through the Cloudflare network by selecting the fastest and most reliable routes. By reducing latency and packet loss, Argo enhances website performance and user experience.

```
# Enabling Argo Smart Routing
1. Log into your Cloudflare dashboard.
2. Select the applicable domain.
3. Navigate to the 'Traffic' tab.
4. Enable Argo by toggling the switch.
5. Monitor improvements in response time and latency statistics.
```

Argo Smart Routing differs from traditional routing by utilizing real-time insights from Cloudflare's global private backbone, leading to expedited and optimized data travel compared to public routes.

HTTP/2 Prioritization: Optimized Multiplexing

HTTP/2 introduces multiplexing, which allows multiple requests and responses to be sent concurrently over a single TCP connection. Proper prioritization within HTTP/2 is integral to ensuring critical resources are delivered first.

Cloudflare enhances HTTP/2 performance by prioritizing requests dynamically, adapting in response to changing network conditions and resource availability.

```
# Enabling HTTP/2 Prioritization
1. Access the Cloudflare dashboard for your domain.
2. Navigate to the 'Network' settings.
3. Ensure 'HTTP/2' is enabled.
4. Fine-tune prioritization within worker scripts if necessary.
```

By coordinating HTTP/2's multiplexing capabilities with strategic prioritization, you ensure that vital resources, especially those critical for initial page rendering, are served with precedence, thereby improving perceived page load times for end-users.

Custom IP Firewall Rules: Enhanced Network Security

Managing network traffic through Cloudflare's customizable IP Firewall allows for precise control over incoming and outgoing traffic to and from your network. This offers a pragmatic approach to mitigate security threats and manage access controls effectively.

IP Firewall Rules can be used to:

- Block, challenge, or allow traffic from specific IP addresses or countries. - Protect resources from malicious activities. - Enforce organizational access policies.

```
# Example: Creating a rule to block traffic from a specific country
1. Log into your Cloudflare dashboard.
2. Go to your domain's 'Security' tab.
3. Open the 'Firewall' section.
4. Create a rule: If visitor's country equals 'CN', then Block.
5. Save and apply the rule.
```

Such rules enhance security by preventing undesirable traffic, thus reducing potential attack vectors and preserving server resources for legitimate users.

Load Balancing and Failover Strategies

Cloudflare's Load Balancing not only manages server loads but also provides failover capabilities to ensure uninterrupted service availability. It uses latency-based routing and health checks to dynamically allocate traffic, optimizing bandwidth and minimizing downtime.

```
# Configure Load Balancing with failover
{
  "name": "Main Load Balancer",
  "origins": [
    {"name": "Primary Server", "address": "192.0.2.1"},
    {"name": "Secondary Server", "address": "192.0.2.2"}
  ],
  "fallback_pool": {"name": "Backup Pool"},
  "monitor": {
    "type": "http",
    "path": "/healthcheck",
    "method": "GET",
    "interval": 60
  }
}
```

Configuring load balancing with Cloudflare ensures that traffic is efficiently distributed among server resources and provides automatic redirection to backup servers during unexpected outages, maintaining continuous service availability.

Optimizing Global Network Distribution with Anycast

Anycast routing skews traditional DNS lookups by drawing from a distributed set of IP addresses in different locations, collectively acting as a single cohesive address point. Cloudflare's implementation of Anycast ensures network requests reach a proximate data center, optimizing latency and strengthening redundancy.

```
# Enabling Anycast DNS distribution
1. Log into your Cloudflare account.
2. Activate options in regions requiring minimal response times.
3. Monitor performance via Cloudflare Analytics.
```

By utilizing Anycast, traffic is dynamically routed to the nearest available data center, mitigating latency issues and maintaining robust network uptime.

Reducing Latency with TCP Optimization

Optimized TCP configurations allow for reduced connection times and improved network efficiency. Cloudflare offers dynamic TCP optimization, which enhances the transmission window, attempts to reduce connection setup time, and decreases error rates.

```
# TCP settings adjustment for performance gains
1. Evaluate TCP Fast Open and Enable
2. Adjust maximum segment size (MSS) for larger payloads.
3. Configure initial congestion window (IW) for rapid initial requests.
```

Such configurations translate into faster initial packet delivery and reduced round-trip times, thereby lowering server response times.

Advanced WebSocket Management

WebSockets facilitate bi-directional and persistent communication channels over HTTP/2, essential for real-time applications. Cloudflare ensures efficient handling and security of WebSocket traffic.

```
# Enable and optimize WebSocket connections
1. Identify WebSocket endpoints.
2. Adjust Cloudflare settings to support persistent connections.
3. Implement WebSocket-specific firewall rules.
4. Monitor performance and refine parameters based on use-case feedback.
```

Optimizing WebSocket management increases efficiency in handling real-time data streams, maintaining responsive applications across variable network conditions.

Diagnostic and Monitoring Capabilities

Monitoring network performance provides insights critical to maintaining optimized operations. Cloudflare Analytics delivers metrics on request/response times, geographic distribution, and threat detection.

```python
# Sample Python code snippet for retrieving and analyzing Cloudflare logs
import cloudflare

def analyze_traffic_stats(api_key, domain):
    client = cloudflare.Cloudflare(api_key)
    data = client.get_traffic_statistics(domain)
    for record in data['requests']:
        print(f"Time: {record['time']} - Hits: {record['hits']}")

# Assume 'api_key' is predefined
analyze_traffic_stats(api_key, 'example.com')
```

Using such analytics, administrators can make data-driven decisions about bandwidth allocation, security enhancement, and predictive scaling.

By implementing these advanced network optimizations within Cloudflare, organizations can effectively reduce latency, improve resource distribution, bolster security, and ensure sustainable growth of web operations. This collaborative orchestration of flexibility, innovation, and precise configuration provides a competitive edge, aligning network performance with evolving digital demands and user expectations seamlessly.

275

10.4 Advanced Security Configurations

In the digital landscape, robust security mechanisms are essential to safeguarding web assets and data integrity. Cloudflare offers a range of advanced security configurations, including Rate Limiting, Firewall Rules, and Security Level settings. This section delves into these features, providing in-depth analysis and guidance on their configuration to enhance web security infrastructures effectively.

- **Rate Limiting: Controlling Request Rates**

Rate Limiting protects applications from abusive or excessive requests, which could lead to Denial-of-Service (DoS) attacks or server performance degradation. Cloudflare allows administrators to define thresholds on the number of requests from an IP address within a specified timeframe.

```
# Setting up Rate Limiting in Cloudflare
1. Log into the Cloudflare dashboard.
2. Select the domain and navigate to the 'Firewall' section.
3. Choose 'Tools' and then 'Rate Limiting'.
4. Create a new Rate Limit:
   - Enter a URL pattern (e.g., *example.com/API/*).
   - Set the threshold (e.g., 100 requests per minute).
   - Define an action (e.g., block or challenge).
5. Save and apply the configuration.
```

This protective measure is crucial for APIs and other entry points susceptible to automated abuse, maintaining performance without compromising accessibility for legitimate users.

- **Firewall Rules: Tailored Traffic Management**

Firewall Rules provide granular control over HTTP request management, allowing one to block, challenge, log, or allow requests based on various parameters, including IP address, country, HTTP headers, and more.

```
# Custom Firewall Rule to Block Threatening IPs
1. Access the Cloudflare dashboard and select the domain.
2. Under 'Security', choose 'WAF (Web Application Firewall)'.
3. Navigate to 'Firewall Rules'.
4. Create a new rule with conditions:
```

276

```
  - If 'IP Source Address' equals 198.51.100.1, then Block.
5. Save and enable the rule.
```

Such targeted rule enforcement prevents malicious access attempts, increasing the site's resilience against unauthorized entry or disruption attempts.

• Security Level Settings: Adjustable Protection Layers

Cloudflare's Security Level settings are pivotal in tuning the sensitivity of automated security responses to perceived threats, ranging from 'Essentially Off' to 'I'm Under Attacki.

```
# Adjusting Security Level
1. Log into your Cloudflare account.
2. Navigate to the 'Firewall' section.
3. Under 'Security Levels', choose the appropriate setting:
   - Low: Minimal security.
   - Medium: Balanced security.
   - High: Comprehensive threat mitigation.
4. Apply changes and review traffic impact.
```

These settings provide dynamic protection levels, increasing or decreasing automatic defenses based on current threat conditions and site risk tolerance.

• Bot Management: Automated Threat Detection

Cloudflare's Bot Management identifies and mitigates suspicious bot activity while allowing beneficial bots like search engines. Algorithms analyze traffic patterns and apply heuristic approaches to discern potential threats.

```
# Configuring Bot Management
1. Access the 'Security' tab in Cloudflare dashboard.
2. Navigate to 'Bot Management'.
3. Enable detection and set desired actions (e.g., challenge or log).
4. Monitor bot activity through Cloudflare Analytics.
5. Adjust heuristics and thresholds to align with legitimate user activities and reduce
     false positives.
```

Advanced machine learning models identify harmful bot behaviors, maintaining site integrity and user experience.

• DDoS Protection: Infrastructure Resilience

Distributed Denial-of-Service (DDoS) attacks aim to overwhelm a system with traffic. Cloudflare offers automated DDoS mitigation through always-on protection protocols embedded within its global network.

```
# Enabling DDoS Protection
1. Cloudflare's DDoS protection is automatically enabled for all domains.
2. No additional setup is required.
3. Monitor threat reports via the dashboard.
4. Optionally fine-tune automated responses using custom Firewall Rules.
```

Cloudflare's infrastructure handles significant traffic surges without manual intervention, absorbing attacks at the edge before they impact your server.

- ## Secure Sockets Layer (SSL): Data Encryption

SSL encrypts data in transit between the user and the server, safeguarding sensitive information from interception and tampering.

```
# Enabling SSL/TLS in Cloudflare
1. Navigate to 'SSL/TLS' in the Cloudflare dashboard.
2. Select a suitable SSL/TLS mode (e.g., Full or Full (strict)).
3. Apply settings to ensure encrypted connections.
4. Configure HTTP Strict Transport Security (HSTS) if needed:
   - This enforces secure connections, redirecting HTTP to HTTPS.
```

Using SSL not only protects data integrity and privacy but also enhances trust, with modern browsers often flagging non-HTTPS sites as non-secure.

- ## Access Management with Cloudflare Access

Cloudflare Access regulates who can access specific resources using identity-aware zero trust security protocols.

```
# Cloudflare Access Configuration
1. Visit the 'Access' tab on Cloudflare dashboard.
2. Set policies using identity providers (e.g., Okta, Azure AD).
3. Define user roles and apply relevant access permissions.
4. Set up multi-factor authentication (MFA) for additional security.
```

Access limits are critical for controlling internal resource exposure, particularly for sensitive applications or development environments.

- ## Audit Logs and Security Monitoring

278

Continuous monitoring and logging are fundamental to maintaining a secure environment. Cloudflare's logging features provide comprehensive records of security events and policy adherence.

```python
# Python script example for analyzing security logs
import cloudflare

def fetch_security_logs(api_key, domain):
    client = cloudflare.Cloudflare(api_key)
    logs = client.get_audit_logs(domain)
    threat_events = [log for log in logs if log['action'] == 'SecurityThreat']
    return threat_events

# Assume 'api_key' is predefined
security_threats = fetch_security_logs(api_key, 'example.com')
for threat in security_threats:
    print(f"Detected threat: {threat['description']} at {threat['timestamp']}")
```

Strategically leveraging these logs helps identify patterns of suspicious activity, allowing for timely intervention and policy adjustment as new threats emerge.

- **Enhancing Threat Intelligence**

Cloudflare integrates detailed threat intelligence data, offering insights into global threat landscapes and emerging attack techniques. This data aids in proactively reinforcing security measures.

Maintaining an updated security configuration is pivotal, as malicious actors continuously refine their methodologies. Through Cloudflare's suite of advanced security configurations, organizations can erect formidable defenses against a myriad of cyber threats, thereby preserving the integrity, confidentiality, and availability of their web assets in an increasingly hostile digital environment. By leveraging these sophisticated tools, organizations are better positioned to respond to, and recover from, security incidents with minimal disruption.

10.5 Troubleshooting Connectivity Issues

Connectivity issues in web environments can stem from various factors, ranging from DNS misconfigurations to SSL handshake failures.

Cloudflare provides a comprehensive set of tools and methodologies designed to diagnose and resolve these issues, ensuring seamless access and uninterrupted performance for users. This section explores effective techniques to identify and troubleshoot common connectivity problems, focusing on DNS resolution errors and SSL handshake disruptions.

Analyzing DNS Resolution Errors

DNS resolution is a critical part of the web connectivity process, translating human-friendly domain names into machine-readable IP addresses. Issues with DNS resolution can manifest as website inaccessibility, prolonged load times, or incorrect content delivery. Utilizing Cloudflare's DNS diagnostic tools can aid in pinpointing and resolving these issues effectively.

```
# Common Symptoms of DNS Resolution Issues
- Error messages such as "DNS_PROBE_FINISHED_NXDOMAIN" or "Server IP
    address could not be found".
- Intermittent site availability.
- Delayed domain propagation or updates not reflecting promptly.

# Steps to Diagnose DNS Resolution Issues
1. Use the Cloudflare dashboard to view DNS settings.
2. Confirm that all DNS records are correctly configured.
3. Employ DNS lookup tools (e.g., 'nslookup' or 'dig') to validate record visibility.

# Example: Using 'dig' to diagnose a DNS issue
$ dig www.example.com +trace
```

The output of this command provides detailed traversal of the DNS resolution path, allowing identification of points where resolution failures may occur.

Resolving DNS Misconfigurations

Misconfigurations are common sources of DNS resolution issues. Ensuring that DNS records, such as A, AAAA, CNAME, and MX, are correctly set and propagated is essential in maintaining proper functionality. Cloudflare's interface allows for simple editing and updating of these records.

```
# Correcting DNS Record Misconfigurations
1. Verify that the domain's nameservers are pointing to Cloudflare's servers.
2. Ensure that DNS entries match actual server IP addresses.
3. Check that CNAME records are properly linked and not conflicting with other
    record types.
4. Re-propagate DNS changes via the Cloudflare dashboard.
```

280

```
# Example: Adding an A record in Cloudflare
Login to Cloudflare -> Select domain -> DNS app -> 'Add Record' -> Type: A, Name:
    example, IPv4 Address: 192.0.2.1
```

Correcting such misconfigurations promptly resolves many DNS-related connectivity issues, restoring expected service access.

Addressing SSL Handshake Failures

An SSL handshake involves communication between the client and server to establish a secure connection. Failures in this process can occur due to certificate issues, protocol mismatches, or network security settings.

```
# Symptoms of SSL Handshake Failures
- Browser error messages like "SSL_ERROR_HANDSHAKE_FAILURE_ALERT" or "
    ERR_SSL_PROTOCOL_ERROR".
- Lack of secure connection icon in browser URL bar.
- Delayed or blocked secure site access.

# Steps to Diagnose SSL Issues
1. Check Cloudflare SSL settings (SSL/TLS mode, certificate status).
2. Use command-line tools (e.g., 'openssl s_client') to test SSL connections.

# Example: Testing SSL connection using OpenSSL
$ openssl s_client -connect example.com:443
```

Output from this command reveals potential problems in certificate validity, issuer trust, or cipher suite negotiations that may disrupt SSL handshakes.

Troubleshooting SSL Certificate Problems

SSL certificate issues can hinder successful handshakes. Ensuring that certificates are valid, correctly installed, and not expired is vital.

```
# Resolving SSL Certificate Issues
1. Confirm that the SSL certificate is correctly installed on the server.
2. Ascertain certificate chain completeness by ensuring intermediate certificates are
    included.
3. Renew expired certificates.
4. Adjust browser and server supported protocols and cipher suites if non-standard
    configurations are used.

# Example: Renewing SSL Certificate in Cloudflare
Navigate to SSL/TLS -> Edge Certificates -> 'Order SSL Certificate' -> Review and
    approve the process.
```

By addressing these certificate-specific problems, the likelihood of successful SSL handshakes is maximized, fostering secure connections.

Network Path and Latency Analysis

Latency or diminished connectivity can stem from network path in-efficiencies. Network path analysis tools help identify slow or failing routes, allowing for optimization or correction.

```
# Utilizing Traceroute for Path Analysis
1. Use traceroute ('tracert' on Windows) to view network path taken by packets.
2. Identify slow responders or unreachable hops.

# Example: Using traceroute on a domain
$ traceroute example.com
```

```
Example output:
1  192.168.1.1 (192.168.1.1)  1.001 ms  0.923 ms  0.981 ms
2  <intermediate nodes> ...
n  destination.com (203.0.113.0)  28.789 ms  28.712 ms  29.045 ms
```

Such results facilitate pinpointing particular segments of the route that may introduce latency, guiding stakeholder decisions on rerouting or re-strategizing network architecture.

Utilizing Monitoring Tools for Real-Time Analysis

Real-time monitoring tools offered by Cloudflare, along with external services, can provide insights into ongoing connectivity issues.

```
# Cloudflare Analytics for Connectivity Monitoring
1. Log into Cloudflare and access the 'Analytics' tab.
2. Review data on latency, DNS resolution errors, and SSL handshake success rates.
3. Cross-reference metrics over time to detect persistent or emerging issues.

# Example: Using Python to automate analytics data retrieval
import cloudflare

def monitor_latency(api_key, domain):
    client = cloudflare.Cloudflare(api_key)
    analytics = client.get_domain_analytics(domain)
    for record in analytics['latency']:
        print(f"Timestamp: {record['timestamp']} - Latency: {record['latency']} ms")

monitor_latency(api_key, 'example.com')
```

These insights offer a clearer depiction of the network's health, en-abling proactive measures before issues impact user experience.

Engaging Support and Community Resources

When internal troubleshooting falls short, Cloudflare support, along with community forums and documentation, can be invaluable resources in seeking solution-oriented guidance.

```
# Steps to Engage Cloudflare Support
1. Prepare detailed problem description with specific error codes/messages.
2. Document diagnostic steps taken and provide relevant logs or snapshots.
3. Contact Cloudflare support via dashboard or email.
4. Participate in community forums for peer insights and potential solutions.

# Cloudflare Community Usage Example
Visit the Cloudflare Community at: https://community.cloudflare.com/
Search for similar issues and participate in discussions.
```

Leveraging these additional resources extends problem-solving capabilities, often uncovering novel solutions based on broader experiences and expertise.

By systematically addressing connectivity issues through empirical diagnostics and strategic problem-solving rooted in Cloudflare's tools, connectivity stability and performance can be preserved, enhancing the reliability and accessibility of web domains. The continuous application of these principles fosters robust network resilience, capable of meeting varied and dynamic demands in today's interconnected digital environment.

10.6 Debugging Cache and Performance Problems

Effective cache management and performance optimization are crucial for maintaining efficient and high-performing web applications. Caching reduces server load, decreases latency, and improves user experience. However, when cache systems encounter problems, they can become bottlenecks. Cloudflare offers robust tools and strategies for diagnosing and resolving cache-related and performance issues. This section provides detailed insights into identifying, analyzing, and remedying caching inefficiencies and performance bottlenecks.

Understanding caching mechanics is important before delving into debugging. Caching stores copies of web content on edge servers closer to users, reducing the need to fetch the original content from the origin server.

```
# Basic Caching Process
```

1. User requests a webpage or resource.
2. Cloudflare edge server checks if the resource is cached.
3. If cached, the edge server serves the content directly.
4. If not cached, the request is forwarded to the origin server.
5. The origin server responds, and the edge server caches the response for subsequent requests.

Understanding this sequence aids in identifying where disruptions may occur and implementing appropriate corrective measures.

Cache misses occur when a requested resource is not found in the cache, resulting in longer load times and increased origin server load. Identifying and resolving the causes of cache misses is essential for optimized performance.

- **Symptoms of Cache Misses**

    - High server load due to unnecessary request handling.
    - Inconsistent content delivery speeds.
    - Increased latency for non-cached resources.

- **Techniques for Identifying Cache Misses**

    - Use Cloudflare Analytics to examine cache hit and miss ratios.
    - Employ browser developer tools to inspect cache headers (e.g., Cache-Control, Expires).
    - Review Cloudflare's browser diagnostics to corroborate cache status.

- **Example: Using browser tools (e.g., Chrome DevTools)**

    - Open DevTools (F12 or right-click, Inspect).
    - Go to the 'Network' tab.
    - Reload the page and examine each resource.
    - Look for 'cf-cache-status' in the headers (HIT, MISS, EXPIRED).

Resources consistently resulting in cache misses require deeper analysis to ascertain corrective strategies, such as adjusting cache-control directives or leveraging custom caching rules.

Fine-tuning caching policies directly impacts performance. Cloudflare allows the creation of custom Page Rules that dictate cache behaviors tailored to specific content characteristics.

```
# Creating a Caching Page Rule in Cloudflare
1. Log into your Cloudflare account and select the domain.
2. Go to the 'Page Rules' tab.
3. Click 'Create Page Rule'.
4. Define a URL pattern (e.g., *example.com/assets/*).
5. Set 'Cache Level' to 'Cache Everything'.
6. Adjust the 'Browser Cache TTL' to a suitable duration.
7. Save and apply the rule.
```

Page Rules enable refined control over caching strategies, ensuring that static resources are reliably served from cache while dynamic content can be freshly fetched from the origin server as needed.

Content updates necessitate cache invalidation to ensure users receive the most up-to-date information. When cache purge processes fail, stale content can persist, negatively affecting user experience.

```
# Steps for Purging Cache in Cloudflare
1. Log into your Cloudflare account.
2. Access the domain's 'Caching' settings.
3. Select 'Purge Cache'.
4. Choose to 'Purge Everything' or specify individual files.
5. Confirm the action, and observe content updates.

# Example: Utilizing API to automate cache purging
import cloudflare
import requests

def purge_cache(api_key, domain, files):
    headers = {
        'Content-Type': 'application/json',
        'Authorization': f'Bearer {api_key}',
    }
    data = {"files": files}
    response = requests.post(f"https://api.cloudflare.com/client/v4/zones/{domain}/
        purge_cache", headers=headers, json=data)
    return response.status_code, response.json()

domain_id = "your_zone_id"
api_key = "your_api_key"
files_to_purge = ["https://example.com/asset1.jpg", "https://example.com/asset2.js"]

status_code, response = purge_cache(api_key, domain_id, files_to_purge)
print(f"Cache purge status: {status_code}")
```

Automating cache purges helps maintain content accuracy, supporting seamless user experiences during content updates or deployments.

While caching addresses numerous performance concerns, deeper networking or client-side aspects may also require attention. Analytical diagnostics help pinpoint underlying issues impacting performance.

```
# Using 'Cloudflares Performance Analytics
1. Review load time metrics across demographics and geographies.
2. Analyze content loading waterfall charts for sequential delays.
3. Evaluate server response times to identify bottlenecks.

# Example: Automated Performance Monitoring
import cloudflare
import time

def monitor_performance(api_key, domain, interval=60):
    client = cloudflare.Cloudflare(api_key)
    while True:
        performance_data = client.get_performance_metrics(domain)
        print(f"Time: {time.ctime()} - Load Time: {performance_data['load_time']}
            ms")
        time.sleep(interval)

api_key = "your_api_key"
monitor_performance(api_key, 'example.com')
```

This monitoring provides real-time insights into performance metrics, facilitating proactive adjustments to configuration and architecture in response to observed trends.

Integrating Cloudflare's capabilities with additional performance monitoring tools, such as Google PageSpeed Insights or GTmetrix, further elucidates potential improvements.

```
# Best Practices for Comprehensive Performance Analysis
1. Combine Cloudflare metrics with PageSpeed Insights to assess overall speed and
    recommendations.
2. Utilize GTmetrix for detailed report generation highlighting potential performance
    improvements.
3. Inspect waterfall views for resource load order and identify critical path
    opportunities.

# Leveraging API for PageSpeed Insights Integration
import requests

def get_pagespeed_insights(url, key):
    response = requests.get(f"https://www.googleapis.com/pagespeedonline/v5/
        runPagespeed?url={url}&key={key}")
    return response.json()

api_key = "your_google_api_key"
page_url = "https://example.com"
insights = get_pagespeed_insights(page_url, api_key)
print(f"Page Speed Score: {insights['lighthouseResult']['categories']['performance']['
    score']}")
```

Synthesizing findings from various tools enhances the depth of analysis and supports comprehensive strategy development for addressing performance challenges.

By diligently addressing cache and performance issues through the analytical frameworks and strategies provided by Cloudflare, web administrators can ensure optimized resource distribution, minimal latency, and a superior user experience. This sustained commitment to performance excellence not only enhances usability and engagement but also promotes higher conversion rates and user satisfaction in a competitive digital landscape.

10.7 Monitoring and Logging for Troubleshooting

Monitoring and logging are essential components of any robust network and web infrastructure. Cloudflare offers comprehensive tools for monitoring and logging that facilitate troubleshooting of potential issues. These tools enable administrators to track performance metrics, identify security threats, and analyze network patterns. In this section, we explore effective strategies for leveraging Cloudflare's capabilities in monitoring and logging to diagnose and resolve issues efficiently.

- Real-time monitoring and historical logging provide valuable insights into the operational health and performance of a web service. By continuously tracking and recording data, stakeholders can pinpoint anomalies, understand trends, and trigger alerts for potential problems before they escalate.

```
# Key Benefits of Monitoring and Logging
- Early detection of performance degradation.
- Identification of security threats and breaches.
- Improved decision-making based on data-driven insights.
- Capacity planning and optimization based on trend analysis.
```

These practices form the backbone of effective troubleshooting and system optimization by supplying factual, time-stamped evidence for postmortem analysis and ongoing improvement.

- Cloudflare provides a robust set of monitoring tools designed to offer visibility into your network layer, application traffic, and security posture. These tools include Real-Time Traffic Analytics, Security Activity Monitoring, and Performance Metrics.

```
# Setting Up Real-Time Traffic Analytics
1. Log into your Cloudflare account.
2. Select the relevant domain.
3. Navigate to the 'Analytics' section.
4. Activate Real-Time Traffic Analytics by configuring dashboards and alerts.
```

Real-time analytics capture live traffic data, allowing administrators to monitor site activity as it happens, facilitating the swift identification and remediation of abnormal patterns.

- Proactive alert configurations are indispensable for immediate awareness of emergent issues. Cloudflare allows thresholds and conditions to be set for alerting whenever predefined metrics deviate from expected norms.

```
# Example: Creating Alerts for Unusual Traffic Spikes
1. Go to 'Alerts' under the Cloudflare dashboard.
2. Define metrics and thresholds (e.g., requests per minute exceeding a specific count).
3. Set communication channels (e.g., email, SMS) for alerts.
4. Deploy the alert to stay informed of critical performance variations.
```

Alerts enable rapid response and immediate investigation, minimizing potential damage caused by unrecognized incidents in real-time.

- Cloudflare offers extensive logging solutions that capture detailed records of requests and responses. By logging full HTTP transactions, administrators can perform in-depth analysis post-incident or for regular performance audits.

```
# Accessing Logs for In-depth Analysis
1. Enable Logging in Cloudflare for the desired domain.
2. Choose log data retention policy and destination (e.g., Cloudflare Enterprise
      LogShare, third-party SIEM).
3. Extract logs for analysis using tools or APIs.

# Example: Using LogShare via API
import requests
import json
```

288

```
logShareApiUrl = "https://api.cloudflare.com/client/v4/accounts/{account_id}/logs/
    received"
headers = {
    "X-Auth-Email": "your-email@example.com",
    "X-Auth-Key": "your-auth-key",
    "Content-Type": "application/json"
}

response = requests.get(logShareApiUrl, headers=headers)
logs = json.loads(response.content)

for log in logs['result']:
    print(f"Timestamp: {log['EdgeStartTimestamp']}, Status: {log['
        EdgeResponseStatus']}")
```

Log analysis offers clarity in understanding how users interact with web resources, highlighting potential issues with content delivery or security protocols.

- Traffic analysis involves monitoring user access patterns and identifying anomalies or inefficiencies. Using programmable interfaces such as Cloudflare Workers, customized scripts aid in managing and optimizing network traffic.

```
# Example: Cloudflare Worker for Custom Traffic Analysis
addEventListener("fetch", event => {
    event.respondWith(handleRequest(event.request))
})

async function handleRequest(request) {
    const url = new URL(request.url)
    const startTime = Date.now()
    const response = await fetch(request)
    const endTime = Date.now()
    const responseTime = endTime - startTime

    // Log or perform additional analysis on response time
    console.log('Request to ${url.pathname} took ${responseTime}ms')

    return response
}
```

By incorporating such custom functionality, administrators can derive additional insights into request handling and response timing, identifying potential bottlenecks and tuning performance accordingly.

- While Cloudflare provides robust native tools, integrating third-party solutions can enhance the scope and depth of monitoring

289

efforts. This integration can include platforms specializing in application performance management (APM), security information and event management (SIEM), and more.

```
# Integrate Cloudflare data with third-party tools
1. Use Cloudflare APIs to export data to SIEM/Log management platforms (e.g.,
   Splunk, Datadog).
2. Configure Webhooks or REST interfaces for automated data imports.
3. Develop dashboards correlating data for comprehensive visibility.

# Sample integration using Datadog API
import datadog

options = {
    'api_key': 'your_datadog_api_key',
    'app_key': 'your_datadog_app_key'
}

datadog.initialize(**options)

from datadog import api

# Example: sending a custom Cloudflare metric to DataDog
api.Metric.send(metric='web_requests.latency', points=135, tags=["source:cloudflare"])
```

Such integrations facilitate enhanced data correlation and visualization, combining several sources of information into a cohesive narrative for troubleshooting.

- Conducting thorough post-mortem analyses following incidents or performance glitches is crucial for ensuring long-term improvements. Documentation of findings informs future strategic vision and highlights procedural gaps.

```
# Documenting a Post-Mortem Analysis
1. Summarize the incident —cause, impact, and recovery timeline.
2. Analyze historical logs and metrics to identify root cause.
3. Develop an action plan to prevent recurrence.
4. Review monitoring configuration to ensure coverage of identified issues.

# Example Template for Post-Mortem Review
"""
Incident Summary:
- Date and Time of Incident
- Affected Services
- Duration and Resolution

Root Cause Analysis:
- Detailed Timeline of Events Leading to Incident
```

```
- Data Correlation and Analysis

Preventive Actions:
- Steps Implemented
- Future Monitoring Configuration Adjustments
"""
```

Continuous improvement methodologies, fueled by systematic documentation and data insights, create a feedback loop that evolves an organization's capacity to respond to new challenges.

Monitoring and logging are foundational to understanding and managing web infrastructures efficiently. By leveraging Cloudflare's comprehensive toolset for ongoing observation, logging, alerting, and integrations with external platforms, organizations harness data-driven processes that bolster troubleshooting efforts and performance optimization strategies, providing seamless, reliable, and secure online experiences to users.